Russian views
of Pushkin

Alexander Pushkin

Portrait by O.A. Kiprensky, 1827

One of the most popular pictures of Russia's national poet is this portrait, painted in 1827 by O.A. Kiprensky. Watched over by a statuette of Erato, the classical muse of poetry, Pushkin himself is depicted romantically – in tartan cloak and nonchalant cravat, with sensitive gaze and hair à la Byron. An odd feature is the poet's slightly ferine hand.

Russian views of Pushkin

Edited and translated by

D. J. RICHARDS

and

C. R. S. COCKRELL

Willem A. Meeuws – Publisher – Oxford – 1976

© D. J. Richards and C. R. S. Cockrell, 1976

ISBN 0 902672 18 5 Hardback
ISBN 0 902672 19 3 Paperback

Published by Willem A. Meeuws, Oxford, 1976

Printed in Great Britain by Kingprint Ltd.,
Richmond, Surrey

FOREWORD

'Translators are the post-horses of enlightenment' (Pushkin).

This collection of 26 essays presents for the first time to the English-speaking reader the Russian view of Pushkin as it has developed over the last one and a half centuries. In their choice of essays the editors' concern was twofold: firstly, to give examples from each of the most important stages in the development of Russian criticism of Pushkin; and secondly, to ensure that the essays, taken as a whole, should reflect the range and many-sided nature of Pushkin's genius. The collection is intended to be of interest not only to the academic student of Russian but also to the general reader. The original Russian is cited only when its inclusion seemed essential for a full understanding of the critic's point (in the essays by Solovyov and Eikhenbaum).

The editors would like to express their gratitude to Mrs Julia Loewy for treating both the manuscript and themselves with such good-humoured fortitude.

University of Exeter.

D.J.R.
C.R.S.C.

CONTENTS

Introduction		i
Gogol	A Few Words on Pushkin (1834)	1
Belinsky	The Works of Alexander Pushkin (1844)	7
Herzen	The Development of Revolutionary Ideas in Russia (1851)	19
Annenkov	Pushkin. Materials for his Biography (1855)	27
Dobrolyubov	Alexander Sergeevich Pushkin (1858)	37
Grigoriev	The Development of the Idea of Nationality in our Literature since the Death of Pushkin (1862)	45
Pisarev	Pushkin and Belinsky (1865)	55
Turgenev	Speech on Pushkin (1880)	63
Dostoevsky	Pushkin (1880)	73
Merezhkovsky	Pushkin (1896)	89
Solovyov	The Significance of Poetry in Pushkin's Verse (1897)	101
Shestov	A. S. Pushkin (1897)	107
Aikhenvald	Pushkin (1908)	121
Blok	The Poet's Role (1921)	127
Eikhenbaum	Problems of Pushkin's Poetic Style (1921)	135
Gershenzon	Reading Pushkin (1923)	147
Tomashevsky	Interpreting Pushkin (1925)	153
Mirsky	The Problem of Pushkin (1934)	163
Vinogradov	Pushkin's Style (1934)	171
Lezhnev	Pushkin's Prose (1937)	177
Shklovsky	A Society Tale: *The Queen of Spades* (1937)	187
Vinokur	Pushkin as a Playwright (1939)	197
Frank	Lucent Sorrow (1949)	207
Stepanov	Paths of the Novel (1959)	225
Slonimsky	The Fairy-tales in Verse (1963)	235
Blagoi	Pushkin's Laughter (1968)	243
Index		257

INTRODUCTION

From a literary, let alone a psychological point of view Pushkin is, like all great writers, a highly complex phenomenon. He was magnificently unique, but also a transitional figure in the development of Russian literature. His roots lay deep in the aristocratic French literature of the eighteenth century, yet he exercised a dominating influence on Russian nineteenth-century literature, of which he has been called the father-figure, even though much of this literature evolved as a conscious reaction against some of the poet's most cherished aesthetic values. His countrymen regard him as their national poet, yet outside Russia he is relatively unknown. And even among those Russian critics – the vast majority – who do not dispute Pushkin's eminence there is a wide measure of disagreement over the precise nature of his artistic achievement and of his role in the history of Russian literature.

By descent, upbringing and temperament Pushkin was an aristocrat (albeit an impoverished one) and moreover a member of the Russian aristocracy of the early nineteenth century when that class was dominated by the cultural values of the French *ancien régime*.

On his father's side the family traced its descent from a forbear who served with Alexander Nevsky in the thirteenth century, while Pushkin's earliest recorded ancestor on his mother's side, his maternal great-grandfather, the Ethiopian Ibrahim Hannibal, was a distinguished servant of Peter the Great who gave him among other rewards the country estate of Mikhailovskoe which eventually came into the poet's possession. Although impoverished, Pushkin was no repentant nobleman. Throughout his life the poet possessed, it seems, an inborn sense of social superiority. Although in his mature years he would admit to having earlier adopted a somewhat exaggeratedly aristocratic pose in imitation of Byron, he never felt anything but pride and gratitude for his '600-year old nobility'.

From an early age Pushkin moved in the highest Russian social and intellectual circles. As a young boy he had been allowed to sit in at gatherings in his parents' house of some of the leading Russian *littérateurs* of the day. From the age of 12 to 18 he was educated at the newly founded Lycée in Tsarskoe Selo where the most brilliant sons of the Russian nobility were to be prepared for posts of high responsibility in the service of the state. Even before leaving school he was admitted to membership of Arzamas, one of the leading literary societies of the period. Later he married a beautiful and socially eligible woman and, willingly or not, spent his last years in close attendance at the court of Tsar Nicholas I.

Pushkin's aristocratic background found expression not only in his writing but also in the style and panache of much of his way of life, from the precise elegance of his handwriting and the more casual elegance of his attire to the dashing vigour of his social life. In his youth Pushkin shared many of the young Onegin's foppish tastes and, like his hero, indulged himself in that exhausting round of dancing, womanising, gambling and duelling which was the fashion among young aristocrats of the period. Tolstoy, it is true, called Pushkin 'a man of letters' *[literator]*, assigning him disparagingly to the same class as Turgenev and Goncharov, in contrast with Lermontov and himself, but for Gogol the poet was very much a highly disconcerting man of the world who seemed to be frittering away his life and his genius at society balls.

During the early years of the nineteenth century when Pushkin's literary values were formed Russian literature was a preserve of the aristocracy and Pushkin gladly associated himself with the aristocratic standards and attitudes which held sway. 'We can be justly proud,' he writes for instance to Bestuzhev in 1825, 'that though our literature yields to others in profusion of talent, it differs from them in that it does not bear the stamp of servile self-abasement. Our men of talent are noble and independent... our writers are drawn from the highest class of society. Aristocratic pride merges with the author's self-esteem...' And in the same year he wrote in a similar vein to Ryleev: 'Don't you see that the spirit of our literature depends to a certain extent on the social position of the writers..?'

At the same time Pushkin's early literary triumphs seemed to reflect that effortless superiority which has been held to be one of the supreme distinguishing characteristics and virtues of the ideal aristocrat. All Russians know, for instance, how Derzhavin, the great court poet of Catherine II, was enraptured by the schoolboy Pushkin's recitation of his *Reminiscences of Tsarskoe Selo* and how five years later Zhukovsky, the leading poet of the early nineteenth century, sent Pushkin his portrait inscribed with the dedication, 'To the conquering pupil from the conquered master in memory of the notable day on which he completed his poem *Ruslan and Lyudmila*, 1820, March 26, Holy Friday.'

By the middle of the following decade, as writers and critics from other classes (most notably Gogol and Belinsky) came to the fore, the social flavour of the Russian literary world had changed quite markedly, causing Pushkin some discomfort. 'There was a time', he writes for instance in 1834, 'when literature was an honourable and aristocratic profession. Now it is a lousy market...' Though Pushkin was compelled to compete in the lousy market in order to support himself and his extravagant family, it is easy to sense where his literary and social sympathies lay.

It is of course impossible to determine precisely the origins of Pushkin's (or anyone else's) mature literary style. Doubtless much derives from nature as well as from nurture — and neither of these is susceptible to accurate measurement. However, if one accepts that the values of his particular social environment exercised an influence on Pushkin's aesthetic judgments, then it follows that the poet owed a considerable debt to France.

In Russian polite society at the end of the eighteenth and the beginning of the nineteenth centuries French aristocratic manners were imitated. The French language was spoken (many Russian nobles had only a defective command of their native tongue) and among the cultivated the literature of France was read more widely than that of Russia itself, while moreover much Russian literature was produced in imitation of French models. Pushkin was brought up to speak French as well as Russian and throughout his life he continued the practice of reading French literature which he had begun as a boy in his father's extensive library. The poet's knowledge of French — which he used for much of his correspondence — was excellent, and indeed in a letter of July 1831 to Chaadaev he claimed it was a more familiar language to him than Russian. According to Annenkov the poet's dying words were spoken not in Russian, but in French (*'Il faut que j'arrange ma maison'*).

The influence of the French language on Pushkin's prose was considerable. Gallicisms are found in his Russian and so much of the structure of his sentences was conditioned by French habits (and by a certain conscious imitation of Voltaire's style) that when Prosper Mérimée translated *The Shot* and *The Queen of Spades* he found that entire paragraphs went straight into his native language. 'I think that Pushkin's prose construction is entirely French. I mean French of the eighteenth century,' he wrote in 1849 to his Russian friend, S.A. Sobolevsky, '... I sometimes wonder whether you boyars do not first think in French before writing in Russian.'

At the same time, Pushkin's debt to France was much more than a purely linguistic one. His immediate experience of French classical literature and his indirect experience of the culture of the pre-revolutionary French aristocracy as it found reflection in contemporary Russian society probably contributed much to that formal grace and that classically aristocratic spirit which are perhaps the distinguishing features of Pushkin's mature style.*

It is perhaps also worth noting at this point that Pushkin's knowledge of German was comparatively slight and, unlike many subsequent Russian nineteenth-century literary figures, he was not influenced to any significant extent either by the ideas or by the style of the German metaphysicians whose writings contributed so much towards shaping the cast of the Russian intellect during the second quarter of the century. To be more precise, he seems to have been actively hostile to this influence. 'You reproach me concerning *The Moscow Messenger* and German metaphysics,' he wrote to Delvig in March 1827. 'God knows how much I hate and despise the latter, but what can one do?...'

In any event, whatever the precise origins of Pushkin's style, its essential characteristics are clearly marked and remain constant through all the vicissitudes of the poet's literary career and through all the many genres in which his work appeared. As Maurice Bowra put it:

> Pushkin is in fact a classical writer... Pushkin's Russian was largely confined to the language of educated people and conformed almost inevitably to the standards of elegance which the eighteenth century had sanctified... Of course, he made many inventions and greatly enriched the language of poetry, but he remains a classical poet in his finish, his neatness, his balance, his restraint.

---

* In his book on Pushkin written while he was in England in the 1920s Mirsky suggests that 'on the whole the French have failed to appreciate Pushkin's work, probably for the very reason that he excelled them in all the qualities which they regard as peculiarly their own'!

INTRODUCTION

The same point had been made earlier by Maurice Baring in his Introduction to the *Oxford Book of Russian Verse* (1925):

> As to his form, his qualities as an artist can be summed up in one word, he is a classic. Classic in the same way that the Greeks are classic.

Russian critics of Pushkin also share this view. Turgenev is by no means alone in speaking (in the lecture reproduced in the present volume) of Pushkin's 'classical sense of proportion and harmony'.

It is clear too that Pushkin himself was consciously guided by these classical stylistic canons. 'True taste', he writes, for instance, in a note published in 1827, 'consists not in the instinctive rejection of this or that word or turn of phrase but in a sense of proportion and appropriateness'. And two years earlier we read in his unpublished essay *On Classical and Romantic Poetry:* '... a difficulty overcome always brings us pleasure – that of loving the measure and harmony characteristic of the human intellect.' 'Precision and brevity' Pushkin considered 'the most important qualities of prose', and in a draft note of 1826 the poet describes 'calm' (which he contrasts with ecstasy) as 'an absolute condition for beauty'.

Associated with this predilection for cool simplicity, harmony and elegance – this geometrical quality of mind – was a wonderfully light touch. More than any other writer in the history of Russian literature (Lermontov is perhaps his only rival), Pushkin possessed that facility of genius, the ability to make the most complex exercise appear easy. No better illustration of this supreme gift exists than *Evgenii Onegin* in which the intricately structured fourteen-lined stanzas flow and dance with an apparently total ease and naturalness. In this, as in other respects, the comparison of Pushkin's poetry with the music of Mozart is still as valid as it is familiar. At the same time Pushkin was of course highly intelligent, in the sense of possessing an agile analytical brain, and the combination of this sharp mind with his sense of elegance and light touch inevitably found expression in those flashes of wit with which both his verse and his prose abound.

Pushkin's powers of observation, insight and analysis are almost proverbial (indeed some of his lines have become proverbs) and this gift is reflected in that universal responsiveness and comprehension which have attracted comment from Russian critics. Had he been born thirty years later and been brought up in a different intellectual climate, Pushkin's talent for insight and analysis might have developed like Tolstoy's but, a true child of his age, Pushkin's response to the world was primarily an aesthetic one. The day when the artist would be a preacher, a rebel, or even a pervert had not yet arrived. Tomashevsky, arguing against the common tendency to 'interpret' Pushkin, explains in an essay included in the present volume that 'for Pushkin himself every thought was to be judged as an artistic theme, from the point of view of its aesthetic potential.' It was not literature's function, according to Pushkin, to serve moral or didactic ends. 'The aim of poetry is poetry', he wrote to Zhukovsky in 1825 and repeated the same view in a review essay published six years later: 'Poetry which by its higher and free nature should have no goal other than itself...' Critics too, Pushkin asserted, should be motivated, not by a variety of extra-literary considerations, but by a pure love of art and by the disinterested desire to discover the beauties and blemishes in works of literature. Even if a little evidence exists that towards the end of his life Pushkin was adopting a morally less neutral attitude towards literature, it still remains incontrovertible that his aesthetic sensibility remained, as always, far stronger than any moral impulse and that this quality, more than anything else, distinguishes him from the vast majority of Russian writers. 'He possessed', opined Tolstoy in a conversation of 1900 recorded by A. Goldenweiser, 'a more highly developed feeling for beauty than anyone else.'

This amalgam of a classical sense of form, a light touch, a sparkling wit and a highly developed aesthetic sense, which together with his self-confidence make Pushkin a truly aristocratic writer, also mark the poet off from the subsequent Russian nineteenth and twentieth-century literary tradition. Pushkin – perhaps the last of the great European aristocratic poets – belongs to a past age in a way that Tolstoy and Dostoevsky, for instance, do not, and the further that age recedes into the past, the more difficult is the task of comprehending its spirit, and the harder it becomes to appreciate Pushkin on his own terms.

In spite of all this, however, most literate Russians regard Pushkin as their national poet. This judgment often comes as a surprise to even the educated Western European who is likely to be far more familiar with the novels of Tolstoy and Dostoevsky or the plays of Chekhov than with any of Pushkin's works; indeed, he may well have come across the latter's name only in connection with Tchaikovsky's operas.

It is of course hard for foreigners to explain with any confidence what a poet means to his compatriots, but some attempt should be made to understand a little of what Russians appear to have in mind when they think of Pushkin, 'Russia's first love', in the words of Tyutchev.

Pushkin's right to the title of Russia's national poet is justified perhaps primarily by his unique ability to evoke deep emotional responses from the Russian heart. For Russians Pushkin is something very special, possessing qualities which, they feel, only a Russian can fully appreciate. As for instance an anonymous commentator quoted in *The Sunday Times* put it, 'You English cannot know what Pushkin is for us. He is our pride, our hope and our love'.

At the beginning of his essay on Pushkin, included below, Alexander Blok emphasises that the very name of Pushkin evokes pleasant sensations. In spite of the dark aspects which can be found in his work, Russians appear to associate Pushkin above all else with gaiety, sunshine, springtime and childhood innocence; he evokes in them visions of a lost golden age when life was simpler and happier. Russians turn to him for confirmation of their hopes and for support in their sorrows, since he provides a joyful counter to both the harsh reality of Russian life and the Russian tendency to indulge in gloomy speculations. It is no coincidence that Pasternak's hero, Yurii Zhivago, for instance, sheltering in Varykino from the horrors of the Russian Revolution and Civil War, should attempt to renew his faith in life by constantly rereading Pushkin, whose optimism, openness and almost childlike directness he contrasts with the morbid introspection of Gogol, Tolstoy and Dostoevsky.

It is clear from the essays in the present collection that Russian critics (and among them perhaps most notably Gogol, Belinsky and Turgenev) tend to discuss Pushkin's status as the Russian national poet under two main headings: first, the poet's stature in comparison with the literary giants of other nations, and second, Pushkin's undisputed ability to express in his work what might be called the essence of the Russian national spirit.

Many Russian critics argue that Pushkin is the Russian equivalent of other acknowledged national poets* such as Dante, Shakespeare and Goethe. Like them, it is true, he assimilated previous literary traditions and achievements, added to these his own unique genius and laid the foundations for subsequent literary developments in his homeland. He forged much of the modern Russian literary language, set an unsurpassed (indeed largely unemulated) aesthetic standard and introduced a tone of universal sympathy. Numerous Russian men of letters – including writers as diverse in their style and spirit as Gogol and Turgenev, Tolstoy and Dostoevsky, or Bunin and Zamyatin – have testified to their indebtedness to Pushkin and their admiration for him. Turgenev even went so far as to proclaim that he would have sacrificed all his own works to have written a certain four of the poet's lines. Pushkin has clearly been an extraordinarily rich source of inspiration for his Russian literary successors – but it does not necessarily follow from this (as some Russian critics are wont to maintain) that without him there would have been, for instance, no Tolstoy and no Dostoevsky.

If Pushkin's stature *within* the Russian context cannot be disputed, it is by no means obvious that *outside* this context he possesses the same power to move the minds and hearts of men of other nations as do his supreme international rivals – or even as do the greatest of his Russian literary heirs. The argument that Pushkin loses more than they do in translation is not fully convincing: after all the highly individual poetry of Homer, Dante, Shakespeare and Goethe survived even that ordeal. What Pushkin appears to lack in comparison with them is the weight and the obvious originality of the greatest minds. Interestingly enough, the more cosmopolitan of the Russian commentators, such as Turgenev, Solovyov or Mirsky, for example, tend to be less pretentious in their assertions about Pushkin's international status. And indeed a claim like Stepanov's that '*The Captain's Daughter* occupies a prime position in world literature', by distracting attention from Pushkin's individual Russian genius, may do the poet more of a disservice than Mirsky's superficially

---

* Debates conducted in Russian about Pushkin's status as a national poet are liable to become complex, if not confused, because of the semantic range of the two Russian adjectives *natsional'nyi* and *narodnyi*. The latter in particular creates problems of comprehension (and translation) because in various contexts it refers to at least three distinct but overlapping concepts: (i) the nation as a symbolic entity; (ii) the population of the nation as a whole; or (iii) the simple working masses, or 'folk'.

harsh judgment that 'on the scale of world history Pushkin does not mark a new step forward'.

For the majority of Russians, however – critics and ordinary readers alike – the necessarily inconclusive debate about Pushkin's achievements in comparison with those of Shakespeare or Goethe is largely irrelevant. For them Pushkin is 'the father of Russian literature', 'the founder of the Russian literary language', and, most important, the writer who, apart from possessing a captivating aura of gaiety and innocence, embodies for Russians the essence of their national spirit.

Gogol's assessment of Pushkin as the Russian national poet in this sense of the term has rarely been disputed:

> The countryside, soul, language and character of Russia are reflected in him with the purity and the spotless perfection with which a landscape is reflected through the convex surface of a lens... From the very first he was a national poet because the true expression of national spirit rests not in the description of peasant costume, but in the very spirit of the people.

In spite of the strong French influence to which he was subjected in his upbringing – or perhaps that influence paradoxically provided a firm platform and an appropriate perspective from which he could observe Russia – Pushkin heard the Russian language and saw Russian life with an unprecedented and unsurpassed clarity.

Of course the time was ripe for this achievement. At the beginning of the nineteenth century the belated development of a Russian national consciousness was starting to gather pace. A growing national pride which had been boosted by Russia's role in the defeat of Napoleon coincided with the fashionable predilection of the European romantic movement for examining each nation's historical roots and cultural heritage. Born at the very end of the eighteenth century, Pushkin was both a product of this new national spirit in Russia and a leading contributor to it in the field of literature.

Russian eighteenth-century literature could boast of little that was purely Russian: like the rest of Russian aristocratic culture, it limped behind European fashions, aping European genres, conventions, poses and idioms. With Pushkin Russian literature suddenly found a new life. 'In his verses', wrote Dobrolyubov, 'we heard for the first time the living Russian language and saw for the first time our authentic Russian world'.

Like a new Adam, Pushkin looked upon Russian life with a penetrating and apparently innocent eye and described his visions with a freshness and vigour which still charm today. Many of his depictions and insights became *topoi,* not only for subsequent Russian writers, but for countless ordinary readers, who find their own experiences in Pushkin and see the world through Pushkinian spectacles. A vivid account of this process is provided in Bunin's novel *Arsenev's Life.* In a chapter devoted to describing the impact of Pushkin on his youthful imagination, the semi-autobiographical narrator cites various verses from the poet which struck deep chords within him and emphasises the intimate correspondence between his own reactions and Pushkin's lines: 'How many emotions he evoked in me! And how often my own emotions and everything amidst which and by which I lived found a companion in him!'

Russian readers of Pushkin are struck by both the range and the depth of the poet's understanding of Russian life. In a famous judgment for which Pisarev took him to task Belinsky described *Evgenii Onegin* as 'an encyclopedia of Russian life'. Pisarev is right when he points out that Pushkin almost completely ignores the political and economic realities of the day, the vital concerns of the peasantry and the growing urban middle class, and the many serious intellectual debates conducted during the period the work describes, but in spite of this Belinsky's remark is far from absurd: the poet's novel in verse provides an astonishingly full gallery of contemporary portraits, interiors and landscapes, a lively account of numerous Russian habits, customs and beliefs, and an accurate record of the way many ordinary Russians of the day lived and thought. More important than this documentary quality of *Evgenii Onegin,* however, is of course Pushkin's magical facility for discerning in Russian life and embodying in a brilliant literary form those features which strike fellow Russians (his readers) as both quintessentially typical and touchingly poetic.

The same facility informs not only Pushkin's other works set in contemporary Russia (including his lyrics), but also the works he set in historical times, whether in dramatic form *(Boris Godunov),* in verse *(The Bronze Horseman),* or in prose *(The Captain's Daughter).* Here the poet recreates, in a wholly convincing way for Russians, not merely the events but, more profoundly, the underlying essence and the enduring spirit of the Russian past.

INTRODUCTION

Pushkin's appreciation of the Russian national spirit is for Russians further demonstrated by the poet's feeling for the Russian folk tradition, elements from which figure prominently *inter alia* in the early *Ruslan and Lyudmila* and the later fairy-tales in verse.

In discussions of the latter (as, for example, in Slonimsky's essay in the present volume) Russian critics usually refer to the poet's nanny, Arina Rodionovna, from whom much of the poet's knowledge of Russian folklore is said to derive and who, more generally, provided the boy Pushkin with his first insights into the nature of the ordinary uneducated Russians who formed the vast bulk of the country's population. Soviet critics, who for political reasons must exaggerate Pushkin's alleged sympathies with the 'broad masses', have naturally given particular prominence to Arina Rodionovna's role in the poet's development – sometimes to the extent that she has seemed to bear on her frail shoulders almost the entire weight of Pushkin's Russianness.

The subject-matter, settings and inspiration of Pushkin's works are, however, clearly not exclusively Russian: indeed, in his creative sympathies the poet ranges so widely that some Russian critics extol primarily his universal responsiveness, his ability to comprehend and recreate the atmosphere and spirit of other peoples, present and past. Critics who recognise and value this gift but also want to preserve their image of Pushkin as an incarnation of the Russian national spirit are then driven to the curious and highly dubious argument propounded in the present volume most passionately by Dostoevsky. This argument – a plain assertion that a single exceptional case is also typical – maintains that precisely a spirit of universality is the uniquely Russian virtue and achievement; in other words, Pushkin, we have to believe, in both his obvious Russianness and in his obvious non-Russianness is being equally Russian!

Pushkin's own opinions of his Russian homeland, like his literary roots and inspirations, were characteristically complex. On the one hand he seemed to feel an almost maternal affection for his country's language, its culture, its history and its destiny, but on the other he could write of his utter contempt – as in his letter to Vyazemsky of May, 1826:

> Of course I despise my country from head to toe, but I am irritated when a foreigner shares my view. How

can you, who are free to go wherever you like, stay in Russia? If the Tsar grants me *freedom,* I won't stay a month. We live in miserable times, but when I imagine London, railways, steamships, English journals or the theatres and brothels of Paris, my remote Mikhailovskoe induces in me a sense of melancholy and rage.

Pushkin's relationship with the Tsar and his attitude to the institution of autocracy were ambivalent and he expressed at various times during his comparatively short life liberal (if not revolutionary) and conservative (not to say reactionary) views. But Pushkin was not really a political animal; he was above all and *par excellence* an artist and it is to his art rather than his politics that attention must be directed.

The central paradox of Pushkin's art remains the unique and remarkable relationship between its form and its content: even those works which strike his compatriots as quintessentially Russian are couched in a style which, perhaps French in inspiration, is markedly un-Russian in its formal elegance. It might seem hardly unfair to claim that Pushkin's works are Russian *in spite of* their form, or that, conversely, they are un-Russian *in spite of* their content; and indeed at least tacit support can be given to such a formulation both by those many critics who discuss the subject matter of Pushkin's works without reference to their form and by those (far rarer in Russia) who analyse the poet's formal structures and devices while ignoring his content. Pushkin's supreme artistic achievement, however, must be seen to be his masterly integration of these two disparate elements to create a wondrous higher harmony and unity. It is a harmony and unity which make Pushkin's work neither Russian nor (let us say) French, but something greater than both, and in responding to his work the reader is moved not only by its Russianness or its Frenchness, not only by its content or its form, taken separately, not only by any individual component elements (intellect or emotion, wit or worship, purity or ribaldry), but above all by that all-embracing aesthetic balance of great classical art which soothes and uplifts because it reminds man of his lost hopes and ideals and provides an earnest of their possible realisation.

Gogol's celebrated remark that Pushkin 'represents a stage to which Russians will have developed in perhaps 200 years' time' is now annoying in its narrow chauvinism and poignant in its

INTRODUCTION

naivety: Pushkin's work represents universal aesthetic ideals, but ideals whose fulfilment is in the modern world becoming ever less likely. On the other hand, as these ideals of harmony and elegance lose their former power over the minds of men, those who still value them turn with greater love and gratitude to Pushkin.

'Literature exists in our country, but criticism still does not', wrote Pushkin in a note of 1829, and the same complaint regularly recurs in the poet's jottings and correspondence throughout the last decade of his short life. Indeed, although Pushkin achieved literary fame during his lifetime, Russian criticism of the poet scarcely began until after his death. Perhaps only two influential essays were produced before the 1840s, Ivan Kireevsky's *Something about the Character of Pushkin's Poetry*, which appeared in *The Moscow Messenger* in 1828, and Gogol's *A Few Words on Pushkin* which was published six years later. (The latter essay is given in its entirety in the present collection). Both essayists strove to sketch the general characteristics of Pushkin's poetry and in so doing stressed several points from which few subsequent critics were to dissent. Kireevsky, having deplored the lack of critical attention devoted to his subject, traces Pushkin's development from a poet of the Italo-French school, through a period of Byronism to his being a thoroughly Russian poet, loved by his compatriots, reflecting their life in his work, and in step with his day and age. Gogol too celebrates Pushkin's Russianness and at the same time the poet's brilliant technical versatility and his supremely refined poetic sensibility. Pushkin's short lyrics, Gogol claims, are a touchstone for the aesthetic sensitivity of every reader.

Any outline of the development of Pushkin criticism in Russia must acknowledge the value and influence of these two essays, but the principle credit for initiating the subsequent tradition indisputably belongs to Belinsky, the originator of the dominant radical or civic tendency in Russian criticism. With his eleven essays on Pushkin written in the mid-1840s Belinsky provided an extensive evaluation of the poet which has been taken into account by almost every later Russian critic and which also remains to this day a valuable contribution in its own right. The critic places Pushkin in his historical context, seeing him as indebted to the Russian poets who preceded him but as immeasurably superior to them in artistic genius; he comments on the range, power and charm of Pushkin's language and on the poet's universal but primarily aesthetic responsiveness; like Gogol and Kireevsky before him, he stresses Pushkin's realism and Russianness but insists in addition that in spite of his predominantly aesthetic concerns Pushkin is unwittingly a highly moral writer; at the same time, however, Belinsky comments that the poet belonged to a school of art (the conservative, contemplative, classical tradition) whose day was already finished. If Pushkin's chief merit, among many, lay in his supreme artistry, his chief demerit for Belinsky lay in his lack of social and political commitment. (Extracts from Belinsky's fifth essay on Pushkin are given below).

In subsequent years many Russian literary debates were to revolve round this last point: should the artist in general be a devotee of art for the sake of art, or should he be a standard-bearer in the struggle for social and political reform? And should Pushkin in particular be honoured or rebuked for his aesthetic stance?

Both points of view found expression during the 1850s and 1860s. Three of the leading non-radical critics, Annenkov, Druzhinin and Dudyshkin strongly defended the ideal of pure art and praised Pushkin for his aesthetic leanings and his harmoniousness. The most significant work produced by this camp was probably Annenkov's *Materials for Pushkin's Biography* (1855), the first attempt to provide a full picture of the poet's life and work. (An extract from this book is given below).

Among the radical intelligentsia, on the other hand, Pushkin was held in lower esteem during this period than Gogol – who was then regarded as primarily a social satirist, intent on exposing the evils of Russian society. Herzen, who linked Pushkin with the Decembrist movement and credited him with reflecting, at least indirectly, the repressive atmosphere of Nicholas I's Russia, was the most favourably disposed towards the poet; Chernyshevsky and Dobrolyubov took a middle path; while the most violent reaction came from the nihilist theoretician, Pisarev, who dismissed Pushkin as completely irrelevant to the needs of the day and even took issue with Belinsky, arguing that Pushkin was no great artist and certainly not a humanist. (Herzen, Dobrolyubov and Pisarev are all represented in this volume).

The great mid-nineteenth-century debate in Russian intellectual society between the Westernists and the Slavophiles was, perhaps surprisingly, not clearly reflected in Pushkin criticism. The Westernist radical critics naturally approved of

Pushkin's links with the culture of Western Europe, but they also joined with Slavophiles like Grigoriev and Dostoevsky (both of whom are represented below) in extolling the Russian quality of Pushkin's work. The Slavophiles tended to lay more emphasis than the Westernists on Pushkin's apparent empathy with the life of the ordinary people, but neither camp tried to claim the poet as exclusively its own, and the opinion expressed by Grigoriev that 'Pushkin is neither a Westernist nor a Slavophile' broadly remained the standard view of Russian critics of all persuasions.

The middle and late 1860s and the whole decade of the 1870s was a period of extraordinary political, social and economic ferment in Russia, and during these years Russian literature tended to concentrate to an unprecedented degree on the burning issues of the day, the effects of Emancipation and the other reforms of the 1860s, the industrialisation of Russia, education, socialism, the role of women in society, etc., etc. In this atmosphere Pushkin inevitably appeared almost irrelevant, and for some fifteen years comparatively little critical attention was paid to him, though devotees like Turgenev and Strakhov made sure he was not completely forgotten. The latter published a series of essays on Pushkin during this period, extolling the poet as the 'chief treasure of our literature'. For instance, his essay of 1867 with that title opens (echoing Grigoriev's pronouncement, 'Pushkin is our all') with the provocative assertion: 'Our literature is meagre, but we do have Pushkin'.

An important turning-point in the history of Russia's view of Pushkin came in June 1880 when the erection of a monument to the poet in Moscow brought him quite literally back into the public eye. (The project had first been mooted almost twenty years earlier, on the twenty-fifth anniversary of the poet's death in 1862). The two key addresses delivered at the accompanying ceremonies by Turgenev and Dostoevsky (both included in the present volume) did much to revive the Russian cult of Pushkin which had been destroyed by the onslaughts of the nihilists of the 1860s. Turgenev paid tribute to Pushkin's artistic genius and then, true to his Westernist liberal ideals, proclaimed the poet a teacher of moral enlightenment and individual liberation. Dostoevsky, now a militant religious nationalist, asserted that Pushkin's 'universal' qualities were typically Russian and extolled the poet as an expression of the finest qualities of the Russian spirit and as a herald of the messianic destiny of his homeland. As so often in the history of Pushkin criticism, both before and after

1880, these two speeches are ultimately more revealing about the critic than about the poet himself, but they served, nevertheless, to set a common seal of approval on Pushkin which could be accepted by both liberals and conservatives. In any event, the revival of interest in Pushkin during the 1880s found expression in biographies and other studies of the poet which began to appear in considerable quantities.

The late 1880s and the 1890s witnessed the development in Russia of a reaction against many of the trends which had dominated Russian literature and thought since the 1830s. Many non-Marxist Russian thinkers, rejecting the prevailing materialist, positivist and utilitarian trend, turned again to religion and, in many cases, expressed their misgivings about the ideals and aims of the political left.. In literature the symbolists emphasised the primacy of aesthetic over moral considerations, cultivated poetry rather than prose and proclaimed the artist's right to express his purely subjective experiences without reference to any social or political philosophy. The recently revived interest in Pushkin increased further as his values, interpreted by some of the most stimulating minds of the day, were shown – with varying degrees of success – to be appropriate in this new atmosphere. Minsky praised Pushkin's allegedly impartial acceptance of good and evil; Merezhkovsky extolled the poet as a champion of spiritual aristocracy, while Solovyov (opposed to Merezhkovsky) tried to include Pushkin within the framework of his own religious philosophy, stressing that divinely inspired beauty – which was manifest in Pushkin's supreme achievements – was inextricably linked with goodness and truth and would eventually lead mankind to the kingdom of God. (Extracts from essays by both Merezhkovsky and Solovyov are given in this volume). The symbolist poets, Bryusov, Bely, Ivanov and Blok, all studied Pushkin deeply and expressed their findings in memorable publications. Blok's address of 1921, *The Poet's Role,* is included in the present volume. In this same turn-of-the-century mould are the impressionist critic Aikhenvald and the social philosopher Gershenzon, both of whom are also represented by essays in the present collection.

The centenary of the poet's birth in 1899 helped to maintain the literate public's interest in Pushkin. 1899 and the years immediately following saw a marked increase in the number of publications devoted to Pushkin's life and work and also witnessed the institution of various academic projects which eventually came together in the Academy of Sciences' Pushkin House, which was founded in 1905.(Shestov's essay in the present collection was written for this Pushkin centenary).

Not that no voices were raised against the growing cult of Pushkin. The adherents of Futurism – a modernist poetic movement founded in 1910 under the leadership of Khlebnikov – called for the rejection of the entire Russian cultural heritage. In their 1912 manifesto, entitled *A Slap in the Face of Public Taste,* the futurists (who included Mayakovsky among their number at this time) recommended that Pushkin, together with Tolstoy and Dostoevsky, be 'thrown overboard from the steamship of modernity.'

At the same time the pre-revolutionary Russian Marxists naturally found little inspiration in Pushkin. Plekhanov, it is true, defended the poet's aesthetic leanings as progressive in their time, but pointed out, quite fairly, that the working masses, i.e. the peasant serfs, meant nothing to Pushkin. Lenin, who analysed Tolstoy quite perceptively and used the great novelist to illustrate various social and economic theses, made almost no public pronouncements about Pushkin, though it is known that he enjoyed the poetry in his private life. Marxist criticism made few serious contributions to Pushkin scholarship until the 1920s.

For all its determination to bring about a radical transformation of Russian society – and indeed ultimately of human nature – the Soviet regime which came to power in October 1917 had no intention of rejecting in its entirety the cultural heritage of the Russian past. As early as December 1917 the decision was taken to promote cheap editions of the Russian nineteenth-century classics and in August of the following year it was resolved that in the main cities of the new republic monuments should be erected to the great scientists and artists of the past, including Pushkin. At the same time, however, the cultural heritage of Tsarist Russia was to point forward rather than back; it had to play its part in the building of a new society. 'Preserving the heritage', wrote Lenin in subsequently oft-quoted words, 'does not imply limiting oneself by that heritage'.

An agreed Soviet view of Pushkin did not emerge overnight. Throughout the 1920s a range of attitudes continued to find expression. At one end of the political spectrum adherents of the old order who had not emigrated continued (at least during the early years of the decade) to propound the views earlier associated with Dostoevsky or with the symbolist poets and idealist philosophers tf the turn of the century; they stressed Pushkin's aesthetic preoccupations, individualism and alleged fatalism. At the opposite political extreme the most fanatical supporters of the new regime *(plus bolcheviste que les bolcheviques)*, most notably the aggressively proletarian writers of the *Proletkult* movement, argued that much of the nineteenth-century literary heritage, including Pushkin's works, was at best useless and at worst actively harmful in the new era.

Two non-political schools which enjoyed a brief flowering in the Soviet Union during the 1920s and brought their doctrines to bear on Pushkin were the Freudian psychologists and the formalist critics. The leading representative of the former was Professor I.D. Ermakov, who in his *Studies in the Psychology of Pushkin's Works* (1923) predictably asserted that Pushkin's primary source of both knowledge and poetic inspiration was erotic experience. The formalist critics concentrated, as their appellation indicates, on the formal qualities of works of literature which they regarded primarily as coagmentations of linguistic devices. This emphasis on form rather than content certainly provided (temporarily) a healthy counterbalance to the tendencies of the main civic tradition of Russian criticism and produced valuable insights into the workings of the Russian literary mind. The formalist school is represented in the present collection by essays of Eikhenbaum and Shklovsky.

At the same time, the serious academic study of Pushkin on the traditional lines followed before the revolution by scholars like Vengerov and Modzalevsky was pursued in the 1920s by critics such as Tomashevsky (represented in the present volume by his excellent, eminently sane essay, *Interpreting Pushkin*) who concentrated on the comparatively unspectacular tasks of careful, detailed research and the editing of texts.

Inevitably the doctrines of Marxism-Leninism exercised a decisive influence on the emergent Soviet school of Pushkin criticism. The chief exponent of Marxian literary criticism in the 1920s was undoubtedly A.V. Lunacharsky, who from 1917 to 1929 occupied the position of People's Commissar for Education in the R.S.F.S.R. His extensive writings included articles on Pushkin. In one of the earliest of these, *Alexander Sergeevich Pushkin* (1922), Lunacharsky propounded the view which was to become a *datum* for all future Soviet Marxist critics – that Pushkin was both a literary giant of world stature ('What was done in Italy by Dante and Petrarch, in France by the giants of the seventeenth century, and in Germany by Lessing, Schiller and Goethe – was done for us by Pushkin') and a turning point in the history of Russia ('In Pushkin the nobleman there awoke not his class – though that class to some extent laid its mark on him – but the people, the nation, the language and historical destiny'). Two significant works of Marxian Pushkin criticism from this early period – when various attempts were made to define Pushkin's class position – were Blagoi's books, *Pushkin's Class-consciousness* (1927) and *The Sociology of Pushkin's Work* (1929), though both of these were subsequently condemned as manifestations of a 'vulgar sociological approach'.

The main lines of Soviet Pushkin criticism were laid down in the early thirties, when the official view of the role of literature in the country was formulated. It is perhaps worth recalling the definition of socialist realism agreed on at the first All-Union Congress of Soviet Writers in 1934.

> Socialist realism which is the basic method of Soviet literature and *literary criticism* [our itals. eds.] requires of the artist a truthful, historically concrete depiction of life in its revolutionary development. At the same time this truthful and historically concrete depiction of reality must be combined with the task of ideologically refashioning and educating the workers in the spirit of socialism...

Two of the characteristic tendencies of Soviet critics – to set Pushkin in his historical context and to present accumulations of detailed information – are directly motivated by the injunction with which this formula opens, while the goal propounded in the second half of the formula is perhaps responsible for the peculiarly impersonal, journalistically didactic tone of much Soviet critical writing.

1934 saw the publication in the Academy of Sciences *Literary Heritage* series of a massive volume (No. 16–18) containing 1000 double-columned pages devoted exclusively to Pushkin. This was an impressive attempt to set out the results of Soviet Pushkin scholarship up to that time and to state policy for the future. Two contributions to this volume are included in the present collection, Vinogradov's *Pushkin's Style* and Mirsky's *The Problem of Pushkin,* which later suffered censure for its provocative and unflattering remarks about Pushkin's allegedly obsequious attitude towards Nicholas I and his court.

The middle and late 1930s witnessed a remarkable increase in the quantity of Soviet publications devoted to Pushkin, many of which were meant to mark the centenary of the poet's death in 1837. The first volume of the massive *Complete Works of Pushkin* (Academic Edition in 17 volumes), for instance, was issued in 1937. (The final volume of this edition appeared in 1949 on the 150th anniversary of the poet's birth). Three items included in the present collection also first appeared at this time, those by Lezhnev, Shklovsky and Vinokur.

Tragically – and by a wicked irony of fate – the Pushkin Centenary celebrations coincided with the height of Stalin's Great Purge which resulted in the arrest and subsequent imprisonment or execution of thousands of Soviet intellectuals, including two of the critics represented in the present volume, Lezhnev and Mirsky.

The second world war inevitably brought the rapidly expanding Pushkin industry to an almost complete standstill, and the bleak early post-war years provided only a slightly more favourable atmosphere for intellectual work. The already severely limited freedom enjoyed by Soviet scholars in general was still further restricted; Pushkin's commentators in particular were hampered by the obligation imposed on them by the political authorities to ignore Pushkin's connections with Western Europe and to portray him as even more of a Russian nationalist than he had been depicted in the 1930s. Only after the death of Stalin in 1953 did Soviet scholars begin again to publish any significant studies of Pushkin on a large scale.

From the mid-1950s critical works on the poet have rolled from Soviet presses in a steady stream. Modern Soviet critics of Pushkin – represented in the present collection by Stepanov, Slonimsky and Blagoi – are indisputably competent scholars. Their factual knowledge of Pushkiniana, often based on the cumulative research of previous years, is sound and extensive, they rarely indulge in unfounded speculations, and their writings are careful, detailed, well-documented and more relaxed in tone than those of earlier decades. It is sad that they are generally marked also by a characteristically Soviet heaviness and a most un-Pushkinian solemnity which informs and instructs but seldom inspires. Belinsky's prophecy that Pushkin would become a classic has been fulfilled in the U.S.S.R. He is a classic who has become an institution, surrounded by ritual expressions of homage and respect, but fortunately also a classic who can be read and enjoyed without the aid of his accompanying critical tradition.

In an essay on Pushkin, *Our Literature's Greatest Treasure,* written as long ago as 1867, Strakhov commented on the wide gulf separating Pushkin from all but the very best of his critics:

> You are struck here above all by the immense disproportion between the object of these opinions and the abilities and methods of the critics. On the one hand you see a huge, profound figure reaching to infinity, a figure reflecting the eternal beauty of the human soul and embodying its ceaseless striving; on the other you see men with microscopically narrow and blind views and with impossibly short rulers and compasses which are supposed to measure and evaluate this great figure. These men are obviously quite unequipped to cope with the task they have set themselves. And that is why their efforts – bold and self-satisfied, but in practice impossible and absurd – produce an impression of madness.

Even if this passage represents an extreme view, an exaggerated appraisal of Pushkin's genius on the one hand and an unjustifiably sweeping condemnation of the critics on the other, Strakhov nevertheless puts his finger on a crucial point which is still valid today, namely that many critical essays on Pushkin are unsatisfying because of a fundamental inequality between poet and critic.

It goes without saying that great writers and their readers or critics are rarely complete equals and no-one expects them to be, but some writers clearly presuppose a less unequal relationship with their audience and a more active participation from them than do others. In this respect Pushkin is very demanding. Whereas Tolstoy and Dostoevsky, for instance, thrust themselves upon the reader (the former by openly hectoring, the latter by slyly insinuating himself) Pushkin is neither frustratingly coy nor crudely overbearing, but direct and straightforward. Of course the aristocratic Pushkin maintains a polite distance between himself and his readers – he is light and elegant, reticent and ironical – but the reader is treated as an equal, as a sensitive, cultivated, informed, intelligent and well-mannered fellow-member of polite society. This means that the reader must make an effort: as in any equal relationship, he must play his part in the process of communication by bringing to it his own knowledge and experience; he must be both sensitively receptive and capable of active response. The passive reader gets little from Pushkin.

The reader who cannot match Pushkin's demands will fail to appreciate him fully – and that is the end of the matter. The critic, however, who cannot respond as an equal to Pushkin, who cannot match Pushkin's experiences or spirit, may nevertheless still feel obliged to write about him – but he will not be able to write with that confidence which comes only from being able both to comprehend an object in its totality and to penetrate to its inner core. In a word, his writing will inevitably and obviously lack authority.*

Indeed it is precisely authority which is missing from the bulk of Pushkin criticism, and its absence is perhaps most clearly reflected in those typical approaches which recur with depressing frequency in essays of both the previous and the present century. Over and over again one meets the following: vague general outlines of the poet's life and work or of aspects of them; wide eulogies (which are often composed largely of familiar and oft-repeated superlatives); loose comparisons of Pushkin with some European writer without any close analysis of either; summaries of the findings of previous researches; attacks on the opinions of other critics; and detailed discussions of trivial minor points. Another commonly encountered but more ambitious tendency, reminiscent of varieties of biblical exegesis, is that of employing carefully selected quotations from Pushkin in order to demonstrate that the poet held certain views, usually those of the critic himself, or – worse still – those of the critic's ideological mentors. All these approaches share in common the failure to come directly to grips with Pushkin and his work.

If these typical practices stem from an apparent lack of *intellectual* authority, another common tendency would seem to result from an ironic failure of *aesthetic* response: no-one who had

---

* At the same time, the magnitude of the critic's task should not be underestimated. Ideally he is required to play two roles which normally are mutually exclusive, those of lover and arbiter. Emotionally he should become deeply involved with the work of art, while intellectually viewing it quite dispassionately. Without emotional involvement his judgments are likely to be dry; without impartial analysis his reactions may well be unbalanced.

INTRODUCTION xxiii

truly caught and been infected* by the wonderfully light and beautifully balanced Pushkinian spirit could unselfconsciously indulge in the incongruous absurdity of discussing the poet in articles or books of interminable length, elephantine weight and unrelieved earnestness. Some of the most depressing examples of this practice have emerged from the labours of what has been tellingly labelled 'the Pushkin industry' in the Soviet Union. (A monument to the best and the worst features of this sector is provided by the huge *Literary Heritage* volume 16–18 of 1934).

The long and heavy Russian critical article blossomed in the nineteenth century with the rise to literary dominance of the *raznochintsy*, the non-aristocratic, politically radical, somewhat provincial intelligentsia. Pushkin's own critical essays and those of his circle are as concise and polished as *The Tales of Belkin*, and it is not surprising that Prince Vyazemsky, for example, should have chided Belinsky *inter alia* for the prolixity of the latter's critical prose. Of course, the more intelligent and sensitive of the early radical or civic critics were keenly aware of the incongruity between Pushkin's light touch and their own heavy hands, but justified their unaesthetic approach on moral, social and political grounds. Chernyshevsky, for instance, explained:

> In order to disseminate among the public any, even the simplest and truest opinions, it is essential to express them very insistently and doggedly, with a passionately animated enthusiasm, without tiring of the repetitions which are boring for the critic himself but necessary for the mass public, without shunning a detailed analysis of books and opinions which are important only for their extrinsic significance, i.e. for their influence on the public rather than for their intrinsic interest as works of art...

Pushkin and his literary friends, Chernyshevsky continues, had no desire to communicate with a wide audience:

> They set themselves the goal of being satisfied with the quiet sympathy of a few readers whom they regarded as an elite and proudly considered that the quality of their audience compensated for its size.

---

* Tolstoy's term. Tolstoy, it will be recalled, defined critics as people who had *not* been infected by art.

Chernyshevsky's points are highly significant and still of relevance today. Between the early years and the middle of the nineteenth century Russia experienced, as Turgenev put it, a transition from a literary epoch to a political one, and the function and scope of both literature and literary criticism underwent a radical change. As moral and political concerns took priority over aesthetic preoccupations and prose superseded poetry as the principle vehicle for literary expression, literature came to be regarded – in the eyes of the radical intelligentsia at least – less as an art form and more as a weapon to be used in the struggle waged by the liberation movement. The principle role of literature, according to the influential civic critics, was to awaken the dormant social conscience of Russia, to enlighten the politically benighted populace and (in extreme cases) to call – as openly as the censorship permitted – for revolution.

Moreover, that political epoch whose beginning Turgenev dated in the 1830s or 1840s has not been supplanted. Indeed, in the USSR its characteristics are even more pronounced. That which in the nineteenth century was a freely chosen heretical stance has become the official policy of the state, with the consequence that literature and literary criticism are now officially *obliged* to pursue ultimately political goals. The aims which Pushkin criticism was to pursue in the USSR were clearly defined in the foreword '*From the Editors*' to the *Literary Heritage* volume 16–18 of 1934:

> Our task is to master everything in Pushkin's heritage which is healthy, vital and revolutionary, everything which can be used in building the culture of a classless society.

In other words, what has been demanded of Soviet critics is a uniform, partial and fundamentally non-aesthetic view of Pushkin which might serve non-literary ends, not a complete picture of the poet, ideological warts and all. Almost no-one could be less Soviet than Pushkin, yet in practice Soviet critics must constantly try to represent the individualistic, aesthetically-minded, French-educated aristocrat as something relevant to their contemporaries. Their admitted failure to produce a satisfactory biography of the poet on Marxist-Leninist principles ironically highlights the inner contradictions of this prescribed goal.

Professional literary critics are seldom either sensitive and original thinkers or experienced men of the world, and it will be a rare one who has the capacity to respond to Pushkin's work in that spirit of free equality which alone can be the basis of true comprehension and authoritative commentary. Much literary criticism in all languages is little more than (in the words of E.M. Forster) 'a higher form of gossip.' Not surprisingly, some of the most convincing writing on Pushkin has over the years stemmed less from critics and more from fellow writers or from men whose chief interest has lain outside the field of literature. Gogol, Turgenev, Dostoevsky and Blok, for instance, bring their personal experience of literature to their reading of Pushkin, and even their oddest views are expressed with an inner conviction which commands respect. Herzen writes about Pushkin, as he does about everything, with the authority of a powerful and balanced intellect married to a sensitive soul. Pisarev, whose professed respect for fine literature was minimal, stands in no awe of the poet and writes with a rarely equalled verve and sparkle, while the idealist philosophers Solovyov and Frank both produce – almost as casual asides from their main scholarly pursuits – essays on Pushkin which are memorable for their confident blend of clear-sightedness and sensitivity. In comparison with these essays the efforts of all but the very best of the professional critics (such as Belinsky – for all his long-windedness – or Tomashevsky) appear fragmentary, tangential and slightly superficial.

In the last analysis, of course, the gulf between Pushkin and his critics is above all further testimony to the poet's genius. Its existence also reaffirms that reading critical essays can never be a substitute for an immediate acquaintance with the original works of art. The primary purpose of the present volume is to provide an introduction to Russian *criticism* of Pushkin, but if in addition to this it inspires readers to turn again to the *works themselves* of Russia's national poet, the editors will have achieved a more important end.

GOGOL

A FEW WORDS ON PUSHKIN

N. V. Gogol (1809–52), one of the greatest of nineteenth-century Russian writers, is also perhaps the most enigmatic. The traditional view of him as the founder of the 'naturalist' school of literature – a view first expressed by Belinsky and still held by Soviet literary critics – is by no means a universal one. Other critics, particularly from the West but also from Russia, have seen Gogol as being the very opposite of a 'realist', concerned not with unmasking the social evils of Tsarist Russia but with projecting his own subjective fears and anxieties into the world around him. As the author of *Dead Souls*, *The Government-Inspector* and *The Overcoat*, however, his place in Russian literature is assured. In this article *A Few Words on Pushkin*, written in 1834 and published in the first part of his *Arabesques*, Gogol was the first writer to point to Pushkin's profound significance as a great and truly national poet.

When you hear the name of Pushkin the idea of a Russian national poet at once springs to mind. And indeed there is not a single one of our poets who is superior to him and who has a greater right to be called national: it is a right which is decidedly his. In him can be found, as if in a lexicon, all the rich diversity, strength and sensibility of our language. More than anyone else, it was he who widened its frontiers and showed us just how wide was its range. Pushkin is an extraordinary phenomenon – perhaps a unique manifestation of the Russian spirit: he represents a stage to which Russians will have developed in perhaps 200 years' time. The countryside, soul, language and character of Russia are reflected in him with the purity and the spotless perfection with which a landscape is reflected through the convex surface of a lens.

His biography is completely Russian. He has the delight in life and in freedom for which Russian people sometimes strive in moments of abstraction, a delight which revealed itself during his early years. Fate cast him, as if by design, to the borders of Russia, to that typically Russian majestic part of the country where Russia's uniform immensity is arrested by cloud-capped peaks and everywhere the presence of the South can be felt. He was deeply affected by the mighty, snow-covered ranges and warm, sunny valleys of the Caucasus; infused with the strength of its spirit, he broke through the last chains shackling the wings of his thought. The free, poetical way of life of the daring Caucasians, their skirmishes and swift, irresistible raids fascinated him; and he began to write with the power, swiftness and boldness which were to have such an impact on Russia, a Russia that was only just awakening to an awareness of literature. He depicts with lightning strokes the fight between the Chechen and the Cossack; the writing glistens with the gleam of swords and moves more swiftly than the battle itself. He alone is the poet of the Caucasus: his whole being is in love with it, radiates with the magnificent landscape, the southern sky, the beautiful valleys of Georgia and the magnificent nights and gardens of the Crimea. This is why perhaps his works contain that extra richness and fervour when he is writing about the south. He subconsciously poured all his strength into them, and this is why his works imbued with the spirit of the Caucasus, the untrammelled life of the Circassians and the Crimean nights had such a marvellous, magical power: even those people who lacked the taste and sufficient spiritual qualities to be able to understand them, were astonished by them. Audacity and daring are immediate qualities which inspire the hearts of everybody but especially of young people, who still thirst only after the unusual. There was not a single poet in Russia with such an enviable fate as Pushkin: no-one's fame spread as quickly. People took it upon themselves, both opportunely and inopportunely, to declaim, sometimes to mutilate, particularly scintillating extracts from his longer poems. There was already something electrifying about his name; and all the idler scribbler needed to do to ensure that his work was sold out was to put Pushkin's name to it.*

---

* A large number of absurd poems have appeared under Pushkin's name. This is the usual fate of a talent which has achieved widespread fame. It is all quite amusing at first but later, as you leave your youth behind you and see no end to these stupidities it becomes irritating. *A Cure from Cholera* and *First Night* and suchlike works have been attributed to him.

From the very first he was a national poet, because the true expression of national spirit rests not in the description of peasants' costume but in the very spirit of the people. A poet can be a national poet even when he is describing a totally different world, provided he sees it with the eyes of his native element and with the eyes of his own people, and that he feels and talks in a way with which his compatriots can identify. If we are to talk of the qualities which distinguish Pushkin from other poets, then they are to be found in the extraordinary speed and skill with which he can describe and encompass something in just a few strokes. His epithets are so apt and so bold, that they sometimes replace whole descriptions; his pen flies across the page. One of his shorter poems is always worth a whole long narrative poem. There is hardly another poet of whom it can be said that he was able to endow a short poem with such majesty, strength and simplicity.

But his final narrative poems, written at a time when the awesome majesty of the cloud-capped Caucasus had already been hidden from view and he had exiled himself to the depths of Russia, with its unremarkable flatness, and was devoting himself more fully to an exploration of the life and *mores* of his fellow-Russians as evidence of his desire to become a completely national poet – these poems no longer possess the same striking qualities of brilliance and dazzling audacity which characterise his work whenever Mt. Elbrus, the Circassians, the Crimea or Georgia appear.

It is not so difficult, I think, to explain why this is so. Astounded by the audacity and magic of his descriptions, all his readers, both educated and uneducated, vied with each other in demanding that he turn his attention, in his poetry, to historical, Russian themes, forgetting that it was impossible to depict the calmer, much less impassioned Russian way of life in the same colours which he had used for the Caucasus and its inhabitants with their free existence. The mass of the public, as representatives of the nation, has very strange desires. 'Show us as we really are, in complete authenticity', they shout. 'Show us the deeds of our ancestors, just as they really happened.' But should the poet try, in obedience to the public's bidding, to depict everything as it really is and as it really happened, then they will at once exclaim: 'This is feeble and weak, it wasn't like this at all'. The mass of the people are like a woman who asks an artist to paint a completely life-like portrait of her: but woe betide him, if he is unable to hide all her blemishes! Russian history has acquired colour and life only during its most recent phase, as an Imperial power; before this the character of the nation was for the most part colourless, generally unaware of the diversity of passions. The poet is not to blame; but the people have this very understandable tendency to exaggerate the deeds of their ancestors. There were two courses open to the poet: he could extend and exalt his style, impart strength to that which was inherently weak, and speak fervently about things which did not really contain much fervour. This was the way to win a mass of followers, the mass of the people, and also the way to wealth. Or he could remain faithful to a single vision of truth: to exalt that which was worthy of exaltation, to use sharpness and audacity only where they were relevant and to be peaceful and calm when events were quiet. But if he did this, then it was farewell to the crowd! It would not gather around him at all, save perhaps when his theme was itself so incisive and so grand that it could not fail to evoke general enthusiasm. The poet did not choose the first course, because he wished to remain a poet and because everyone who feels the slightest spark of sacred mission within him possesses a shrewd insight which does not allow him to demonstrate his talent in such a way. No-one would dispute the fact that the primitive mountain-dweller, dressed for battle, as free as the air, his own judge and master, is much more colourful than any magistrate and even if he has burnt down an entire village, he still evokes in us much more interest and sympathy than our magistrate does, with his worn tobacco-stained frock-coat, his certificates and forms, innocently dispatching all manner and kind of people, serfs as well as freemen, to all ends of the earth. But both of them are part of our world; they must both have the right to our attention although, quite naturally of course, the less often anything is seen, the more forcibly it strikes our imagination, and the fact that a poet prefers the commonplace to the exotic is nothing more than a miscalculation – a miscalculation as far as the mass of the public is concerned, but not as far as he himself is concerned. He will not in any way demean himself; on the contrary, perhaps he will enhance his own standing, but only in the eyes of genuine critics. An incident from my childhood occurs to me here. I had always felt a passion for art, and I was much taken up by a landscape which had a dead tree in the foreground. At the time I was living in the country; amongst my neighbours were connoisseurs of art and critics. One of them looked at the picture, shook his head, and said, 'A good artist chooses a fine-looking live tree, with green leaves, and not a dead one'. As a young child, I was irritated when I heard such criticism, but afterwards I distilled the wisdom contained in it: to know what the public likes, and what it dislikes. Those works of Pushkin which breathe the Russian countryside are as quiet and as peaceful as the countryside itself. Only the person who bears within himself the essence of Russia, for whom Russia is the motherland, and whose emotions are sufficiently sensitive and mature to appreciate the superficially colourless Russian songs and spirit, only he is able really to understand Pushkin's works. For the more commonplace the theme, the greater the poet needs to be in order to extract the unusual from it and, moreover, to ensure that the unusual is completely authentic. Have his final narrative poems been correctly assessed? And what about *Boris Godunov?* Has anyone defined or understood this great and profound work, encased in its inward, mysterious poetry, and rejecting any coarse and superficial colourfulness which the public generally find attractive? They have not been correctly assessed anywhere in print at least and remain untouched to this day.

In his attractive anthology of small-scale works Pushkin is unusually versatile and shows a side to him that is broader and more evident than in the longer narrative poetry. Some of these shorter poems are of such scintillating brilliance that anyone can understand them, but most of them, the best moreover, seem too ordinary for the public to understand them; you must possess an over-refined sensitivity and taste to a degree which raises you above those who can appreciate only clearly-defined and large-scale features. For this you need to a certain extent to be a sybarite, someone who has long since eaten his fill of coarse, heavy food and who now eats and enjoys small birds no larger than your thumb, whose taste seems extremely strange, vague and unpleasant – at least to those used to peasant food. This collection of short poems is a whole series of brilliant pictures. Here is that crystal-clear world so redolent of features known only to the ancients, in which nature is reflected as vividly as in a silvery stream, where dazzling shoulders, white arms, or an alabaster neck encircled by dark curls, translucent clusters of grapes, or myrtles and a canopy of trees flash past the eyes. There is everything here: delight, simplicity, momentary intellectual heights, embraced by the cold light of the reader's inspiration. There are no cascades of eloquence or of verbosity for its own sake, in which every phrase derives its strength and deafening force precisely from its conjunction with the other phrases, and in which separate phrases become feeble and weak. This is not eloquence, but poetry: without superficial brilliance, everything is simple and chaste, filled with an internal brilliance which does not instantly reveal itself; everything is as laconic as pure poetry always is. There are few words, but they are so precise that they embrace everything. Each word has its own infinity of space; each word is as boundless as the poet himself. This explains why you read these short works again and again, a privilege not accorded to works whose main theme is glaringly obvious.

I have always found it curious to hear these works criticised by many people with the reputation of experts and literary critics, whose opinions I had always trusted until I heard their views on this subject. It is possible to see these short works as a touchstone, on which to test the taste and the aesthetic sensibility of the critic analysing them. What a strange suggestion! No-one, it seemed, could have failed to understand them! They are so exalted and yet so simple, so colourful, so fervent, so sensuous and yet, at the same time, they have such a childlike purity. How can they not be understood! But, alas, it is an indisputable truth, that the more the poet becomes a poet, the more he depicts feelings which only poets are familiar with, the smaller becomes the crowd surrounding him, until finally there are so few that he is able to count his true followers and critics on his fingers.

BELINSKY

THE WORKS OF ALEXANDER PUSHKIN

V. G. Belinsky (1811-48) was a key figure in the development of Russian nineteenth-century thought. One of the first representatives of the radical intelligentsia, he initiated the dominating civic tendency of modern Russian literary criticism. His major critical work was perhaps the cycle of eleven essays on Pushkin, published in *Notes of the Fatherland* (1843-6), which laid the foundations for much subsequent critical analysis of the poet. Many of Belinsky's principal points (couched in the critic's customary passionate and prolix language) are made in the present extracts taken from the fifth of these essays (1844). Pushkin is set in the context of both European and Russian literature, and his unique position in the latter is strongly emphasised: he was the first Russian poet with a finely developed aesthetic sense and the first to depict contemporary life realistically. At the same time, however, although the poet's moral stature is extolled, Pushkin's lack of socio-political commitment is seen as a bar to his being a truly modern writer according to Belinsky's lights.

It was Pushkin's vocation to be the first Russian poet who was a genuine artist, the first to give Russia poetry as art and as literature rather than as merely a fine language of sentiment. Naturally, he could not have achieved this alone. In our previous essays we outlined the entire course of *belles-lettres* in Russia, indicating the origin and the development of her poetry and the part played in this process by Pushkin's predecessors, and also the latters' individual merits. Let us here repeat the comparison made earlier – that all these poets stand in relation to Pushkin as rivers great and small are related to the sea into which they flow. Pushkin's poetry was this sea. To continue the comparison, the sea is bigger and more important than the rivers, but without the rivers it could not have been formed. Such a comparison cannot be insulting to the poets who preceded Pushkin, particularly if we remind the reader that Zhukovsky's poetic career reached the high point of its development and produced its richest, most mature and finest fruit during Pushkin's lifetime, while Batyushkov was lost to literature in the prime of his life and power. In order to expound our thesis as clearly and as convincingly as possible, we devoted an entire essay to analysing not only the schoolboy poems of Pushkin's childhood but also the poems of Pushkin's youth which reflect the influence of the preceding school. These verses are incomparably inferior to those in which he was later to reveal his individual genius, but they are at the same time far superior to the models under whose influence they were written. In our essay we noted that in the first part of *The Poems of Alexander Pushkin* (1829) there were more pieces written under the influence of the preceding school than in the second part, whereas in the third part there were none at all; but even in the first part almost half the items were already fully independent poems by Pushkin. This first part contains poems written between 1815 and 1824; they are arranged chronologically, and with every year one can see Pushkin becoming less a pupil and an imitator – albeit one who surpassed his teachers and models – and more an original poet. The second part contains pieces written between 1825 and 1829, and only in the poems of 1825 can a slight influence of the old school be traced; in the pieces from the subsequent years this has disappeared completely. Reading the poems influenced by the earlier school, one feels and sees that poetry existed in Russia before Pushkin; but if one chooses to read only his original poems, it is not that one disbelieves, rather one completely forgets that poetry existed in Russia before Pushkin: so original, so new and so fresh is the world of his poetry!..

And what poetry! In it a classical plasticity and a strict simplicity combine with a fascinating play of romantic rhyme; in it all the acoustic wealth and all the power of the Russian language appear in their astonishing plenitude. Pushkin's verse is as tender, sweet and soft as the murmur of a wave, as viscous and thick as resin, as vivid as lightning, as transparent and pure as crystal, as fragrant and sweet-scented as spring, and as strong and powerful as a sword-thrust from the hand of a knight. It has a seductive and inexpressible charm and grace, it has a blinding lustre and a roscid tenderness, it has a wealth of melody and a harmony of language and rhyme, it has all the voluptuousness and all the rapture of creative dreams and poetic expression. If we were to characterise Pushkin's verse in a single word we would say that it is a supremely *poetic, aesthetic and artistic* verse – that is the secret of the power of all Pushkin's poetry.

When you read Homer you see the greatest possible fulness of artistic perfection, but it does not absorb your entire attention, you are not amazed by this alone: you are more struck and engaged by the ancient Hellenic philosophy in which Homer's poetry is bathed and by the ancient Hellenic world itself. You are in Olympus among the Gods and in battle with the heroes; you are charmed by this noble simplicity, and by this elegant, patriarchal and heroic age of a nation which once represented the whole of humanity; but the poet himself remains for you, as it were, outside, and his artistry seems to be something which inevitably belongs to the poem, and so it never occurs to you to pause and marvel at him. With Shakespeare you are also struck, not by the artist, but by the penetrating connoisseur of the human heart and the observer who comprehends the whole world; his artistry is somehow acknowledged without words and explanations. In the same way, when considering a great mathematician, people indicate his contributions to science without speaking about the astonishing power of his ability to grasp objects and combine them in infinite permutations. With Byron's poetry your heart is above all gripped in awed amazement at the colossal personality of the poet, his titanic boldness and the loftiness of his feelings and thoughts. From Goethe's poetry emerges a poetically contemplative thinker, a powerful lord and master of the inner world of man's soul. Reading Schiller's poetry, you bow with love and veneration before a tribune of mankind, a prophet of humanity and a passionate worshipper of the great and the morally beautiful. In Pushkin, on the other hand, you see above all an artist, equipped with all the charms of poetry, summoned to art for the sake of art, interested in and filled with love for everything and therefore accepting everything. From this stem all the merits and all the shortcomings of his poetry – and if you look at him from this standpoint you will doubly enjoy his merits and will condone his shortcomings as the necessary consequence and obverse of these very merits...

Pushkin's vocation is explained by the history of our literature. Russian poetry is an imported, not a native growth. Any poetry must be an expression of life – in the widest sense of that word, embracing the whole physical and moral world. Only thought can lead poetry to this point. But, in order to be an expression of life, poetry must first of all be poetry. Art gains nothing from a work which may be described as *intelligent, true and profound, but prosaic*. Such a work is like a woman with a generous heart but an ugly face: one can wonder at her, but one cannot fall in love with her; yet a little love, rather than wonder, would give more happiness not only to her but also to the man whose wonder she has aroused. Non-poetic works are fruitless in all respects, whereas semi-prosaic works are useful for society and individuals, but even for this purpose they are only semi-effective. When the origins of poetry are remembered, when poetry appears not as the fruit of a nation's life but as the fruit of civilisation, then the first task, if it is to develop fully, is to work out poetic forms, since, we repeat, poetry must first of all be poetry and only then express this or that notion. That is the reason for Pushkin's being as he was, and that is why he could not have been otherwise. Before him we had not the slightest premonition of what art is, art as one of the absolute categories of the human spirit. Before him poetry was no more than an eloquent exposition of fine sentiments and thoughts, which did not constitute its soul, but served only as a suitable means to a worthy end, like ceruse and rouge on the pallid face of that old hag, the truth. This dead concept of using poetic form to express moral and other ideas gave rise to so-called *didactic poetry* and achieved expression in the following lines of Merzlyakov which appear to have been taken from Tasso:

> Thus a doctor to the lips of a sick child
> Brings a goblet, full with sweets to the brim;
> The happy child, captivated, drinks the bitter cure.
> The deception has given him life, the deception is salvation!

Our Russian poetry before Pushkin was indeed a gilded pill, a sugar-coated medicine. Consequently, flashes of true, inspired and creative poetry appeared in it only occasionally here and there, and these flashes were submerged in a flood of rhetoric. Much was done for the language and for verse, and something was done for poetry too, but poetry as poetry – that is, poetry which, while expressing this or that notion and developing this or that philosophy, remains above all poetry – such poetry did not yet exist. Pushkin was summoned to be a living revelation of its secret in Russia. And since his mission in the service of Russia was to conquer and master for ever poetry as art so that subsequently Russian poetry would be able to express any tendency and any philosophy without fear of ceasing to be poetry and turning into rhymed prose, it was only natural that Pushkin had to be an artist to the exclusion of other things.

Once again: we had poets before Pushkin, but not one was a genuine artist. Pushkin was the first Russian poet to be an artist. Therefore, even the first immature works of his youth, such as *Ruslan and Lyudmila*, *The Robber Brothers*, *The Prisoner of the Caucasus* and *The Fountain of Bakhchisarai* marked with their appearance a new epoch in the history of Russian poetry. Everyone – not just the educated, but even many barely literate people – saw in them not simply new poetic works, but a completely new sort of poetry for which they had not seen any model in Russian and of whose existence there had never been the slightest hint. And all literate Russia read these narrative poems; they circulated in exercise books, copied out by young girls devoted to poetry, by schoolboys surreptitiously under their desks, and by assistants behind the counters of shops and stores. And this happened not only in the capital cities, but also in the most remote places. At this moment people suddenly realised that the difference between poetry and prose was not just a matter of rhyme and metre, and that poetry too, in its turn, might be either poetic or prosaic. This meant no longer seeing poetry in something external but in its inner essence. Should a poet immeasurably greater than Pushkin emerge in Russia today, his appearance could not create an equal stir or evoke such widespread passionate enthusiasm, because after Pushkin poetry is no longer an unprecedented, unheard-of thing. And for the same reason even a poet ceding nothing to Pushkin in talent, indeed even one surpassing him in this respect and like him primarily an artist, might achieve an only too modest success today.

If the above-mentioned first narrative poems of Pushkin already reflect clearly that artistry which so sharply distinguishes them from the works of earlier schools, then there is yet more artistry in Pushkin's original lyrics. The early narrative poems have already lost much of their former charm for us; we have already outlived and so gone beyond them; but the lyrics stamped with Pushkin's creative originality are just as charmingly beautiful today as they were when they first appeared. This is quite understandable: the narrative poem demands a maturity of talent which only experience of life can give – and there is no such maturity in *Ruslan and Lyudmila, The Robber Brothers* and *The Prisoner of the Caucasus*, while in *The Fountain of Bakhchisarai* Pushkin succeeds only artistically. But youth is the best age for lyrical poetry. The narrative poem demands a knowledge of life and people, it demands the ability to create characters and, consequently, the ability to dramatise; the lyric poem demands richness of feelings – and when is man's bosom richest in feelings if not in the days of his youth?

The secret of Pushkin's verse lay not in the art of 'fusing obedient words into harmonious metres and locking them with ringing rhymes', but in the secret of poetry. Inherent in Pushkin's soul was above all that poetry which is to be found not in books, but in nature and in life; inherent in it was the art whose seal is impressed on 'the full creation of glory'. Reason is the spirit or the soul of life; poetry is life's smile, its radiant gaze reflecting the play of quickly changing sensations. There are women who are endowed by nature with a rare beauty but whose strictly regular features suggest a certain dryness and whose movements lack grace. Such women can after their own fashion be dazzlingly brilliant and evoke wonder, but their appearance never makes any heart beat with mysterious agitation, their beauty never inspires love – and beauty without the grace of love lacks life and *poetry*. In the same way, both nature and life would evoke only cold wonder were they not steeped in poetry; without poetry, only the dank cold of the grave – not love – would emanate from them. True, the heavenly bodies form harmonious spheres; yet it is not that feature alone which elevates the soul of the man who contemplates them, rather is it the poetry of their mysterious sparkle and the wonderful beauty in the lively play of their fiery pale rays. In their harmonious movements Pythagoras not only saw mathematics in action but also heard the music of the spheres. If the sun only warmed us and shone, it would be no more than a gigantic torch or a huge stove, but it pours out onto the earth its bright, happily quivering and joyfully playful rays – and the earth greets these rays with a smile which contains an inexpressible charm and an elusive poetry...

Nature comprises more than organic forces; she is also full of a *poetry* which more than anything else bears witness to her *life*. Her perpetual movement, the swaying of her forests, the trembling of a silvery leaf lovingly caressed by a ray of sunlight, the murmur of a brook, the wafting of a breeze which stirs the golden harvest –

all these things are bathed for man in a mysterious lustre and in them he seems to hear living voices, now sad and solitary like the notes of an Aeolian harp, now merry and joyful, like the song of a lark rising up to the heavens... Man himself is even more full of poetry. Why do you want to kiss the child noisily playing in the meadow? Why are you so captivated by his eyes which shine with pure happiness, his blissful smile and lively, high-spirited movements? Worn by life, experience and everyday cares, old and wise, what have you in common with this almost unconscious creature who understands nothing? As you hurried on important business with a worried frown, why did you suddenly stop on the meadow, forgetting your important affairs, to look on this child with a tender smile? Why did your forehead become smooth and clear as worry left for a moment? And why did a smile of happiness momentarily light up your morose expression, like a ray of sunlight penetrating through a chink into a dark cellar to tremble on its damp floor?.. Because the sight of this child made you aware of the poetry of life... And look at this beautiful young woman. In her features you see no definite expression; she is no personification of sentiment, soul, goodness, love, self-denial, or elevated thoughts and aspirations; in other words, nothing in this face signifies any firmly imprinted moral quality; it is simply beautiful, sweet and animated with life; that is all. You are not in love with this woman and feel no desire to be loved by her; you calmly wonder at the charm of her movements and the grace of her manner – and yet in her presence your heart somehow beats faster and a gentle happy harmony suffuses your soul... Why is this, if not because beauty in itself is a quality and a merit – indeed a great one? Truth and virtue are excellent and precious, but beauty too is excellent and precious, and the latter is as valuable as the former; it cannot replace the former, but all in equal degree constitute spiritual needs of man. That is why in their poetic polytheism the ancient Greeks deified not only truth, knowledge, power, wisdom, courage, justice and chastity, but also beauty, companied by the Graces of love and desire. According to their religious philosophy which was full of poetry and life, the goddess of beauty possessed a mysterious girdle:

> It contained every charm:
> In it were love and desires, friendships and requests,
> And flattering words which seized the minds even of
> the men of reason.

And in order to express the irresistible power of Homer's poetry to influence the soul and heart of man the Greeks said that he had stolen Aphrodite's girdle...

Pushkin was the first Russian poet to possess this girdle of Cypris. Not only every line of his verse, but every sensation, every feeling, every thought and every picture he drew are full of inexpressible poetry. He viewed nature and reality from a particular point of view, and this point of view was an exclusively poetic one. Pushkin's muse was an aristocratic maiden in whom seductive beauty and spontaneous grace combined with elegance of tone and a noble simplicity and whose fine inner qualities were developed and even further heightened by a virtuosity of form which she so mastered that for her it became second nature...

Pushkin's poetry is astonishingly true to Russian life, whether it is depicting the Russian countryside or Russian characters, and for this reason common opinion dubbed him a Russian national poet and a poet of the Russian people. That seems to us to be only half true. A poet of the people is one who is known to all the people, as for instance France knows her Béranger; a national poet is one who is known to all the even slightly educated classes, as for instance Germans know Goethe and Schiller. Our people do not know a single one of their poets; to this day they sing to themselves 'Not the white snows' without suspecting for a moment that they are singing verse rather than prose. Consequently, from this point of view, it would be ridiculous even to speak about applying the phrase 'of the people' to Pushkin or to any other Russian poet. The adjective 'national' is even wider in its significance than the phrase 'of the people'. By 'the people' we always understand the mass of the ordinary population, the lowest and basic stratum of the state. By 'the nation' we mean the entire people, all classes, from the lowest to the highest, who all together constitute the body politic. A national poet expresses in his work both the fundamental, impersonal and indefinable substantial element which is usually represented by the mass of the people and also the formulated significance of this substantial element which is developed in the life of the most educated strata of the nation. A national poet is a wonderful thing! Turning to Pushkin, we will say regarding this question of his nationalness that he could not help reflecting in himself the life of the people geographically and physiologically since he was not only a Russian but moreover a Russian endowed by nature with genius.

However, in that which is called the popular or national quality of his poetry we see rather his extraordinarily great artistic sensitivity. He possessed to the highest degree that sensitivity to the rhythm of life which is one of the chief qualities of an artist. Read his marvellous dramatic poem *The Water Nymph* – it is packed full of authentic Russian life; but read his equally marvellous dramatic poem *The Stone Guest* – and in the same way in its portraits of the country-side and in the customs of its heroes it breathes the air of Spain; read his *Egyptian Nights* – and you will be transported to the very heart of the life of the moribund ancient world. We could adduce many more such instances of Pushkin's astonishing ability to feel at home in numerous highly diverse spheres of life, but these three will suffice. And what does this prove, if not his artistic versatility? If he could portray so authentically the countryside and the customs of countries which he had not even seen, were his depictions of Russian subjects not bound to be strikingly authentic? In order to pursue this question more thoroughly we must introduce a fairly lengthy extract from Gogol's essay, *A Few Words on Pushkin:* [Here Belinsky quotes the first two thirds of Gogol's essay from 'When you hear the name of Pushkin...' to '... They have not been correctly assessed anywhere in print at least and remain untouched to this day'.]

All this is very true, particularly the definition of a national poet:

> A poet can be a national poet even when he is describing a totally different world, provided he sees it with the eyes of his native element and with the eyes of his own people and that he feels and talks in a way with which his compatriots can identify.

And, if you like, from this point of view, Pushkin was more a Russian national poet than any of his predecessors...

We have already stated that reading Pushkin must have a strong influence on the cultivation, development and education of refined and humane feelings in a man. Indeed, *pace* our literary old-believers, our dry moralists and our hard, anti-aesthetic philosophisers, no-one, no single Russian poet has gained such an indisputable right as Pushkin to be the educator of young, mature or even elderly readers (provided the latter once possessed and have not entirely lost a grain of aesthetic and humane feeling) because in Russia we know no poet with talent who is more *moral* than Pushkin. The old-believers still cannot forget Lomonosov, or Sumarokov, or so-and-so, or so-and-so, etc. As regards the moralists and the philosophisers (among whom you will find many limited, though kind and well-meaning people, but rather more Pharisees and Tartuffes) when they inveigh against Pushkin as an immoral poet, they usually like to refer either to the playfully erotic poems of his youth and to *Ruslan and Lyudmila*, which contains not a few instances of poetic licence, or to the poems *The Demon* and 'Vain gift, chance gift'. Yet they do not hold the former tendency against Derzhavin, the author of *The Miller* and numerous fairly free anacreontic poems, since in spite of these they consider him an outstandingly 'moral' poet. In the same way they admire Bogdanovich's *Psyche* and do not think of finding it 'immoral'. How then is Pushkin guilty in their eyes? This they do not understand themselves, and so let us leave them alone. Concerning *The Demon*, we shall have more to say below about the Pushkinian demon's not being one of the most dangerous and about his being a little imp rather than a demon. Let us add to this only that, without being a demonic poet, Pushkin had the right to experience pangs of doubt and could not help sometimes experiencing them, since only shallow, petty, dry and dead natures can be completely free of such pangs. The poem 'Vain gift, chance gift' is nothing more than the outcome of one of those difficult moments of moral apathy and spiritual despair which are inevitable – as moments – for any strong living nature, but this poem is by no means an expression of the general tendency of Pushkin's poetry; rather is it a chance contradiction of his poetry's general tendency...

Pushkin's poetry reflects primarily a poetic contemplation of the world and unconditionally recognises the existing state of the world as, if not always consoling, at least always necessary and rational; consequently it bears a character which is contemplative rather than reflective and gives an appearance more of feeling or of contemplation than of thought. Pushkin's muse is humane through and through and is capable of suffering deeply at the dissonances and contradictions of life, but she gazes on them with a certain self-renunciation *(resignatio)*, as if acknowledging their fateful inevitability and without bearing in her soul any ideal of a better life or any faith in the possibility of its realisation. This view of the world issued from Pushkin's inmost nature, and Pushkin owes to this view the elegant smoothness, the gentleness, the profundity and the loftiness of his poetry, but at the same time this view lies at the root of the shortcomings of his poetry. However that may be, Pushkin belongs in his outlook to a school of art whose day is completely finished in Europe and which even in Russia cannot produce a single great poet. A spirit of analysis, an irrepressible impulse towards enquiry and passionate convictions, which are full of love and hate, have now become the life-blood of all true poetry. That is how time has outstripped Pushkin's poetry and deprived a large proportion of his works of that topical and lively interest which is possible only if works of art represent a satisfactory response to the disquieting and painful questions of the day...

HERZEN

ON THE DEVELOPMENT OF REVOLUTIONARY IDEAS IN RUSSIA

Alexander Herzen (1817-70) was perhaps the broadest and the most gifted of the Russian nineteenth-century thinkers and publicists. He first attracted attention by a series of articles on science and philosophy and by a clumsy though topical novel, *Who is to Blame?* (1846). In 1847 he emigrated to Western Europe where he produced his most celebrated works — the journal *The Bell*, which though officially banned was widely distributed in Russia, the scintillating essays *From the Other Shore*, and his panoramic autobiography, *My Past and Thoughts*. Herzen published very little literary criticism and when he did it would contain a considerable measure of political and social comment. Thus, in the present extract from *On the Development of Revolutionary Ideas in Russia* Herzen argues that Evgenii Onegin is a typical product of the repressive atmosphere of his age and that Pushkin's personal fate provides another illustration of the misfortune which was likely to befall any talented individual in tsarist Russia. The extract ends with Herzen's famous martyrology of Russian poets. *On the Development of Revolutionary Ideas in Russia* appeared in 1851, first in German and then in French.

Pushkin could not be more truly a national poet, and yet he is easily comprehended by foreigners. He rarely mimics the popular language of Russian songs, but expresses his thoughts as they spring to his mind. Like all great poets, he is always on the level of his reader: he may expand to become gloomy, threatening or tragic; his verse may roar like the sea, or sough like the forest in the path of a gale, but he always remains serene, light and sparkling, and eager for delights and excitement. The Russian poet is everywhere down-to-earth. There is nothing morbid in him, no trace of the exaggerated psychological disorder or abstract Christian spirituality which one meets so often in German poets. His muse is no pale, hysterical creature, wrapped in a winding-sheet, but a woman of passion, with an aura of health, too rich in genuine emotions to need to seek artificial ones and unhappy enough without inventing artificial misfortunes. Pushkin was by nature pantheistic and epicurean, like the Greek poets, but his soul contained also a completely modern element. When he withdrew into himself he found in the depths of his soul the bitter thought of Byron, that corrosive irony of our century.

Pushkin has been seen by some as an imitator of Byron. The English poet certainly had a strong influence on the Russian, and none of us can ever emerge from communing with a strong and attractive personality without experiencing his influence and becoming more mature under his light. If a spirit we respect confirms by his approbation certain things hidden our hearts, we feel a fresh inspiration and a new understanding. But such a natural reaction is a long way from imitation. After his early poems, in which Byron's influence is strongly felt, Pushkin becomes more and more original with each new work. While remaining full of admiration for the great English poet, he was neither his dependant, nor his parasite, neither his *traduttore* nor his *traditore*.

At the end of their careers the distance between Pushkin and Byron was very great – and for the one simple reason that Byron was profoundly English while Pushkin was profoundly Russian, and moreover a Russian of the St. Petersburg period. Pushkin was acquainted with all the sufferings of civilized man, but he also had a faith in the future which Western man had already lost. Byron, a great free individual, a man increasingly isolated in his independence and increasingly enveloped in his arrogance and his proud scepticism, became more and more gloomy and unrelenting. He could see no immediate future; weighed down by bitter reflections and disgusted by the world, he handed over his fate to a tribe of Slavonic-cum-Greek pirates whom he mistook for the Greeks of the Ancient World. Pushkin, on the contrary, grew more and more composed, immersed himself in the study of Russian history, collected material for a monograph on Pugachov, wrote the historical drama *Boris Godunov* and developed an instinctive faith in the future of Russia; the triumphant and victorious cries which impressed him so strongly in his childhood, in 1813 and 1814, resounded again in his heart; for a while he was even carried away by that St. Petersburg patriotism which boasts of the number of its bayonets and is based on cannons. This arrogance is of course just as unpardonable as Byron's excessively aristocratic pose, but its cause is obvious. Sad as it is to admit it, Pushkin's patriotism was very strong. Some great poets have been courtiers – witness Goethe, Racine, etc. Pushkin was neither a courtier nor a supporter of the government, but the brute force of the state appealed to his patriotic instinct, and in consequence he shared the barbaric impulse to answer arguments with cannon-balls. Russia is a slave partly because she finds poetry in material force and sees glory in being a bogy to other nations.

People who say that Pushkin's *Evgenii Onegin* is *Don Juan* in Russian dress understand neither Byron nor Pushkin, neither England nor Russia. They are judging by the external form. *Evgenii Onegin* is Pushkin's most important work which absorbed half his life. The poem emanated from the period with which we are concerned, maturing in those sad years which followed December 1825. Can one possibly believe that such a work, a poetic autobiography, is a simple imitation?

Onegin is neither Hamlet, nor Faust, nor Manfred, nor Obermann, nor Trenmor, nor Karl Moor. Onegin is a Russian; he is possible only in Russia; he is inevitable in Russia, and encountered there round every corner. Onegin is an idler, because he has never occupied himself with anything; he is superfluous in the sphere in which he finds himself and lacks the character to escape from it. He is a man who has tempted life to the point of death and who would like to try death, so as to see whether it is better than life or not. He has turned his hand to everything, but taken nothing to its conclusion; the more he has thought, the less he has done; at twenty he was already old and he is rejuvenated by love when he begins to age. He has always been waiting for something, like all of us, because no man is insane enough to believe in the persistence of the existing state of affairs in Russia... Nothing came, and life passed by. The Onegin type is so national that he can be found in every novel and every poem which has enjoyed the slightest degree of success in Russia, and not because we wanted to copy the type, but because we constantly see him next to us and within ourselves.

Chatsky, the hero of a celebrated comedy by Griboedov, is Onegin-*raisonneur*, his elder brother.

Lermontov's Pechorin is his younger brother. Onegin appears even in minor works, perhaps exaggerated or incomplete, but still recognisable. If it is not he, then it is at least an imitation of him. The young traveller in Count Sollogub's *Tarantas* is a limited and ill-bred Onegin. The fact is that we are all more or less Onegins, unless we prefer to be officials or landowners.

Civilisation is ruining and bewildering us. It is civilisation which makes us a burden to others and to ourselves. Civilisation is rendering us idle, useless and capricious; we oscillate between eccentricity and carousing, squandering without any regrets our fortune, our heart and our youth and ever craving for fresh pursuits, sensations and amusements – like the dogs of Aix-la-Chapelle in Heine, who to dispel their boredom beg the passers-by to bestow on them the favour of a kick. We try everything – music, philosophy, love, the military arts, mysticism – in order to distract ourselves and to force ourselves to forget the enormous void which oppresses us.

The two extremes of civilisation and slavery which have been forcibly brought together without any padding between them grind us to pieces, internally and externally!

We are given the broadest education; we have been infected with the desires, aspirations and sufferings of the modern world, and at the same time we are told, 'Remain slaves, silent and passive – or else you are lost'. As a reward we are left the right to fleece the peasants and to dissipate in the casino or the cabaret the taxes which we levy on them in blood and tears.

A young man meets nothing of vital interest to him in this world of servility and petty ambition. And this is the society in which he is condemned to live, since the ordinary people are even more remote from him. 'Society' consists at least of fallen beings of the same species as himself, whereas he and the ordinary people share nothing in common. Our traditions were so thoroughly destroyed by Peter I that no human power is capable of reuniting these two classes – at least at the present time. We are left with the choice between solitude or struggle, but we have insufficient moral strength for either. That is how men become Onegins – unless they perish in brothels or in the casemates of some fortress.

We stole civilisation, and Jupiter means to punish us as relentlessly as he set about tormenting Prometheus.

Beside Onegin Pushkin placed another victim of Russian life, Vladimir Lensky, Onegin's converse. We see intense suffering next to chronic suffering. Lensky is one of those virginal, pure natures who cannot acclimatise themselves to their corrupt and insane surroundings, who have welcomed life, but can imbibe nothing more from the impure soil except death. Expiatory victims, young and pale and with the brand of fate on their foreheads, these youths pass before our eyes like a living reproach and penitence, and leave even blacker the night in which 'we move and have our being'.

Pushkin drew Lensky's character with the tenderness we feel towards the dreams of our youth and towards our memories of the time when we were full of hope, purity and ignorance. Lensky is the last cry of Onegin's conscience, because Lensky is his youthful ideal. The poet saw that there is nothing for such a man to do in Russia and he has him killed at the hand of Onegin who loved him and who, even as he aimed, did not want as much as to wound him. Pushkin himself was frightened by this tragic end and hastens to comfort the reader by depicting the banal life which would have awaited the young poet.

Next to Pushkin stands also another Lensky – Venevitinov, an ingenuous poetic soul, strangled at the age of twenty-two by the coarse hands of Russian life.

Between these two types – between the dedicated enthusiast and poet and, on the other hand, the weary, embittered and useless man, between Lensky's grave and Onegin's boredom – stretches the deep and muddy river of civilised Russia, with its aristocrats, bureaucrats, officers, gendarmes, grand-dukes and emperor – a dumb and formless mass of baseness, obsequiousness, bestiality and envy, a formless mass which draws in and engulfs everything: 'That abyss', as Pushkin puts it, 'where, dear reader, you and I all bathe.'

Pushkin made his *début* with revolutionary verses of great beauty. Alexander I exiled him from Petersburg to the southern borderlands of the Empire. The new Ovid spent the years 1819 to 1825 in the Tauric Chersonese. Separated from his friends, remote from political activity and placed amidst a magnificent but untamed nature, Pushkin, as a poet first and foremost, withdrew into his lyricism. His lyrics are phases in his life, they are the biography of his soul. In them are to be found traces of everything which stirred this ardent soul – truth and error, the passing enthusiasm of a moment, and deep, enduring loyalties.

Nicholas I recalled Pushkin from exile a few days after hanging the heroes of 14 December. He hoped to destroy the poet in the public eye through this favour and to subdue him through acts of kindness. Pushkin returned and could not recognise either Moscow or Petersburg society. His friends were no longer there, and people hardly dared even utter their names; conversation was only about arrests, searches and exile; the atmosphere was one of gloom and intimidation. He briefly met Mickiewicz, that other Slav poet, and they shook hands silently as if in a graveyard. The storm was raging over their heads: Pushkin had just returned from exile, while Mickiewicz was departing into it. Their meeting was dismal, but they did not understand each other. The lectures which Mickiewicz gave at the Collège de France revealed the disagreement which existed between them. The time for a Pole and a Russian to understand each other had not yet come.

Continuing the comedy, Nicholas appointed Pushkin a gentleman of the bedchamber. The latter took the point and did not appear at court. So he was given the choice: either to take himself off to the Caucasus or to put on courtier's uniform. He was already married to the woman who was subsequently to cause his downfall. A second exile seemed to him more grievous than his first – and he chose the court. In this lack of pride and resistance, in this dubious pliability one sees the bad side of the Russian character.

When the heir to the throne complimented him on his appointment, Pushkin replied, 'Your Highness is the first to congratulate me on this matter'.

In 1837 Pushkin was killed in a duel by one of those foreign paid assassins who, like the mercenaries of the Middle Ages or the Swiss of our own days, are prepared to hire out their sword to the service of any despotism. He fell at the height of his powers, before finishing his songs and before saying everything which he had to say.

Apart from the court and its entourage all Petersburg wept. Only now did it become obvious how great a popularity Pushkin had acquired. As he lay dying, a dense throng crowded round his house for news of his progress. Since this was only a few yards from the Winter Palace, the Emperor could see the crowd from his windows. He was consumed with jealousy and deprived the public of the poet's funeral: Pushkin's body, escorted by gendarmes and police, was furtively transported through the frosty night, not to his own parish, but to a completely different church; there a priest hastily read the office for the dead, and a sleigh carried the poet's body to a monastery in the province of Pskov where his estate was situated. When the deceived crowd made its way to the church where the corpse had first been taken snow had already covered all traces of the funeral procession.

In Russia a terrible dark destiny is reserved for anyone who presumes to raise his head higher than the level traced by the imperial sceptre. An inexorable fate pushes the poet, the citizen and the thinker down into the grave. The history of our literature is a martyrology or the register of a convict prison. Even those whom the government has spared perish almost before they have begun to blossom, hastening to abandon this life.

> La, sotto i giorni brevi e nebulosi,
> Nasce una gente a cui l'morir non dole.

Ryleev – hanged by Nicholas I.
Pushkin – killed in a duel, aged 38.
Griboedov – assassinated in Teheran.
Lermontov – killed in a duel, aged 30, in the Caucasus.
Venevitinov – killed by society, aged 22.
Koltsov – killed by his family, aged 33.
Belinsky – killed, aged 35, by hunger and poverty.
Polezhaev – died in a military hospital after being forced to serve 8 years as an ordinary soldier in the Caucasus.
Baratynsky – died after 12 years of exile.
Bestuzhev – died in the Caucasus, still quite young, after forced labour in Siberia.

'Woe betide the nations which stone to death their own prophets!' says the Holy Scripture – but the Russian nation has nothing to fear, since nothing more could be added to its unhappy lot.

ANNENKOV

MATERIALS FOR PUSHKIN'S BIOGRAPHY

As a young man P. V. Annenkov (1812-1887) was closely acquainted with such writers and intellectual figures as Gogol, Belinsky, Herzen, Turgenev and Bakunin. In his literary reminiscences, for which he is perhaps best known, he gave his readers not only valuable and lively portraits of these figures, but also a fascinating insight into the spirit of what he himself called 'the remarkable decade' (1838-1848). In his literary criticism and his views on the function of literature Annenkov was an aesthete: he held that the main criteria for evaluating a work should be aesthetic rather than utilitarian and attacked the civic critics for introducing non-literary elements of only temporary significance into their criticism. Annenkov's *Materials for Pushkin's Biography,* first published in 1855, was the first attempt to give a complete characterisation of Pushkin's personality and work. Our extract, taken from Chapter 8 of this work, is concerned with Pushkin's romantic narrative poems of the early 1820s and with his attitude towards the vexed question of romanticism.

Let us pause here for a moment to make certain observations on all the narrative poems written by Pushkin during these four years (1821-1824), a period which was so full of diverse impressions and so fruitful from a literary point of view. It is interesting to unravel the secret of their origin, the significance which the general public ascribed to them, and the author's reaction to the way they were interpreted and criticised.

The narrative poem *The Prisoner of the Caucasus* was Pushkin's first attempt to create an authentic hero, an attempt which, as everyone knows, was not entirely successful. Incidentally the first person to point this out was Pushkin himself. This is what he wrote to his publisher, hardly before the ink had had time to dry on his manuscript:

> The faults in this story, poem or whatever are so obvious that I was for a long time unable to bring myself to publish it. The simplicity of its ideas comes very close to paucity of invention, the description of Circassian life has nothing to do with the plot and is no more than a geographical article or a traveller's account. The character of the hero is more suited to a novel than a narrative poem, and, anyway, what sort of a character is he? Who will be entertained by the portrayal of a young man, who has lost his sense of emotional response in some misfortune or other about which the reader knows nothing? His inaction, his indifference to the savage cruelty of the Caucasians and to the charms of a Circassian girl may well be very natural, but what is so moving about them? It would have been easy to enliven the tale with an account of events which flowed naturally out of the subject. The Circassian who captured my Russian could have been the lover of the girl who freed him; her parents and brothers could all have had their own parts to play and their own individual characters; but I scorned all this: firstly, out of laziness; and secondly because all these rational reflections only occurred to me when both parts of the poem were already finished and I lacked the courage and will to start afresh... You can see that paternal affection has not blinded me as far as *The Prisoner of the Caucasus* is concerned but I must confess that I am fond of it, without knowing why: it has lines which come right from the heart...

In another letter to one of his friends, V. P. Gorchakov, Pushkin writes about the work with an equally remarkable naivety and frankness:

> Your remarks... are extremely fair – too lenient in fact. Why did my Prisoner not follow the Circassian girl's example and drown himself? As a person he acted very prudently, but prudence is not required in the hero of a poem. The character of the prisoner is a failure and it shows that *I am unable to create romantic*

heroes. I wanted to portray in him that indifference to life and its joys, that premature ageing of soul, which have become the distinguishing features of contemporary youth. It would of course have been better to call the poem *The Circassian Girl* – I did not think of it.

The Circassians, their customs and way of life form the largest and best part of my story; but none of it is connected with anything else and is an *hors d'oevre* in the real sense of the word. In general I am very dissatisfied with my poem and consider it far inferior to *Ruslan* – although the verse is more mature...

It is interesting to observe Pushkin's attempts to clarify a character which his imagination conceived so indistinctly. These traces of his imaginative process, the struggle to clarify an image for ever disappearing under his pen are especially instructive in the case of a writer who was later to become the model for all to follow...

The majestic picture of the Caucasus which Pushkin painted with such a sense of poetic truth and such simplicity astonished even his opponents. They reacted to the new work with moderation... The quiet but astonishingly noble and tender heroism of the Circassian girl delighted the reader and, in the atmosphere of general enthusiasm, Pushkin's critics remained silent. They confined themselves to a few words of advice on how the character of the Prisoner could most advantageously be altered, and, later, to remarks on incorrect style. This latter aspect of criticism always engaged Pushkin's attention. He would collect the remarks on grammar and syntax and would frequently refute them, even in his notes to the second editions of his own poems. Whether as a result of his abiding interest in the Russian language or of a sly desire to show the extent of his reviewers' taste and knowledge, he painstakingly, if not comprehensively, collected the philological curiosities to be found in criticisms of him...

Seven years after the first appearance of *The Prisoner of the Caucasus* Pushkin said of it: 'It is all very weak, immature and incomplete, but there is much that has been truthfully captured and expressed.' This was a repetition of what he had said on the day the work had appeared.

In the criticism of *The Fountain of Bakhchisarai*, to which we now turn, a great deal was said about the influence of Byron on our poet. And indeed, the character of Girei, just like that of the Prisoner, has much in common with the typical Byronic hero, although, on closer examination, it is easy to see Pushkin's individual creative talent appearing through the imitation. The alien temper and cast of mind involuntarily imposed on both these characters can be explained by Pushkin's almost constant involvement with Byron's works during this period.

Those people who were able to observe closely the gradual unfolding of Pushkin's natural genius knew very well why he should have worshipped the English poet with such obvious delight. Byron was a sign-post pointing the way towards new and distant horizons and leading Pushkin away from the French road which had been guiding him during his first years as a writer. Of course, everything that was subsequently to be expressed about the general mood of the age, or about the spirit of European literature, had some truth in it; but the most immediate reason for Byron's influence on Pushkin lay in the fact that he alone presented Pushkin with a contemporary pattern for his work. Pushkin read German only with great difficulty; the scales were weighted in favour of the English poet. From him Pushkin drew his respect for his own imagination, which he had viewed before in a somewhat light and superficial manner; from him he learnt the value of his work and his own creative talent. Byron placed a mighty tool in his hands: and with it Pushkin was subsequently to fashion images from the world of poetry which were totally unlike his teacher's finest conceptions. After three years' close involvement the Byronic mood and Byronic devices disappeared entirely from Pushkin; all that remained was his own developing talent – something which almost always arises from a relationship between two true poets! It is impossible to say even that Byron was the only influential figure during this evolution of Pushkin's artistic talent. Side by side with Byron stood A. Chénier whom Pushkin admired almost as much. Pushkin was the first Russian to speak about Chénier, and he was of course one of the first people in Europe really to understand the charm of Chénier's tender lyrics, especially the classical poems, in which mere panache was replaced by a genuine elegance. When we remember that this was the time when Lamartine's elegies were being greeted with shouts of acclamation, we can clearly see just how little attention Pushkin paid to such noises generally, even if they came from afar... Some of Pushkin's friends were publishing Lamartine and writing with fervent conviction about him, but Pushkin showed not the least response to their enthusiasm. It is a fact that, for a very long time, Pushkin was the only Russian to admire Chénier's works, and that Chénier played a part in Pushkin's life equal to that of Byron. They were both pointers to his own, emerging talent, stages by which he rose to the full flowering of his genius.

On the appearance of *The Fountain of Bakhchisarai* all the divergent strands of critical opinion in Russian literature merged into a single chorus of praise for the unprecedented harmony of language, the opulent beauty of verse and descriptive passage, which were the poem's distinguishing features. Critics saw in it the apotheosis of the Russian language, and it was only the author's subsequent development, which showed that Russian poetry could become even more perfect. The only criticism was expressed in a few hesitant remarks on the new work's lack of action and movement *(Son of the Fatherland,* Part 92). The poem's origin is sufficient to explain its compressed, almost anecdotal form. Pushkin simply transposed into verse a story told by a beautiful woman. In a well-known letter from the Crimea, he writes of his first visit to Bakhchisarai: 'I had already heard about the strange memorial to the lovelorn Khan. K. described it to me in a very lyrical way, calling it *la fontaine des larmes*'. Later on he wrote from Odessa: 'I am glad that my *Fountain* is such a success. Its lack of form is not my fault. I superstitiously transposed into verse the tale of a young woman:

> Aux douces lois des vers je pliais les accents
> De sa bouche aimable et naive.

I wrote it, incidentally, for myself alone, but am publishing it because I need the money'. And the money came; the poem was published in 1824 in Moscow by Prince Vyazemsky, and the entire edition was bought up by a group of booksellers for the sum of 3,000 roubles.

In Pushkin's papers there exists an unpublished poem which he had at first intended to use as an introduction to the larger work. Discarded during the final correction of the text and subsequently completely forgotten, it confirms the testimony of the letter on *The Fountain's* origin.

> My tale will be a sorrowful one!

> When, long ago, I first heard
> Of this legend of love,
> My heart grew cold amidst the sounds of joy
> And I forgot for a moment the exultation
> Of the magnificent orgies.
> But then emotion after emotion
> Followed each other in quick succession!
> In place of happiness – a quiet melancholy,
> In place of sorrow – an intoxicating joy.

It is easy to understand why the rendering of the story into verse had of necessity to omit its dramatic development and preserve merely the tone and vividness of impression with which the poet himself was struck on listening to it. The poem, incidentally, was at first called *The Harem* but, as the author remarks in his notes, 'The melancholy epigraph (which of course is the best part of the work) captivated me'. This epigraph, which appeared in the second edition of the poem in 1827, was taken from the Persian poet, Saadi: 'Many, like me, have seen this fountain; some have journeyed further, while the others have gone for ever.'

There still remains one more observation to be made about *The Fountain of Bakhchisarai*. Pushkin's emotions were always of an uncompromising and courageous nature. If, on the one hand, he could easily surrender himself to a genuine passion, he nevertheless, on the other, was incapable of indulging in endearments or of playing with emotions. We know that he used to advise his close friends to rid themselves as soon as possible of vague, languishing desires and to go out on to the high road of life, inspired by a definite aim. His innate desire for cheerfulness and strength was reflected in his language. Everyone will agree that in *The Fountain of Bakhchisarai*, for all its transports of delight, there is nothing that is effeminate, feeble or laboured. When an adjective, which seemed too bold, was replaced, Pushkin wrote to his publisher:

> I do not like to see in an ancient and proud language any traces of European affectation or French refinement; strength and simplicity become it far more; I am moralising from an inner conviction, but I write differently, out of habit ...

We cannot pass over in silence the polemics evoked by Prince Vyazemsky's introduction to the poem. Prince Vyazemsky's introduction under the title, *Instead of an Introduction: A Conversation between the Publisher and a Classicist from the Vyborg Quarter or from Vasilevsky Island,* which preceded the poem, included a refutation of all the criticisms of the classicists, amongst whom there were still some powerful figures. As if foreseeing their objections, the author of the article stated that the poem's real movement resided in its language, in the flow of its story, that there was a poetical clarity and form in its descriptive passages, and that it was enough to see a beautiful building without having to analyse its structure. The most significant section of the article, however, lay in its view of romanticism. The author evidently saw Pushkin's use of local colour, *la couleur locale,* so highly praised by the French aesthetic critics of the time, as evidence of his romanticism...

The whole argument about classicism and romanticism has come to us from France and on the way it has lost, it seems, its serious and academic side. It was of course the Germans who, in the last century, laid the foundations for subsequent disputes with their comparative critical analysis of different literatures: ancient, Eastern and old European. This critical analysis cleared the way for the two great German poets, Schiller and Goethe; elsewhere however it was never completely understood or appreciated, and gave rise to the sort of purely *imitative* literature which, not so long ago, was still considered the highest stage of art. We received only second-hand definitions of romanticism, from France, and neglected any original work on the subject, which was the only way the essence of the matter could have been explained. This is the reason for the rootlessness and lack of any real content which characterised so many articles published in Russia during this period on a subject which divided literature into two hostile camps. Very often, for example, the critics would view the question of romanticism as some kind of curious novelty, almost as news of an unexpected occurrence, and they would discuss it in such terms. It became the custom to view such a question quite arbitrarily, to see it purely according to the fortuitous personal impressions of the author or critic. Thus many saw romanticism as sheer wilfulness on the part of someone who found the positive laws of art tedious, and they defined it essentially as a combination of *'gloom and sensuality, of rapid narration and total lack of action, of ardent passions and cold indifference'* (*European Herald* 1824, No.4). Others upheld the right of talent and genius to disregard established theories, and explained the new tendency as an expresssion of exalted joy *'in which a person is so carried away by his sensations of delight that he cannot but give expression to what he feels'* and added: *'The secret of so-called romantic poetry lies in the vague uncharted depths of the human heart'* (*Moscow Telegraph* 1825, No. 5). Others again saw the essence of romanticism in the use of local colour and indigenous folk elements, on which point, however, nobody was ever very explicit, lacking any clear understanding of the meaning of indigenous. We could give other examples in support of our view, but we will confine ourselves to those already cited. The whole matter was further clouded by the need for an immediate assessment of contemporary literature. There were those Russian romantic writers who were enraptured by the epic poetry of Kheraskov and his followers, the so-called classical romantics, whose views were reflected in Prince V. Odoevsky's Journal *Mnemozina* and there were those romantic writers who reproached Zhukovsky for his liking for folk legends, and for the dreamlike quality and nebulous vagueness of his poetry. Pushkin very wittily and aptly compared this last group to a small child who bites the breast which suckled him simply because he has cut his teeth. Pushkin himself was unable to rid himself of his own friends' capricious interpretations, and was forced to explain the meaning of his poems to his followers, who were completely taken aback by the unexpected content and literary devices. *The Lay of Oleg the Wise,* Chapter 1 of *Onegin* and *The Gipsies* were accompanied by similar commentaries. We shall be discussing these works at greater length in due course, but now we shall simply cite an extract from Pushkin's letter on *The Lay of Oleg the Wise,* in which he was compelled to explain its meaning:

> It seems you don't like Oleg – this is a mistake. The old prince's feeling of brotherly love for his steed and his concern for its fate are signs of a touching simplicity of heart, and in the very simplicity of the incident there lies a great deal of poetry.

Our poet would have to resort to such commentaries even for those critics who were most ardently acclaiming romanticism.

It is interesting to see Pushkin's attitude to the two hostile camps and his innermost conception of this literary argument. At the time nobody yet realised that his works would make this argument an anachronism, and that they would replace both these concepts of romanticism and classicism with a new and much higher concept of creativity and art which sought its own laws, from within itself. He conceived the essence of the matter very simply, holding the view that the difference between the two types of work lay only in their *form* and saying that if people tried to differentiate them according to the *spirit* in which they were written, then it would be impossible to avoid contradictions and false interpretations. This is what he wrote, for himself, about the question with which Russian literature was then so preoccupied:

> Our critics are still not agreed on a clear difference between the classical and the romantic types of literature. For our confusion on the subject we are indebted to the French journalists, who generally assign to Romanticism everything that they consider is characterised by visionary idealism and Germanic ideology or based on popular superstition and legend. This is a most imprecise definition. A poem might possess all these characteristics and yet still belong to the classical type. To this type must be assigned those poems, whose *forms* were known to the Greeks and Romans or of which they have left us models. If, instead of the form of a poem, we take as a basis the *spirit* in which it was written, then we shall never arrive at a clear definition. A hymn by Pindar naturally differs in spirit from an ode by Anacreon, Juvenal's satire from that of Horace, and *Gerusalemme Liberata* from the *Aeneid* – but they all belong equally to the classical type. Which poems belong then to the romantic type? Those which were unknown to the Ancients and those whose earlier forms have been changed or replaced by others.

This simple and ingenuous definition reveals Pushkin's general lack of enthusiasm for theoretical subtleties, which he was to show many times during the course of his life. Whereas he was able to make very penetrating remarks about individual works, including his own, the laboured intellectual process, which abstract theories of art demand, was quite alien to his nature. Very often he simply felt an idea to be true and would jot it down in his notebook without fully exploring its significance. Here is an example of this:

Pushkin was called a Romantic and he himself used the same term about himself, but at the back of his mind he meant something completely different. In his letters to his friends, for example, he constantly used the expression *romantic work,* but he clearly meant simply a creative work which did not belong to any particular system or one-sided view. He never found an alternative way of expressing his real thoughts; nor, probably, did he ever look for one. For him, this universally familiar and accepted word signified a concept, which, at the time had occurred to only very few people. In his letters on *Boris Godunov* we shall see that, by the term 'romantic tragedy', he meant the totally free manifestation of the creative spirit in the sphere of art. Again and again, for example, he wrote: 'I wanted to write something truly *romantic'.* On another occasion, he said: 'An important matter! I have written a tragedy and am very pleased with it, but I am afraid of publishing it – our timid tastes will not tolerate true *romanticism...* Everything I have read about romanticism has been beside the point'. Behind these simple remarks it is possible to discern his philosophy underlying a work of art; but he never analysed his thoughts, leaving their full expression to the works themselves. And indeed, they clearly revealed laws on which a true theory of art must be based and which made Pushkin the true mentor and guide of aesthetic taste in society...

DOBROLYUBOV

ALEXANDER SERGEEVICH PUSHKIN

At the age of twenty-one N. A. Dobrolyubov (1836–61) succeeded Chernyshevsky as the principal critic of the most famous Russian nineteenth-century literary journal, *The Contemporary* which had been founded by Pushkin in 1836. Dobrolyubov shared his predecessor's materialist aesthetics and followed him in using literary criticism as a vehicle for discussing the state of Russian society. His essay *Alexander Sergeevich Pushkin* (1858) first appeared, however, in another journal, *The Russian Illustrated Almanac,* under the pseudonymous signature of N. Laibov. Here Dobrolyubov repeats the views of Belinsky about Pushkin's realism and significance for Russian society but makes a more original contribution when he goes on to analyse the mood of restless discontent which he detects in the works of Pushkin's last years.

Pushkin's significance is enormous, not only in the history of Russian literature, but also in the history of Russian enlightenment. He was the first to teach the Russian public to read, and that was his supreme service. In his verses we heard for the first time the living Russian language and saw for the first time our authentic Russian world. Everyone was charmed and captivated by the powerful music of this unprecedented poetry. Before him Russian poets had extolled to order with their hired rapture various triumphal illuminations, festivals and other events about which they themselves had no conception and for which an entire nation had no concern. Then, having delivered themselves of this buffoonery, these worthy individuals turned their attention to humane ideas, but generally saw them as completely divorced from life and began to build a utopian edifice on unprepared ground. In this way literature ran to sentimentality: ignoring real calamities, people would weep over fictional woes; while bowing down to the dominant vice, they castigated imaginary vices and crowned ideal virtues. Realising eventually the fruitlessness of this lachrymal tendency, at the beginning of the century our poetry found itself confessing that the real world was not as handsome as it had been painted. But then poetry found consolation for us in another, ethereal and misty world among shades, spectres and other apparitions. Poetry mourned for something, dimly and languidly hymned something, including the misty distance, and strove after something unknown. Among earthly subjects it deigned to hymn only *elevated* sentiments or erotic revelry. In his early years Pushkin paid tribute to each of these tendencies, but quickly managed to free himself from them and establish his own original poetry in Russia. Brought up in a family and in real life, attending school at a time when, after the events of the war with Napoleon, Russians were beginning to reach self-awareness, and enjoying the opportunity of coming into contact with all classes of Russian society, Pushkin was able to grasp the true needs and the true character of our national life. He looked closely at Russian nature and at Russian life and saw that they contained much which was genuinely good and poetic. Fascinated by this discovery, he proceded to depict reality, and the multitude rapturously welcomed these wonderful creations in which they heard so much which was familiar to them, which they had long seen, but which they had never realised contained so much poetic charm. And Pushkin responded to everything which manifested Russian life, he surveyed its every aspect, traced it in every degree and in every part, without devoting himself exclusively to any one thing. We do not consider this diversity and lack of a clearly defined tendency an especial merit of the poet, as have certain others, but we are convinced that it was a necessary phenomenon belonging to the age. Thus it was with science, when the first Russian scholar to reveal to us what science really is had to be himself a chemist, and a physicist, and a historian, and a political economist, and an orator and, moreover, a poet as well. Thus it was at the beginning of our poetry, when in one man were combined a writer of odes, a fabulist, a satirist, a composer of elegies, tragedies and comedies, etc. Thus it was now too at the discovery of reality: here was another new unexplored world, and it was hard to bring oneself to select any one thing in it. We had to try many different paths before holding to any one of them. Everything attracted and everything seemed so beautiful that sweet sounds of delight burst forth of their own accord from the poet's youthful breast. And the multitude listened to him with reverent love: for them this verse and these images were a radiant remembrance of what they had up to that moment dared to think of only as prosaic banalities and everyday annoyances which it was advisable to keep away from. And the significance of Pushkin's poetry lies precisely here: he directed people's thoughts towards those objects which ought to occupy them and diverted them away from everything misty and spectral and morbidly dreamy in which earlier poets had found their ideal of beauty and of every perfection. Therefore, it should not seem strange that in Pushkin we are so *charmed* by our poor world and so little disturbed by its imperfections. In his day it was important to show again that which is good in the world, so as to bring people down to earth from their castles in the air. The time for strict analysis had not yet come, and Pushkin could not summon it into being prematurely. Besides, that would have been quite useless: a select few would have understood him at the time, but the mass of the people would have remained faithful to its daydreams. Today, however, Pushkin's verse has prepared the form in which higher creations have subsequently been able to appear and his influence on the public has made them more capable of receiving and understanding these creations. The public have already understood the value of life from Pushkin's mellifluous verses and now the bitterest indignation against the trivial vulgarity of life will nudge people towards reform rather than carrying them away from earthly reality into supernal spaces.

That is how we today regard the historical significance of Pushkin's poetry. But in his own time it was impossible to grasp this clearly, and he himself was not fully aware of his mission. It could not of course have been otherwise: as a poet, Pushkin himself was bound to be captivated before the rest of Russia by those things with which he captivated others; as a poet of a particular time and nation, he was bound to belong primarily to his own time and nation. He was not one of those titanic natures who, recognising their own rational superiority and satisfied only by their own power, stand above the multitude in their solitary greatness, refusing to stoop to the multitude's level of comprehension or to attract its sympathies. No, Pushkin walked on a level with his age. In spite of his assertions of contempt for the crowd, he pleased them; otherwise there would be no way of explaining the enormous success he enjoyed among the public. The public never rewards with its peculiar love the man who stands above its level of comprehension. Geniuses who are in advance of their age are appraised by posterity.

But even Pushkin did not always follow his own rule:

> Why argue fruitlessly with the age?
> Custom is a despot among men.

His richly endowed, ardent and noble nature did not always submit to the demands of circumstances. Looking more closely into the subjective nature of Pushkin's poetry, we can go even further and say that we see there a constant searching which is not satisfied by reality. His lyrics are full of sad longing, and if this sad longing is not profound, if it is immediately dispersed by a forced smile, then the reason is to be found mostly in the light spirit of the poet's theoretical education under which he could not even seriously ask himself what idea might lie at the root of his sad impulses. But now we can understand the poet's sad longing more easily than he could himself. We have seen that there was in his life a period when every impression was new to him:

> When those sublime emotions,
> Freedom, glory and love,
> And the inspired arts
> So strongly stirred the blood.

The picturesque scenery of the Caucasus and the Crimea soon provided him with a substitute for all inner questions. Discarding every external aim and every extraneous aspiration, he enclosed himself within the sphere of pure artistry. He fulfilled his task magnificently. In vain did he try to justify himself by claiming that serving the muse allowed no worldy vanity. In vain did he hurl a contemptuous cry at the crowd:

> Be gone! What concern
> Of the peaceful poet are you?

In vain, because it was not the crowd, but his own inner awareness which troubled his noble soul, and these agitations are strongly reflected in his works. They appear only for brief moments, but they possess all the greater significance for us since on each occasion the poet in no way resolves his doubts and sufferings, but tries to dismiss them with a joke or an effort to forget them. In this way his feeling of sad longing repeatedly returns with renewed force and allows us to see that he was not satisfied with his role of carefree artist. 'I understand the pettiness of life', he says, 'and I am little attached to it...' He calls the world empty and fears lest his soul should grow cold in this world which deadens rapture. He regrets his youth:

> But it is sad to think that in vain
> Youth was given to us...
> That our best desires
> And our fresh dreams
> Have faded away in rapid succession.

He trembles and curses as he recalls his past life and suffers at the thought that he has outlived his dreams. He languishes under this pain, saying,

> There is no goal before me,
> My heart is empty, my mind is idle,
> And I am wearied by the melancholy
> Of life's monotonous sound.

His last elegies are full of a burning, joyless sorrow. He senses that life will not give him any peace and says:

> My path is joyless. The future's surging sea
> Forebodes me toil and sorrow.

And what despair is reflected in those notes of hope with which he tried to console himself:

> But, O my friends, I do not want to die;
> I want to live, in order to think and suffer;
> And I know that there will be delights for me
> Among sorrows, cares and tribulations:
> At times again I shall revel in harmony,
> I shall dissolve into tears over a fantasy...

What a wretched consolation! Only a man who has lost all faith in real happiness can dream about enjoying fantasies. And this deliberate desire to deceive himself is Pushkin's chief shortcoming. He found no way out of his doubts and exclaimed:

> Dearer to me than ten thousand base truths
> Is the deception which ennobles us

and achieved a state of calm... but not for long.

During the last period of his life he found a steadier calming influence – in religion. This of course was to lead to complete reconciliation; this was the end of the agonised struggle. We regard as unfounded the opinion of those who surmise that Pushkin would have eventually appeared to us in a new, as yet unseen light, bearing the fruits of a new original development. No, exhausted by life's battle, he had reached the end of his journey. He could have given us many new works of the highest artistic quality, but it was impossible to foresee any new, higher development in the character of his poetry.

But, having regard to his conception of art as an end in itself, Pushkin was able, nevertheless, to understand also his obligations towards society. In his *Monument* he places to his own credit not his artistry, but the fact 'that he aroused kind feelings with his lyre, that through the living charm of verse he was of use and called for mercy for the fallen.'

Let us note too that to Pushkin belongs the idea behind *The Inspector General* and *Dead Souls,* and that he inspired Gogol to work on those themes. This shows that in his heart there always lay an awareness of what our society needed.

In the images which Pushkin himself created it is in fact possible to see certain hidden thoughts which are in strong accord with his mood of eternally dissatisfied anxiety. His Onegin is not simply a society fop; he is a man with great strength of soul, a man who understands the emptiness of the life to which fate had called him but lacks sufficient strength of character to pull himself out of it. His Aleko is also a sort of Onegin who has run away from society to join the gipsies, with the same praiseworthy intention with which Krylov's wolf ran off to Arcadia. And the poet describes with obvious love the gipsy encampment and the simple life and customs of the gipsies, as if trying to deceive his own emotion. But Aleko finds sorrow and treachery even here. Of course it is his own fault rather than the fault of those he joined and whose happiness he destroyed, but the poet seems to be glad of this opportunity to console himself with the thought that there is no happiness anywhere on earth. Thus he writes his sad epilogue:

> But there is no happiness even among you,
> Poor children of nature,
> Even under your tattered tents
> There dwell tormenting dreams.

For the sake of his own peace of mind he is unwilling to comprehend even the image which he himself created.

We had no intention of producing an analysis of all Pushkin's works and so the reader will not of course accuse us of completely ignoring many of the poet's wonderful creations. But it is impossible to limit oneself to simply a few words in speaking about them, and the bounds of our article are quite narrow. Besides, if we were to launch into a detailed account, we could of course add nothing new after the remarkable essays on Pushkin which Belinsky wrote for *Notes of the Fatherland* between 1843 and 1846. We have limited ourselves simply to general remarks about the character of Pushkin's poetry, especially his lyrics, which offer the greatest opportunity to follow the direction and spiritual development of the poet himself and, having reread him, we can now say with full respect to his glorious name: Pushkin exercised a beneficial influence by directing the people's gaze onto the path which others were to tread. He did not express the full significance of all Russian nature and life, but on the other hand, from the standpoint of form, he created out of them everything which could be created without touching their inner content. And this is why after Pushkin the mere portrayal of an object could no longer satisfy; after him poets were required to make sense of the phenomena they described, to capture in their work not merely the visible distinctive features of an object but also its innermost nature. These demands led to the emergence of a new period of literature, the most complete expression of which we see in Gogol, but the origin of which was already latent in the poetry of Pushkin.

GRIGORIEV

THE DEVELOPMENT OF THE IDEA OF NATIONALITY IN OUR LITERATURE SINCE THE DEATH OF PUSHKIN

A. A. Grigoriev (1822–1864) was a leading Russian critic of the mid-nineteenth century. A close friend of Dostoevsky, Grigoriev took up a position very akin to that of the Slavophiles. This article, *The Development of the Idea of Nationality in Our Literature Since the Death of Pushkin,* published in Dostoevsky's journal *Time* in 1862 and given here in extracts, clearly shows Grigoriev's basic position as a literary critic. As in his other works on Pushkin, Grigoriev emphasises the writer's links with the 'soil' and with the Russian people and sees Pushkin as the crystallisation of specifically Russian traits as opposed to alien European types and ideas. Pushkin is an *intuitive* as well as an intellectual artist and it is precisely this intuitive and irrational element which makes him a true poet 'of the people'. Grigoriev writes in an unattractive, prolix style but the originality of his thought and his contribution to Pushkin criticism cannot be doubted.

To anyone like P.Ya. Chaadaev, who has looked boldly and honestly on Russian life, its past and present, from a Westernist point of view, and who is not blinded by essentially false analogies, Russian life must seem as empty, as monotonous and as sad as the Kirghizian steppe. And yet such a point of view did not suddenly appear, like a *Deus ex machina*. The seed of such a critical view was sown long ago in the consciousness of our greatest figures; from time to time, it burgeoned in the greatest of them all, Pushkin, now in the form of an ironic reconciliation with reality, as in the well-known stanza from the missing chapter of *Onegin,* now as a poem which he himself called *Caprice:*

> Come over here, my red-faced critic,
> Sit down by me, my pot-bellied cynic,
> Always so ready to mock our languid muse...

a poem, which for all its joking tone, contains in embryonic form many of the attitudes our literature was subsequently to adopt to reality: Lermontov's view, expressed with such vital bitterness,

> I love my country, but with a strange love,
> My reason cannot fathom it...

and the stories of the 1840s with their consistently and deliberately unpleasant portrayals of an unhealthy and uncivilised society in which the best people were condemned to perish; Ogaryov's plaintive cries,

> Tell me then! What else is there to do
> In this sad land of ours,
> Save for the wife to keep home,
> Or the husband to go hunting..?

and the gloomy, joyless views of that great analyst of the 'banality of the banal'; the depressing cloudy-grey light which sentimental naturalism throws on life; and finally, almost all Nekrasov's poems up to his most recent one – up to, that is, *Village News,* which by the way is very difficult to call a poem at all – all these are in essence nothing more than a development of Pushkin's *Caprice,* that is to say, a consistent development and exegesis of the point of view briefly expressed by Pushkin in his *Caprice...*

But Pushkin was the only complete person in our literature, the only person who fully represented all the facets of our national physiognomy.

For him the bitter and joyless contemplation of reality was no more than a brief moment of awareness, and certainly not something which would express itself in sharp bursts of critical reaction, as in the case of Lermontov, or anything which would distort an impartial and direct view of life, as in the stories of the 1840s. However much Pushkin's impartiality led people to accuse him of indifference or lack of principle, he was first and foremost an artist, half-consciously and half-subconsciously a tremendous life-force, a 'hero' in the sense that Carlyle uses the word heroism, a force, which influenced not merely the present but also the future. He was blessed with an instinctive feeling and love for Russian life. And despite the view which has emerged recently, denying his significance as a truly national poet, a view conceived by intellectuals who have come to know Russian life only through books, this is an undoubted truth, confirmed by the tenor of his writing in *Boris Godunov, The Water Nymph, The Bridegroom, The Drowned Man,* in his fairy-tales *The Fisherman and the Fish, Kuzma Ostolop,* the extract on *The She-bear,* etc., and, what is more important, by the tenor of his overall attitude in *The Captain's Daughter, The Tales of Belkin* and other works. Even in the days when, in his own expression, he was pursued by his muse who galloped with him, like Leonora, through the moonlit mountains of the Caucasus, when, as he says,

> I ... sang
> To the Caucasian maiden, my ideal,
> To the slave-girls from the banks of the Salgir,

when his heart was filled with images of the Prisoner, Aleko, Girei and other martyrs to the passions of this world, even then this sensitive being responded with an astonishing sense of truth to the reality which surrounded him, and even while reacting to this encroaching sense of reality with semi-comic, semi-serious repugnance:

> Pah! The prosaic ravings
> And assorted rubbish of the Flemish school...

he was able to weave poetry of tremendous originality out of this same reality ('Winter. What can we do in the country? ...', 'Frost and sun, heavenly day...', 'How long have I left on this earth...' 'I am sad. Nina, the path I tread is boring...', *The Devils...*) Then of course there is the purely Russian figure of Tatyana, still the only true and complete realisation of a Russian woman, Tatyana who,

> ... Russian in spirit,
> Loved the cold beauty
> Of the Russian winter
> Without herself knowing why,

and in whom the poet's muse appeared as

> ... a provincial girl,
> With a sad, pensive expression,
> And a French book in her hands...

And Onegin himself, who although by no means a 'Muscovite in Harold's cloak', is nonetheless revealed as a Russian by numerous traits in his character... All this still needs to be elucidated and proved, but I am merely indicating something which needs no proof: the yearning unexpectedly expressed by the very same poet who begins his novel by adopting a satirical, or at least humorous attitude towards just such principles ('This is how families are...' and numerous other stanzas), a yearning to be able to depict

> ... the simple words
> Of a father or old uncle,
> The trysting places of children
> Under the old lime-trees, by the stream.

Finally there are *The Tales of Belkin, The Chronicle of the Village of Goryukhino* and *The Captain's Daughter* in which in particular the poet achieves the most astonishing identity with the attitudes of previous generations; *Dubrovsky,* in which only an immediate awareness of the essence of national life could have created, for example, the figure of the blacksmith who, while setting light with stern indifference to the petty officials, clambers into the fire to rescue a cat, lest 'one of God's creatures should perish...'

It can hardly be doubted that these characters and episodes, which I have cited at random, form the nucleus of all the attitudes which our literature has adopted towards the people and their everyday existence, towards our fathers and forefathers, the nucleus of Aksakov's *Family Chronicle,* for example, and of many of Pisemsky's stories, just as *The Undertaker* in *The Tales of Belkin* contains the nucleus of naturalism.

But nevertheless, in Pushkin's complete and all-embracing nature, a purely negative view of life and reality can form only a fragment of the whole... He does not dwell on this fragment but goes further and identifies himself with the figure of Belkin. But even here he does not stop. In identifying himself with the opinions of his fathers and forefathers in *The Captain's Daughter* he is not denigrating or denying the existence of past ideals, for at the same time he is creating *The Stone Guest*...

Pushkin's all-embracing nature and tremendous national significance is shown by the fact that the purely realistic, even somewhat primitive, attitudes of Belkin go hand in hand with a profound understanding and recreation of the ideals of the past which inspired him as a young man, rather than with a renunciation of such ideals...

Pushkin is neither a Westernist, nor a Slavophile: he is a Russian, whose characteristics European culture has helped to shape. Those gentlemen who seek to deny Pushkin's significance as a national poet, always cite the same point, by indicating certain false Karamzinian forms to which even the great poet, in common with everybody else of his time, submitted; for everything that is false in *Boris Godunov*, in particular the figure of Godunov himself, springs from Karamzin. Everything purely Pushkinian (whether it be the feast at Shuisky's, the scenes in the tavern, the battle scene, the scene at the Novodevichii Monastery or at the Place of Execution) is as eternal as the soul of the people itself, or it has both a poetical and universal truth (the fountain scene, for example). Nor should it be forgotten that those who criticise the falseness of certain aspects of *Boris Godunov* evaluate these aspects, not from the standpoint of the people, but by using new theories which have replaced the stereotyped and brilliant forms of Karamzin. And these new theories, as long as they remain simply theories, are just as capable as the stereotyped Karamzinian forms of distorting the artistic representation of life. This has been shown very clearly in Mey's brilliant work *The Maid of Pskov*, in which the Pskov popular assembly is so well and so poetically conceived, in which the anticipation of Ivan the Terrible's arrival and his first appearance is portrayed with such grandeur and truth, in which Ivan himself becomes such a comic figure when he embraces his son and Boris and discusses his policies of state entirely in the manner of Solovyov, in which Ivan is portrayed practically as a tender and soft-hearted figure – the very same Ivan who listed a very large number of unknown and nameless serfs whom the executioner Tomilo had 'dispatched' ('Weigh these names in the scale, O Lord'). Would it have been better if Pushkin had created his *Boris Godunov* according to the latest theories as well ... while they are only theories? The Karamzinian forms are often false, but you do not find in Karamzin false sympathies and antipathies, which diverge as sharply as the most recent theories from the popular memory...

It seems to me that a careful reading and study of Pushkin's *Boris Godunov* should lead people, not to question the poet's national significance, but rather to a sense of amazement at his astonishing national sensitivity, at the greatness of his genius... *Boris Godunov* like all his attempts at drama, is a sketch rather than a brightly coloured painting, but such sketches are striking in their truth and beauty... Probably the poet felt that the real colours were no longer obtainable, that they had in fact vanished for ever in a way of life which had become so separated from all the events of its past history, that one of the characters in our other truly national writer is led to remark: 'This Lithunia has simply dropped on us out of the blue' *(The Thunderstorm)*. Our poet, as a poet, had no desire to paint his sketches in cheerful colours. He desired the truth. Even in *The Water Nymph* where he gave full rein to his fantasy he created in fact only sketches. But do you gentlemen who consider that Pushkin is not a national poet know just how full of majestic life these sketches are? People have tried to put *The Water Nymph* on the stage in the form in which Pushkin created it. But the attempt proved unsuccessful precisely because the sketches in their full form are too compressed and too brief to be realised on the stage. *The Water Nymph,* its original form and content, and even most of its divine poetry, has been made into an opera. Just look how the libretto – Pushkin's poem – in acquiring colour, body and dramatic continuity, overpowers the music, music moreover which is in many ways a remarkable composition, written by an outstanding musical talent. The composer's attempt to give colour and form to these sketches sometimes seems to me, and probably to many other people, an act of insolence!... Every feature in this work of genius stands out in such sharp relief that the music can only suffer!... A strange feeling overcomes you: at times you are ready to be irritated by the music, you would like simply to hear the poetry, which is on a far more exalted plane than the music, but you nonetheless realise that the entire poetic creation is only a sketch, that this sketch can be realised on the stage and become accessible to the general public only if it is supplemented by the use of colours, however inferior in quality they may be.

But if Pushkin's highly artistic sense of truth prevented him from using false colours and forced him to present his material in sketch-form, nothing held back other, not ungifted, sometimes indeed very talented people of his time from using such colours, provided they were effective.

The age, which even the sensitive and, in the realm of art, almost invariably perspicacious Belinsky called the romantically-national era, deceived not only us, the readers, but with the best will in the world, itself. And the source of such self-deception lay in none other than the stereotyped Karamzinian forms. The age believed in these forms, believed in the correctness of the Karamzinian analogy and was highly enraptured by this belief. And, indeed, how could it not be enraptured? We had captured our fugitive national spirit and recreated it evidently in a simple and completely decorous way, we had introduced its idea into our entire history. We naively believed, for example that 'Yaroslav acceded to the throne over corpses', that 'Henceforth (from the reign of John – not Ivan – but John III) our history was to assume a character truly derived from the state', etc. etc., without in any way noticing how laughable these majestic phrases became as soon as they were compared with the chronicles and historical documents or with the wills of the princes themselves, in which the language and concepts are much closer to the present day than to concepts of state and grand, official language... We need only remind ourselves of our child-like delight at the appearance of *Yurii Miloslavsky*... I am not talking about the delight of the readers but of the critics. In the most serious of the contemporary journals, *The Telescope,* a long article appeared in connection with Zagoskin's second novel *Roslavlev* about the historical novel in general; the concept of the Russian national idea in this genre received very naive treatment.

It did not occur to a single person to say that it could all be explained quite simply: by the influence of Walter Scott on the one hand, and of Karamzin on the other.

It was only Pushkin, not only as poet but also as critic, who understood the essence of the matter, but he would express his views in an indirect form, invariably with great success and subtlety. When Zagoskin's *Roslavlev* appeared Pushkin wrote a review of the work in the form of a highly artistic but, sadly, incomplete tale, which restored the correct colours and significance to an event and an age, which had been so distorted in Zagoskin's novel, but even this subtle and artistic piece of criticism became known only posthumously... About the prevailing tendency of the 1830s he kept silent; he himself never subscribed to it and used colours only when he was convinced of their authenticity, as in his *Negro of Peter the Great, The Captain's Daughter* or *Dubrovsky*. He kept silent even when the highly talented Lazhechnikov's attempts started to appear in print, probably because he saw in them a combination of talent, even at times true artistry, with indescribable falseness. When we were all in raptures over the use of 'popular' speech in Zagoskin's novels, Pushkin, with his sure command of idiom (*The She-Bear*), his deep understanding both of the comedy underlying Russian life (*The Chronicle of the Village of Goryukhino*) and of the tragedy (the blacksmith in *Dubrovsky*, Pugachov in *The Captain's Daughter*, Pugachov's feast etc.), did not once permit himself to write a single story which contained 'popular' speech, for he knew that the time had not yet come, that the colours were still not to hand and that there was nowhere they could be obtained until people followed his advice and learnt their Russian from the women of Moscow who baked communion bread (the notes to *Onegin*); he knew that what purported to be popular speech was not popular at all but taken from the nobility, that the feelings such speech reflected were false, and so on. I repeat once again that he used colours only when he knew them to be authentic; and everything that he wrote using such colours is as eternal as the Russian soul, whether it be Tatyana's nurse and the story of her marriage, or Natasha's words in *The Bridegroom*, the speech of the miller's daughter in which even the iambic pentameter is transformed into the rhythm of folk verse, or the crowd scenes in *Boris Godunov*. All this is eternal, all this is as true as if it had been written today by Ostrovsky who knows the Russian character and the popular idiom so intimately. No, it is even better than Ostrovsky, at least when Pushkin expresses it in the language of the Gods, in poetry; it is better, precisely because it is written in such language, its characteristics etched sharply in bronze...

The negative ability to discern falsehood and thereby to avoid not only all falsehood but the least ambiguity of characterisation, to avoid it, of course only when it is impossible to recreate the truth — this ability constitutes just as important a quality in geniuses as their positive qualities. Pushkin was incapable of inventing colours. He was unable, like Karamzin, to borrow alien forms by analogy because he was incomparably more gifted than Karamzin in the spiritual sphere and consequently more farsighted; to take from contemporary life, like the rest of his age, the first colours he came across was also inimical to his artistic conscience. This conscience was such a profound force in him that in his portrayal, for example, of Boris' daughter Kseniya bewailing the loss of her betrothed, he replaced some evidently superb lines of poetry by a passage of prose in the style of a Russian song, as simple and as unadorned as possible ('My beloved betrothed, beloved prince...') he struck out the scene with the two monks, evidently also a superb scene but one which apparently dissatisfied him; he even omitted from the first edition of *Boris Godunov* the irreproachable crowd scene by the Novodevichii Monastery, a scene which appeared only in the posthumous edition and, in the main body of the work, only in the Annenkov edition... Yes, this 'scion of the nobility', who wrote in French (superbly, it should be added) his notes about the historical drama and his *Boris Godunov,* had a feeling of reverential awe for the simple people, a religious fear of misrepresenting them, their way of thinking, their feelings and their idiom... It is clear that the folk tales of his nurse, Irina Rodionovna, evoked a profound response in the sensitive heart of this great man...

PISAREV

PUSHKIN AND BELINSKY

D. I. Pisarev (1840–68), one of the most influential theorists of Russian nihilism, produced the bulk of his writings during the years 1862–66 when he was in prison. Since his supreme criterion of value was practical utility, Pisarev favoured the popularisation of the natural sciences and tended to dismiss much literature – including the greater part of Pushkin's poetry – as worthless. In his essay *Pushkin and Belinsky,* from which the extracts below were taken, Pisarev, himself a brilliant stylist, recognizes Pushkin's formal mastery but argues with wonderfully sustained irony against Belinsky's attempts to establish the high seriousness and universal scope of *Evgenii Onegin*. This essay was first published in 1865 in *The Russian Word* which during the 1860s, under Pisarev's guidance, gradually supplanted *The Contemporary* as the leading journal of Russian radical thought.

The whole of *Evgenii Onegin* is nothing but a brilliant and sparkling apotheosis of a most joyless and senseless *status quo*. All the scenes in the novel are painted in such bright colours, all the dirt of real life is so carefully brushed away, the major absurdities of our social customs are described in such a majestic manner, our minor peccadillos are ridiculed with such an imperturbable geniality, and the poet himself finds life so jolly and breathes so freely that the impressionable reader cannot but imagine himself as the happy inhabitant of an Arcadia which is about to witness the establishment of the golden age.

Indeed, what human suffering did Pushkin manage to observe and consider necessary to carol? First of all, boredom or melancholy; secondly unrequited love; and thirdly... and thirdly... nothing at all. Apparently no other forms of suffering existed in Russian society in the 1820s. At first Onegin is bored because he is too happy and because he has enjoyed too fully all the blessings of life; then Tatyana suffers because Onegin does not want to marry her; and finally Onegin suffers because Tatyana refuses to become his mistress. That is to say, in Russian society during the 1820s there were two capital vices, two vices onto which the greatest poet in Russia considered it necessary to focus his enlightened attention. Firstly, in Russia at that time the blessings of life were too many, so that Russian youths over-indulged themselves on them, upset their stomachs and fell into a state of melancholy. Secondly, Russian men and Russian women were so constituted by nature that they did not always fall in love with each other simultaneously. It would happen, for instance that a woman might be ablaze, while a man had hardly begun to feel warm; later the man is aflame, but the women's passion has already burnt out and is dying away. This inconvenient arrangement used to cause much distress both to enlightened Russian men and to charming Russian women. Pushkin's novel threw considerable light on these two principal sores of Russian life. Once it had been published, the novel's *heroic sweep* made change inevitable and, having carefully considered the sufferings of Onegin and Tatyana, Russian society immediately issued the necessary edicts, firstly to ensure that the quantity of life's blessings should be brought strictly into harmony with the capacity of youthful stomachs, and secondly to ensure that enlightened Russian men and charming Russian women should become inflamed with love simultaneously. Once this equilibrium was duly instituted, melancholy and unrequited love were swept away, the golden age was established in Russia, young men began to partake of life's blessings in reasonable moderation and, thanks to these moderate youths, in due time the maidens were transformed into contented wives and wonderful mothers. But this golden age disappeared like a happy dream and the youthful descendants of the inhabitants of Arcadia look upon the heroic sweep of *Evgenii Onegin* as a quite absurd dream, which, once one has awoken, it is hard to understand, hard even to recall. And these corrupt descendants are beginning to realise that if *Evgenii Onegin* is an encyclopedia of Russian life, then that means that this encyclopedia and Russian life have nothing in common, for the encyclopedia is one thing while Russian life is another.

Following certain obscure traditions and certain profound historical research, one might for instance be led to believe that in Russia of the 1820s there existed that institution which is now known as serfdom. It would be interesting to see how that feature of Russian life is reflected in the encyclopedia. Consulting it, we learn that when Onegin took up residence in the country he replaced the yoke of the old fashioned *corvée* by a light quit-rent and that the peasant thanked fate; we learn that Madame Larina 'beat the maidservants in a temper', 'shaved their foreheads' and 'gave to the former Akulka the name Selina'; we learn that when the maidservants picked berries they were ordered to sing a song 'so that sly lips should not secretly eat the master's fruit'; we learn that 'the peasant, celebrating, renews his journey on his sledge', and the serf boy runs about the yard, 'putting the watch-dog onto a toboggan and pretending himself to be a horse', and that at Christmas time:

> Servant-girls from the whole estate
> Told fortunes for their young mistresses,
> And every year predicted for them
> Military husbands and a campaign.

That is all we can extract from the encyclopedia concerning serfdom. And, truth to tell, these details are bathed in the most rosy light. The landowner eases the peasant's situation; the peasant blesses his fate; and the peasant celebrates the onset of winter – which means he loves the winter, which means he is warm in winter and has plenty of bread; moreover, since the Russian winter lasts at least six months, then that means the peasant spends at least half his life celebrating and in a benign frame of mind. The manservant's son also rejoices and enjoys himself – which means that no-one beats him, he is well fed and warmly dressed and is not turned from an early age into a little cossack who must sit on a wooden horse in the servants' quarters, ready to run and fetch, now a handkerchief, now a glass of water, now a pipe, now a snuff-box. The rosy light darkens a little with the unexpected news that Madame Larina beat the servant-girls; but, in the first place, she beat them only when she lost her temper, and she probably lost her temper only very rarely and with good reason, for had she been liable to lose her temper frequently and injudiciously, then of course the shrewd Onegin, friend and beloved hero of the author of the encyclopedia, would certainly not have described Madame Larina as 'a very sweet old lady'. In the second place, the servant-girls had to be beaten because, as we learn from the same encyclopedia, they were real rogues. They were liable to steal their master's berries, and the mistress of the house, in order to defend the sacred rights of property and to safeguard the villainous servant-girls from an abominable crime, was compelled to rack her seigneurial brains and devise that intricate remedy, dubbed by the encyclopedia 'an enterprise of rural wit', which taught the servant girls to prefer elevated aesthetic pleasures, such as singing, to base material objects, like berries. Thirdly, the servant-girls were clearly not given painful beatings, because neither the beatings themselves nor the girls' memories of them prevented them from spending Christmas singing canticles – which they had the opportunity to perfect in the summer during their frequent encounters with base material objects, i.e. with the berries.

Thus, on the evidence of the encyclopedia, we are fully justified in concluding that serfdom provided much benefit and pleasure to both landowners and peasants. The landowners enjoyed the opportunity to display their generosity, while the peasants enjoyed the opportunity to learn disinterestedly from them, and the servant-girls developed their aesthetic sense and capacity for moral self-control – in a word, all prospered and assisted each other towards self-perfection.

Should you want to know how the most educated stratum of Russian society of the 1820s occupied itself, our encyclopedia of Russian life will tell you that this educated stratum ate and drank, danced and went to the theatre, fell in love and suffered, now from boredom, now from love. Nothing else? you may ask. Nothing else, replies the encyclopedia. That is all very jolly, you may think, but hardly plausible: there must have been other things in Russia at that time. Surely young men thought about their careers and tried to work their way to wealth and distinction? Surely not every individual was satisfied with his lot and lifted no finger to improve it? Surely Onegin cannot have despised people simply because they stamped their heels too loudly during a mazurka? And surely there were people in society at that time who did not veil the thinkers of the eighteenth century in mourning crepe and who could regard Onegin with the same contempt with which Onegin himself regarded Buyanov, Pustyakov and the various other representatives of provincial fauna? To this last question the encyclopedia gives a straight negative reply. At least we see that Onegin looks down on everyone, and that nobody looks at him in that way. All the other questions are left without any answer whatsoever.

On the other hand, our encyclopedia gives us extremely detailed information about restaurants in the capital and about the dancer Istomina who flies about the stage 'like down from the lips of Aeolus'. We learn that jam is served in saucers and bilberry cordial in jugs. We are told that the ladies spoke Russian with grammatical mistakes and we learn what verses were written in the autograph albums of provincial young ladies.We are told that champagne was sometimes replaced in the country by Tsimlyansk wine, that the cotillion is danced after the mazurka, and so on. In short, you find a description of a great many trivial customs, but from these tiny snippets, useful only for the expert antiquarian, you will elicit almost nothing of the physiology or the pathology of society at that time. You will certainly not discover the ideas and illusions by which society lived; nor will you discover what gave it meaning and direction, or what supported its nonsense and apathy. You will not see an historical portrait, but merely a collection of old-fashioned costumes and coiffures, old-fashioned menus and notices, old-fashioned furniture and old-fashioned grimaces. All this is described with extraordinary liveliness and jollity, but it is surely not enough: in order to draw a historical portrait, one must be not only an attentive observer, but a penetrating thinker as well. From the motley of faces, thoughts, words, joys, sorrows, follies and base tricks all round him, the artist must select precisely that which reflects in a concentrated form the whole significance of the given epoch, that which stamps its imprint on a whole mass of secondary phenomena, and that which contains and influences all other aspects of private and social life...

In the work of a thinking writer who has resolved to portray a certain society, figures like Onegin are admitted only as *parenthetic* characters standing in the background, like, for example, Zagoretsky and Repetilov in Griboedov's comedy. In the latter the foreground quite rightly belongs to Famusov and Skalozub, who provide the reader with a key to understanding an entire period of history and who with their typical and sharply defined characteristics explain not only Molchalin's subservience, but also Sofia's foolish sentimentality and Chatsky's fruitless eloquence. In his analysis of Russian life Griboedov reached the extreme limit beyond which no poet can pass without ceasing to be a poet and becoming instead an academic researcher. Pushkin, however, in contrast, did not even begin to approach analysis; with complete sincerity and with a most praiseworthy modesty he says in Chapter 7 of *Onegin:* 'I sing of a young acquaintance and his many whims'. And indeed that is his whole aim. There is no point in asking why he turned his attention to this particular 'young acquaintance' rather than another. He is a poet precisely so that he may act in the realm of his creativity just as his fancy takes him, without having to render account to anyone in the world, not even to himself. And accounting for the whims of this acquaintance is another matter in which he has no interest whatsoever.

If critics and public had understood Pushkin's novel as he himself understood it, if they had regarded it as some harmless and pointless joke, like *Count Nulin* or *The Little House in Kolomna,* if they had not placed Pushkin on a pedestal to which he has not the slightest right and had not forcibly thrust upon him great problems which he could not and did not wish to solve (or even set himself), then I would not have dreamt of shocking the sensitive souls of Russian aestheticians with my disrespectful articles about the works of our so-called great poet. But, unfortunately, the public of Pushkin's day was uncultured enough to mistake excellent verses and brilliant descriptions for great events in their intellectual life. This public copied out with equal enthusiasm both *Woe from Wit* – which is one of our greatest works of literature – and *The Fountain of Bakhchisarai* – which offers nothing whatsoever beyond pleasant sounds and bright colours.

Twenty years later the problem of Pushkin was taken up by that superb critic, honest citizen and remarkable thinker, Vissarion Belinsky. One would have expected such a man to be able to settle this problem satisfactorily and assign to Pushkin that modest place which rightfully belongs to him in our intellectual life. But things turned out otherwise. Belinsky wrote eleven superb essays about Pushkin, in which he scattered numerous highly enlightened thoughts about the rights and responsibilities of man, about relationships between men and women, about love, about jealousy, and about private and public life, but at the end of all this the problem of Pushkin proved to have been completely obscured. It seemed to the readers of these essays – and perhaps even to Belinsky himself – that it was Pushkin who had generated all these remarkable thoughts in his works. They belonged, however, entirely to the critic, and the poet who was being analysed would in all probability not have liked them. Belinsky exaggerated the significance of all Pushkin's major works and ascribed to each of them a serious and profound meaning which the author himself had been quite unable and unwilling to put in them.

In themselves, as independent works of literature, Belinsky's essays on Pushkin played an extremely useful part in the intellectual development of our society, but as eulogies of an old idol and as invitations into an old temple, which contained a mass of food for the imagination but none for the mind, these same essays could and did do their share of damage. Belinsky loved a Pushkin whom he created for himself...

TURGENEV

PUSHKIN

To western readers I. S. Turgenev (1818–1883) is known primarily as a novelist and short-story writer. He was also a dramatist and poet, however, and an interesting and influential literary critic. His speech on Pushkin, which formed part of the celebrations marking the dedication of a monument to Pushkin in Moscow in June, 1880, is marked by its scholarly approach and restrained, tactful tone. His speech provides a fascinating contrast with Dostoevsky's, delivered on the same occasion. The most important difference lies in their overall view of Pushkin's significance as a national writer; on this point Turgenev, unlike Dostoevsky, seems unwilling to commit himself. Indeed he leaves the whole question of Pushkin as a national writer, in the sense of a Russian Shakespeare or Dante, open. Perhaps what emerges most clearly from this speech is Turgenev's love for poetry and for art in which he sees a tremendous liberating force.

Gentlemen!

The erection of a memorial to Pushkin which has had the enthusiastic support of all educated people in Russia, and which so many of our most eminent people, representatives of the landed gentry, government, science, literature and art, have come to celebrate – this act is a measure of the gratitude and love shown by our society for one of its most outstanding members. Let us try to define, in some of its aspects, the meaning and significance of this love.

Pushkin was the first Russian poet who was also an artist. Art, taken in its broadest sense to include poetry, is a fundamental characteristic of mankind in that it recreates and incarnates those ideals which lie at the very roots of human life and defines its essential spiritual and moral features. Art, it is true, is an imitation of what is already implicit in nature, but it is an imitation whose spiritual significance was realised in the very earliest period of human activity as something distinctively human. The stone-age savage scratching the outline of the head of a bear or an elk onto a fragment of bone with his piece of flint ceased to be a savage or an animal. But it is only when a nation arrives at a consciously full and unique expression of its art and poetry through the creative force of a select few, that it can demonstrate its ultimate right to a place in history; it takes on its own spiritual form, its own distinctive voice, it is accepted by other peoples and joins with them in brotherhood. It is not by chance that Greece is called the homeland of Homer, Germany of Goethe, England of Shakespeare. It is not our intention to deny the significance of other manifestations of national life, in the spheres of religion or politics, for example; but the particular characteristic we have just mentioned can be given to a nation only by its art and its poetry. And this is not surprising: the art of a people is its living, individual soul, its thought and its language in the highest meaning of the word; in its fullest expression it becomes the heritage of all mankind even to a greater extent than poetry precisely because it represents the vibrant, thinking human soul, a soul which never dies because it outlives its body, its nation. What remains to us of Greece? Its soul! Both religious and scientific forms outlive those nations in which they have appeared, but by virtue of their general, eternal aspects; poetry and art live on by virtue of their vital individual qualities.

Pushkin, we say again, was our first poet who was also an artist. Two fundamental principles combine in a poet as the one who fully expresses the essence of a nation: the principle of *receptivity*, and the principle of *self-sufficiency* – the feminine principle, and the masculine principle, we might venture to add. Both these principles have assumed a special colouring with us, the Russians, a people who entered the family of European nations later than the rest; we have a two fold receptivity: to our own life and also to the life of other European nations with all its riches – and at times its, for us, bitter fruits. Our spirit of self-sufficiency also has become a special force of its own – uneven and impulsive but one, on occasions, of genius: it has had to fight against both external and internal contradictions. Remember, gentlemen, Peter the Great, with whose nature Pushkin himself felt such an affinity. It was not without reason that Pushkin's feelings for him were of such loving reverence! This two-fold receptivity, which we have just mentioned, was reflected significantly in the life of our poet: first, birth into a house of the ancient nobility, then a foreign upbringing at the Lycée, the influence of contemporary society, imbued with foreign principles; Voltaire, Byron and the Napoleonic War of 1812; and then his retiring into the depths of Russia, his immersion in the life and language of the people, and the famous old nanny with her epic tales... As for the spirit of self-sufficiency, it awoke in Pushkin at an early stage, and quickly shedding its searching, undefined character, turned into spontaneous creativity. He was not yet eighteen, when Batyushkov read his elegy, The swift-moving bank of clouds begins to clear' and exclaimed: The rascal! Look how he's begun to write!' Batyushkov was right: no-one had hitherto written in such a way in Russia. And perhaps, in exclaiming The rascal!', Batyushkov was foreseeing dimly that some of his own poetry and phrases would be ascribed to Pushkin although they had in fact appeared before Pushkin's. 'Le génie prend son bien partout où il le trouve', – as the French say. Pushkin's independent genius – with a few insignificant exceptions – quickly freed itself both from the imitation of European examples and from the temptation to hide under a purely Russian form. To imitate purely national forms, generally, is as inappropriate and fruitless as to submit to foreign influences: the best proofs of this are, on the one hand, Pushkin's folk tales, and on the other, *Ruslan and Lyudmila,* generally considered to be the weakest of his works. Everybody would of course agree with the inappropriateness of submitting to foreign influences. But some people might perhaps argue that unless the poet keeps his own countrymen firmly in focus as a constant aim, he will never become their poet: the people, the ordinary people, will never read him. But, gentlemen, where is the great poet who is read by those whom we call the ordinary people? The ordinary German does not read Goethe, nor the Frenchman – Molière; even the Englishman does not read Shakespeare, and yet Goethe, Molière and Shakespeare are poets of the people in the true sense – they are national poets. Let us permit ourselves a comparison: Beethoven and Mozart, for example, are undoubtedly national composers, and their music is essentially German music; but in none of their works will you find a trace not merely of any debt to German folk-music but even of any similarity with it, precisely because this elemental music became an indistinguishable part of them; it dissolved in their bloodstream just as the theory of their art did – just as, for example, rules of grammar dissolve in the creative process of a writer. In other forms of art, even further removed from everyday existence, and even more inward-looking, the term national becomes meaningless. There are painters such as Raphael and Rembrandt who are national in the universal sense, but there are no painters who are national in the purely local sense. And let us state here by the way that the raising of the banner of purely local nationalism in art, poetry or literature is something which is characteristic only of weak, immature or suppressed and enslaved races. Their poetry must serve other, more important, aims, namely the safeguarding of their existence. Russia, thank heaven, is not one of these; she is neither weak nor enslaved. She has no reason to fear for herself or zealously preserve her sense of independence; aware of her strength, she even welcomes those people who point out her shortcomings.

To return to Pushkin: whether he can be called a national poet, in the sense of a Shakespeare or a Goethe, is a question we must leave open for the time being. But there can be no doubt that he was the creator of our poetic and literary language and we and our descendants can only go along the path which his genius laid for us. From what has just been said you will already have been convinced that we are unable to agree with those albeit conscientious people who maintain that there is no such thing as a genuinely Russian literary language; that we will obtain it only from such salutary elements in our society as the common Russian people. On the contrary, in the language which Pushkin created we find all the conditions necessary for life: a creative Russian spirit and Russian receptivity which have combined elegantly to produce this magnificent language, and Pushkin himself was a magnificent Russian artist.

Yes, precisely that: Russian! The very essence and all the characteristics of his prose reflect the essence and characteristics of our people. The virile charm, strength and clarity of his language, the open-hearted truthfulness, the absence of falsehood and empty rhetoric, his simplicity, frankness and honesty of feeling – all these fine Russian characteristics in Pushkin's works are striking not merely to us, his fellow-countrymen, but also to those foreigners who have had access to him. The judgement of these foreigners is of great value, since it is not the result of patriotic fervour. The famous French writer and admirer of Pushkin, Prosper Mérimée, who once unhesitatingly called the Russian the greatest poet of his age practically within earshot of

Victor Hugo himself, said to us: 'Above all, your poetry seeks truth, and beauty follows naturally as a matter of course; our poets, on the other hand, take the opposite approach: they concern themselves primarily with effect, wit and external brilliance, and the question of authenticity arises only as an afterthought'... 'Pushkin's poetry', he added, 'blossoms of its own accord in some miraculous way out of the most unassuming prose'. It was this same Mérimée who applied the well-known saying *proprie communia dicere* to Pushkin, in acknowledgement of his ability to state the obvious in a totally original way – the very essence of poetry, a poetry in which ideals and reality are reconciled. It was he also who compared Pushkin to the ancient Greeks with their regularity of form and content, with their lack of any kind of didacticism and moral conclusions. Once, I remember, when he had finished reading the last quatrain of *The Upas-tree* he remarked: 'No contemporary poet would have refrained from a commentary here'. Mérimée was also enraptured by the way Pushkin was able to enter immediately *in medias res*, 'to take the bull by the horns', as the French say, and would point to *The Stone Guest* as an example of this.

Yes, Pushkin was an artist of central importance, someone who stood close to the very heart of Russian life, a quality which explains his majestic and unique ability to appropriate alien modes, an ability which foreigners themselves recognise in us, albeit somewhat disparagingly, as one of 'assimilation'. This quality enabled him, for example, to create the monologue in *The Miserly Knight* of which Shakespeare himself would have been proud. Another striking factor in Pushkin's poetic temperament is his characteristic blend of strong, impassioned feeling with unruffled calm, or rather, the essential objectivity of his art, in which the passion and fervour of his subjective personality are reflected only inwardly.

All this is so... But do we have the right to call Pushkin a national poet in the universal sense (two concepts which often coincide) – in the sense we use when we talk about Shakespeare, Goethe or Homer?

Pushkin could not do everything. It should not be forgotten that it fell to Pushkin alone to fulfil two tasks, which in other countries have been separated by at least a century: to establish a language, and create a literature. He was beset moreover by the same cruel fate which has pursued the elite of our nation with such, almost malicious persistence. He was plucked from us before he reached the age of 37. It is impossible to read the words which he wrote in one his letters a few months before he died without a sense of deep sorrow, without a profound, if undirected, feeling of anger: 'My soul has expanded, so that I feel ready to create'. To create! And the idiotic bullet which was to put an end to his burgeoning genius was already being cast! And who knows? – Perhaps another bullet was being cast at the same time, a bullet destined to murder another poet, Pushkin's heir, who had begun his career with those famous, impassioned lines of poetry inspired by the death of his mentor... But we shall not dwell on these tragic circumstances of chance whose very fortuitousness makes them all the more tragic: let us move from darkness into light and return to Pushkin's poetry.

This is not the time or place to pick on individual works; other people will do this better than we can. Let us merely remark that we have inherited from Pushkin's works a whole host of models and types (yet one more clear sign of genius) which were to be fully realised in the literature that was to follow. Remember, for example, the tavern scene from *Boris Godunov* or *The Chronicle of Goryukhino*, or take such figures as Pimen, or the main characters of *The Captain's Daughter* – can they not be seen as proof that the past lived in him as vividly as the present or as his instincts about the future?

But in the meanwhile even Pushkin could not avoid the fate of all true poets and initiators. His contemporaries cooled towards him and succeeding generations grew still more distant from him, ceased to need him or be brought up on him; it is only recently that there has been a noticeable return to his poetry. Pushkin himself had a presentiment that the public would cool towards him. It is well known that during the last years of his life, at the full flowering of his creative talent, he vouchsafed his readers practically nothing, leaving works such as *The Bronze Horseman* unpublished. He could not but feel a certain disdain for a public who had learnt to see him as a nightingale, a singer of sweet melodies... Yes, and how can we blame him, when you remember that a man with the intelligence and perspicacity of Baratynsky, who with others had been asked to sort through Pushkin's papers after the poet's death, unequivocally exclaimed in a letter to an equally intelligent colleague: 'Do you know what astonishes me most about his poetry? The abundance of his thoughts! Pushkin – a thinker! Is this what we were led to expect?' The proof that Pushkin foresaw all of this lies in his famous sonnet *To*

The Poet, 1 July, 1830, which we now beg leave to read to you, although it is of course known to you all... We are unable to resist the temptation to embellish our meagre prose with the rich gold of his poetry...

> Poet! Don't value the people's love!
> Ecstatic praise's momentary uproar will pass,
> You will hear the fool's censure and crowd's cold laughter,
> But stay firm, unmoved and calm.
>
> You are king: live alone. Travel along
> The path of freedom, inspired by a free mind,
> Realising the fruits of your heartfelt thoughts,
> And demanding no reward for your noble work.
>
> Reward lies in you yourself. You are your own best judge,
> Best able to assess what you yourself have done.
> Does it satisfy your rigorous appraisal?
>
> If it satisfies, then let the masses scorn it,
> Let them spit on the altar on which your light burns,
> Let them rock your tripod in childish play.

Pushkin is not being entirely just here however – especially in relation to succeeding generations. The 'fool's censure' and the 'crowd's cold laughter' were beside the point; the real reasons for this coldness lay deeper, and are familiar enough. Let us simply remind you of them. They lay in fate itself, in the historical evolution of society, in the circumstances which gave birth to the transition from a literary epoch to a political one. Quite unexpected and yet perfectly natural aspirations arose, together with unprecedented and irresistible demands; questions appeared, to which answers had to be given... There was no time for poetry or for art. Only inveterate *littérateurs,* with the mighty, turbulent waves of the new epoch sweeping past them, could show an equal admiration for *Dead Souls* and *The Bronze Horseman* or *Egyptian Nights*. Pushkin's conception of the world seemed limited, his zealous regard for our, at times national fame seemed old-fashioned, and his classical sense of proportion and harmony – an unfeeling anachronism. The white marble temples, where the poet-priests served, where there was indeed light – but on the altar, where only incense was burned – these temples had been abandoned for the clamourous market-place which demanded a new broom – and a broom was indeed found. The poet as echo, to use Pushkin's expression, the poet as focal point, a centripetal affirming force, the force of life at rest, gave way to the poet as message-bearer, a centrifugal negating force, the force of life in motion. Pushkin's first and most important critic, Belinsky, was succeeded by others who placed scant value on poetry. We have uttered the name of Belinsky, and although today nobody's praises must ring beside those of Pushkin, you will probably permit us a heartfelt word in honour of this remarkable man when you learn that he was fated to die on 16 May, the birthday of the very poet who was to become for him the highest expression of the Russian genius!. . . But let us return to the development of our idea. Upon Lermontov's untimely death, when Gogol had already captured first place among people's thoughts, there rang out the voice of the poet 'of vengeance and sorrow' to be followed by others pulling the succeeding generations along behind them. If art, in the works of Pushkin, had achieved citizenship, a full awareness of its existence, and a language, it now began to serve other ideals, just as necessary in the social order. Many people saw, and still see, this change as a decline; but we will permit ourselves to remark here that it is only the dead, the inorganic, which declines and decays. The living changes in an organic way – by growth. And Russia is growing, not declining. There is, it seems, no need to show that such a process, like all kinds of growth, inevitably goes hand in hand with illness, painful crises and terrible, at first sight insoluble contradictions; we learn this not only from history in general, but even from the history of each individual. Science itself speaks of necessary diseases. But only short-sighted people, or those who have outlived their time are annoyed by this, bemoaning the albeit relative calm of former times and attempting to return to it and perhaps forcing others to do the same. During those periods of national life which are called transitional, it is the duty of the thinking person, of the true citizen of his country, to go forward despite the difficulty and the mud on the road, without losing sight for a moment of those fundamental ideals which form the basis of the society of which he is an organic part. Ten or fifteen years ago, this event, which we have all gathered here to celebrate, would have been greeted as an act of justice, as a mark of society's gratitude; but there would not perhaps have been the same feeling of unanimity which possesses all of us, regardless of rank, profession or age. We have already indicated with joy the fact that young people are beginning once more to read and study Pushkin; but we should not forget that several successive generations have passed before us, generations for whom the name of Pushkin was nothing more than a name, to be consigned with others to oblivion. It is not our intention, however, to blame these generations excessively: we have tried to show briefly why such an attitude was inevitable. But neither can we not show our joy at this return to poetry. We are particularly happy, because our young people are returning to it, not in a penitent and disillusioned way, worn out with their own mistakes, and seeking refuge and comfort in something they have turned away from. No, rather, we see in this return a sign of a certain satisfaction; we see it as evidence that at least some of the aims for which it had been considered not merely permissible but obligatory to scarifice all irrelevancies, to confine life to a single channel – at least some of these aims have been recognised as completed and the future will see the completion of the rest; and nothing can any longer prevent poetry, with Pushkin as its chief representative, from taking up its rightful position as part of the lawful structure of social life. There was a time when life was reflected only in elegant literature; then there came a time when such literature vanished completely from the stage... the first role was much too broad, the second narrow to the point of non-existence. In finding its natural limits, poetry has established itself for ever. Under the guidance of an old, but not old-fashioned teacher, the laws and methods of true art will, we firmly believe, once again come into their own and – who knows? – perhaps a new, as yet unknown genius will appear who will surpass his teacher and earn in full the title of a universally national poet, a title which we cannot decide to bestow on Pushkin, yet which we do not presume to take from him.

Be that as it may, Pushkin's services to Russia are tremendous and worthy of national gratitude. He gave a final form to our language, which in richness, strength, logic and beauty is acknowledged even by foreign philologists to be inferior only perhaps to that of ancient Greece; all aspects of Russian life are permeated with the images he created, with his immortal music. And finally, it was his mighty hand which was the first to raise high the banner of poetry on Russian soil; and if the dust of battle which was raised after his death clouded this radiant banner for a while, then it is now, as the dust is beginning to settle, that we see this victorious standard shining once more on high. And may this noble bronze face, erected in the very heart of our ancient capital, shine forth and proclaim to future generations our right to be called a great nation, because such a man with all his great contemporaries was born among us! And just as it was said about Shakespeare that he would be read by everybody who had learned to read and write, so we too must hope that all those who come after us and who stand reverently in front of this statue of Pushkin, will show, by such reverence and understanding of its significance, that they, like Pushkin, have become more Russian, more educated and more liberated people; you should not be astonished at this last word, gentlemen! The force in poetry is a liberating one, because it is an uplifting and moral one. Let us also hope that in the not too distant future the descendants of the Russian common people, who today do not read Pushkin, will understand what the name Pushkin means; and that they will echo, this time consciously, the words we heard recently coming unconsciously from someone's lips: 'This is a memorial to a teacher!'

DOSTOEVSKY

PUSHKIN

By the last years of his life, after many vicissitudes and setbacks, F. M. Dostoevsky (1821–1881) had achieved a position of tremendous stature and influence both as a novelist of genius and as a publicist. His famous *Pushkin Speech,* delivered in Moscow in June 1880 at the dedication of a monument to Pushkin, was received amid scenes of wild enthusiasm and acclaim. The speech, which may be regarded as the culminating point of Dostoevsky's career, was of immense significance on two counts: firstly it developed the view, first advanced by Gogol, of Pushkin as a supremely national and prophetic writer; and secondly, much more broadly, Dostoevsky uses the occasion to express his most cherished wish, something which lies at the heart of his creative thought and work: his desire for universal brotherhood and unity. Such a state could be achieved, in Dostoevsky's view, only through Russia and through a Russian writer such as Pushkin, with his unique quality of 'universal responsiveness'.

Gogol said of Pushkin that he was an extraordinary phenomenon, perhaps a unique manifestation of the Russian spirit. To this I would add the idea of prophecy. Yes, there is something indisputably prophetic in this figure which embraces all of us Russians. Pushkin was to appear precisely when we were beginning to achieve a sense of self-awareness, an awareness which was born a whole century after the reforms of Peter the Great, and his appearance helped to cast a bright and guiding light on to the dark road before us. In this sense Pushkin is both a prophet and a guiding star. I will divide the life and works of our great poet into three periods. I am speaking now not as a literary critic and if I touch on Pushkin's creative activity it will be only to illuminate my thought on his prophetic significance and what I mean by this word. I would just like to say in passing, however, that these periods in Pushkin's creative activity do not have, it seems to me, clear divisions between them. The beginning of *Onegin,* for example, belongs in my opinion to his first period, but the work is completed in the second, by which time Pushkin had already discovered his ideals in his native land, ideals which his whole being had assimilated with love and insight. It has also become generally accepted that, during his first period, Pushkin imitated European poets, such as Parny, André Chénier and others, in particular Byron. Without doubt, European poets greatly influenced the development of his genius, and were to continue to do so all his life. Even Pushkin's very earliest poems, however, were more than just mere imitations, for they too expressed the uniqueness of his genius. Imitations can never attain the uniqueness of suffering and the depth of self-awareness which appeared in Pushkin's *The Gipsies,* for example, a poem which I would place in its entirety in his first period. Neither would mere imitations contain such creative power and sense of purpose. In the character of Aleko, the hero of *The Gipsies,* there can already be seen the expression of a completely Russian idea, profound and forceful, an idea which was to attain its apotheosis in *Onegin,* in which practically the same Aleko appears again, this time not in such a fantastic guise, but in a tangibly real and comprehensible form. In Aleko Pushkin's genius had discovered and delineated a specifically Russian character, a historically conditioned type divorced from his own people, an outcast in his own country. Such a type, of course, he did not merely borrow from Byron. It is a faultlessly conceived and completely authentic representation of an indigenous Russian type, one of the longstanding features of our life. These homeless Russian outcasts are still wandering even today, and will probably not disappear for a long time. And if now they no longer seek ideals and peace in nature, in the primitive gipsy way of life, as a refuge from the confused absurdities of the Russian intelligentsia and its society, they still nonetheless turn to the ideals of socialism, which in Aleko's time did not yet exist, and make for fresh pastures where they can work with renewed faith and vigour, believing, like Aleko, that in such a fantastic enterprise they can attain their aims and a happiness which is not merely personal but universal as well. For the Russian outcast needs just such universal happiness to attain peace and will settle for nothing less; all this of course is, as yet, still theory. It is the same Russian type, only the time is different. This man, I repeat, was born a hundred years after the great Petrine reforms into that part of our society, the educated part, which was divorced from the people and from its strength. Oh yes, even then, in Pushkin's day, just as much as nowadays, the vast majority of educated Russians peacefully served their time as government officials, working in the treasury, the railways or the banks, or simply made money by various means, or were scholars and lecturers even – and all this was quite ordered, indolent and peaceful, with regular salaries, card games, and nobody felt the slightest urge to run off to gipsy encampments or anywhere else more suitable to our time. There are many, many people who profess to a little liberalism 'with a touch of European socialism', but who possess nevertheless a placid, good-natured Russianness – but all this is really only a question of time. What does it matter, if one person has not yet experienced the first stirrings of alarm, but the next has already managed to reach the locked door and be crashing against it with his forehead? Everybody who does not take the path of salvation leading to humble communion with the people, can sooner or later expect the same fate. Well, if not quite everybody, then a small number of people who have seen the danger signs would be enough to ensure that their alarm was visible to the remaining vast majority. Aleko, of course, is as yet unable to express his grief and alarm; it is still all expressed in a rather abstract way as a longing for nature, complaints against society, as a yearning for universality, as a tearful yearning for a truth which has somehow vanished and which, try as he may, he cannot find. There is something of Jean-Jacques Rousseau about all this. What exactly this truth is, where and in what form it might appear and when exactly it disappeared, he of course cannot say, but he suffers deeply. This impatient, somewhat unreal man thirsts for temporary salvation in primarily external phenomena; and this is as it should be: the truth, he says, is outside him, perhaps somewhere in another country, in Europe for example, with its firm, historically-based society and with its established social and civil way of life. He will never realise that the truth is above all within himself, and indeed, how can he realise this? He is an outcast amongst his own people, for a whole century he and his kind have forgotten how to work, he has grown up like someone at boarding school in an enclosed world, he has performed strange and unaccountable duties in accordance with his membership of one or the other of the fourteen classes into which educated

Russian society has been divided. As yet he is just a plucked blade of grass flying through the air. He feels this to be so and suffers because of it, often terribly. And what does it matter, if coming from hereditary noble stock and very probably a serf-owner, he should permit himself, as a measure of his privileged position, a tiny fantasy and be attracted to people living 'beyond the law', or if he should become for a time part of the gipsy way of life, and lead a bear round on a chain? It is understandable that a woman, a 'primitive woman' as a poet has said, should be the first to offer any hope of a way out of his anguish and that he should throw himself at Zemfira's feet with a foolish but passionate belief in such a salvation. 'This,' he seems to say, 'is where my answer lies, this is where I may find my happiness, here, in the midst of nature, far from society, here with people who possess neither civilisation nor laws!' And what happens? At his first confrontation with wild nature he is unable to restrain himself from staining his hands with blood. The unhappy dreamer is unfit not merely for universal harmony but even for the gipsies, and they cast him out – without thoughts of revenge, without malice, with a kind of simple majesty:

> Leave us, proud man;
> We are primitive people, without laws,
> We neither torture nor punish.

All this of course is fantasy, but the 'proud man' is exactly and realistically portrayed. Let us not forget that it was Pushkin who portrayed such a character for the first time. Should anything happen in the least degree not to his liking, he is ready to torture and punish out of malice for the wrong inflicted upon him, or, better still, remembering that he is a member of one of the fourteen classes, he will invoke (for this has indeed happened) the law of torture and punishment to avenge such a personal wrong. No, this brilliant poem is no imitation! Underneath it all lies the Russian solution to the problem, 'the accursed problem', according to the beliefs and justice of the simple people: 'Humble yourself, proud man, above all rid yourself of pride. Humble yourself, idle man, and above all devote yourself to honest labour at home, on your native soil'. This is the answer given by the people's sense of justice and reason. 'The truth does not lie outside you, but within; find yourself within yourself, submit and control yourself and you will see the truth. This truth lies not in material things, not outside you nor somewhere over the seas, but first and foremost it lies in self-discipline. By conquering yourself and making yourself submit you will become free, freer than you could ever have imagined, and you will begin to do great things; you will liberate others and you will know happiness, for your life will be fulfilled and you will at least understand your own people and its sacred truth. Universal harmony will not be found among the gipsies or anywhere else, if you yourself remain unworthy of it in your malice and pride and if you ask that life be given to you for nothing without realising that you have to pay for it.' Pushkin's poem strongly implies such a solution to the problem. It is expressed even more clearly in *Evgenii Onegin,* a poem which is not fantastic but which has a tangible realism, in which the reality of Russian life is embodied so fully and with such creative force that its like has not been seen before or since.

Onegin arrives from St. Petersburg – inevitably from St. Petersburg, this was absolutely essential and Pushkin could not omit such a clearly authentic trait in his hero's biography. Let me say once again that this is another Aleko, a fact which is especially evident when he exclaims with a sense of deep melancholy:

> Why am I not, like the assessor from Tula,
> Stricken with palsy?

But when he says this, at the beginning of the work, he is not yet a total fop and man of the world and has not lived sufficiently long to have become completely disillusioned with life. But he too begins to be tormented and alarmed by the

> Noble demon of secret boredom.

In the depths of the country, deep in the heart of his native land he of course does not feel at home. He does not know what there is for him to do and feels like a guest in his own house. During his subsequent melancholy travels around his own country and abroad he, in his indisputably intelligent and sincere way, feels even more alienated from himself. It is true that he too loves his native land, but he does not trust her. Of course he has heard of patriotic ideals but he does not believe in them. He believes simply in the total impossibility of doing any sort of work in his own country and regards those who do believe in such a possibility – there were not many such people then and there are just a few now – with a sad but mocking smile. He killed Lensky simply out of spleen, a spleen which perhaps arose out of a longing for a universal ideal – this seems very probable, an all-too Russian characteristic. Tatyana is different; she is a strong character, deeply rooted in her native soil. She is more profound than Onegin and, of course, more intelligent. With her noble instinct she senses where the truth lies, something which emerges clearly from the final scene of the work. Perhaps Pushkin would have done even better to call his poem after Tatyana rather than Onegin, for she is without doubt the work's main hero. She is a positive creation, not a negative one, an embodiment of positive beauty, the apotheosis of the Russian woman, and it was she whom the poet destined to express the idea of the poem in the famous scene where Tatyana and Onegin have their final meeting. One might even say that such positive beauty has not been recreated in the figure of a Russian woman in our literature – with the exception perhaps of Liza in Turgenev's *Nest of Gentlefolk*. But Onegin's supercilious way of looking at life and people meant that at their first meeting in the depths of the countryside he was unable to see Tatyana for what she really was, in the modest, chaste and innocent young girl standing so shyly before him. He was unable to distinguish the perfection and completeness of this poor girl – indeed, he saw her perhaps as a 'moral embryo'. She a 'moral embryo', and this after her letter to Onegin! If there does exist a moral embryo in the work then it is of course Onegin himself; this is indisputable. And he was totally unable to see her for what she was; what knowledge did he have of the human soul? He remained an abstract person, a restless dreamer all his life. Neither did he see her properly later in St. Petersburg, as a lady of high society when, in his own words, in his letter to Tatyana, 'he was able with his whole being to comprehend her perfection'. But these are mere words: she passed through his life unrecognised and unappreciated; herein lies the tragedy of their relationship. If only during their first meeting in the country there had arrived on the scene from England a Childe-Harold or even, somehow, Lord Byron himself and, noticing her shy, timid charm, had pointed it out to him – oh then Onegin would have been deeply astonished and affected, for these universal sufferers possess at times so much spiritual sycophancy! But this did not happen, and the seeker after universal harmony, having lectured her and having acted with extreme

honesty, set off again with his universal grief, and with his hands
stained with blood shed after a stupid fit of pique wandered
through his native land without noticing it and, bursting with
health and strength, exclaimed:

> I am young and full of life's strength,
> Yet what awaits me? – anguish, anguish.

Tatyana understood this. In immortal lines the poet depicted
her visiting the house of this strange, enigmatic man. I will not
speak here of the artistry, the matchless beauty and the depth of
these lines. Here she is in his study, examing his books and things,
trying to arrive at an understanding of him through them and to
solve her own riddle, and then this 'morally imperfect' being
stops, finally, in a reverie, a strange smile on her lips and with a
presentiment that the riddle is solved, whispers quietly:

> Perhaps he is just a parody?

Yes, she had to whisper this; the riddle had been solved. When
they met again in St. Petersburg a long time afterwards, she knew
him fully. Who, incidentally, was it who said that she had been
corrupted by society and court life and it was precisely her new
worldly understanding of life which partly caused her to refuse
Onegin? No, it wasn't like that. No, this is the same Tanya, just as
we knew her in the country! She is not corrupted but, on the
contrary, deeply depressed by the opulent life of St. Petersburg,
crushed by it and she suffers deeply; she hates her worldly image
and anybody who thinks differently does not understand at all
what Pushkin was trying to say. She says quite firmly to Onegin:

> But I am pledged to someone else;
> To him I will remain faithful unto death.

These are the words of a Russian woman, these are her
apotheosis. In them she expresses the truth of the work. No, I
shall not say a single word about her religious convictions, about
her views on the sanctity of marriage – I shall not touch on this.
But why then did she refuse to go with him despite the fact that
she had told him that she loved him? Was it because she, a
Russian woman, and not a Southern or a French woman, was not
capable of making a decisive step, of breaking her chains or of

sacrificing honour, riches, worldly standing and virtue? No, Russian women are bold, and will boldly follow that in which they believe. She herself had proved this. But she is 'pledged to someone else and will remain faithful to him unto death'. Faithful to whom, to what? To what obligations? To this old general whom she cannot love, because she loves Onegin, and whom she married only because her mother begged her to with imploring tears, 'but her insulted and broken heart contains only despair without a sign of hope or light'? Yes, faithful to this general, her husband, an honest man who loves her, respects her, and is proud of her. Her mother might have begged her, but it was after all she, and nobody else, who gave her consent, it was she who swore faithfulness to him as his wife. She might have married him from despair, but now he is her husband, and her betrayal would cover him with scorn and shame and would kill him. Can anyone really base his happiness on someone else's unhappiness? Happiness resides not in the raptures of love alone but in the higher harmony of the spirit. How can you placate the spirit, if behind you lies a dishonest, pitiless and inhuman act? Is she to run away just because this is where her happiness is to be found? But what happiness is possible, if it is based on another's unhappiness? Imagine that you yourself are erecting the edifice of human destiny with the ultimate aim of making people happy, of giving them, in the end, peace and rest. And then imagine also that to achieve this you need to torment just one human creature, somebody perhaps of no particular worth, even someone ridiculous in some eyes, not a Shakespeare, but simply an honest old man, a young girl's husband – in whose love he believes blindly although he does not know her heart at all, who respects her, is proud of her, who is happy and at peace. And all you need do is shame, dishonour and torment him and erect your edifice on the tears of this broken old man! Would you agree to be the architect of such a building on such a condition? This is the question. And can you entertain for a moment the idea that those people, for whom you erected this edifice, would themselves agree to accept such happiness from you, if its foundations rested on the suffering albeit, let us suppose, of an insignificant being, but nevertheless one who has been pitilessly and unjustly tormented, and, accepting this happiness, would remain happy for ever? Tell me, could Tatyana decide otherwise, with her nobility of soul and with a heart which itself had suffered so much? No! The pure Russian soul reasons in this way: 'It may well be that I alone am unhappy, that my unhappiness runs immeasurably deeper than the unhappiness of the old man, that, finally, nobody, not even this old man, will ever know or appreciate my sacrifice, but I do not wish to achieve happiness by destroying somebody else!' Herein lies the tragedy; it is complete; it is now too late to break out, and so Tatyana sends Onegin away. But people will say, 'Surely Onegin is unhappy; by saving one, she has destroyed the other!' But this is another question, perhaps the most important one in the work. Incidentally, the question why Tatyana did not go with Onegin has its own very characteristic history, at least in our literature; this explains why I have talked at such length about this question. And most characteristic of all is the fact that the moral resolution of this question should have been so long subject to doubt. This is my opinion: even if Tatyana were to become free, even if her old husband were to die and she were to become a widow, even then she would not go with Onegin. Do we have to understand the essence of this character? After all she sees him for what he is: an eternal wanderer who has suddenly met a woman whom he formerly spurned, in a totally new and inaccessible setting – perhaps indeed the setting contains the essential point. This young girl, whom he was once not far from despising, is now the idol of society – that society, which for Onegin is an awesome authority despite all his universal ideals – and this surely is why he throws himself dazzled, at her feet! Here is my ideal, he exclaims, here is my salvation, here is the way out of my anguish, a way out which I failed to see, but 'happiness was so possible, so close!' And just as Aleko yearned for Zemfira, so he yearns now for Tatyana, seeking all the answers in a new burst of whimsical fantasy. Surely Tatyana sees this? Surely she had long since understood him? She knows very well after all, that in essence he loves only his new fantasy and not her, still as meek and humble as ever! She knows that he takes her as something other than she really is, that he does not even love her, that perhaps he does not love anybody, is not capable of loving anybody, despite his anguished suffering. He loves the fantasy, and surely he himself is just a fantasy. Even if she were to follow him, then the next day he would become disillusioned and look mockingly at his enthusiasm. He is rootless, a blade of grass carried by the wind. She is quite different; even in her despair and her suffering awareness that her life has been destroyed there remains nonetheless a firm and unshakable foundation to her whole being. This is the memories of her childhood, of her native land, of the peaceful remote countryside where her chaste and humble life began – and 'the cross and the shade of trees over the grave of her poor nurse'. These memories, these images of her former life are all the more precious to her, they are all that are left to her, and it is they which save her from final despair. And there is more to it than that, much more, for this represents an entire foundation of being, something totally unshakable and indestructible. Here is an indissoluble link with her native country and people, with its religious core. And who is he, what has he to offer? She cannot go with him out of compassion, merely to console him, to bestow on him at least for a time a phantom happiness through a boundless loving pity, knowing full well in advance that the next day he would be mocking at this very happiness. No, there are profound and unyielding beings, who are unable to expose consciously the religious core of their hearts to mockery even out of boundless compassion. No, Tatyana could never have followed Onegin.

And so in *Onegin,* in this immortal and unique poem, Pushkin appeared as a supremely and unprecedentedly national writer. In the most perspicacious and accurate way he struck instantly at the very heart of our essential characteristics, at the heart of the simple people and of society. Having delineated the Russian wanderer as a type, a wanderer who existed then and who still exists today, in being the first to divine with his instinctive genius such a person with his historical destiny and his huge significance for our future, having contrasted him with the figure of a Russian woman embodying a positive and indubitable beauty, Pushkin was, of course, also the first Russian writer to introduce in other works of this same period a whole galaxy of fine, positive Russian types drawn from the Russian people. The chief beauty of these characters lies in their sense of truth, something so definite and real that it is no longer possible to reject them; they stand, as if sculpted out of stone. May I remind you once again that I am speaking not as a literary critic, and therefore I shall not begin to clarify my ideas with a particularly detailed discussion of these works of genius. One could write for example a whole book about the Russian monk-chronicler in order to show the full importance and significance of this marvellous Russian character, drawn by Pushkin from the Russian soil, portrayed, sculpted and placed before us for ever in his humble and indisputably majestic spiritual beauty, as a witness to that majestic spirit of national life which can depict images of such obvious truth. This type is a given fact, it cannot be refuted or claimed as mere fantasy and idealisation on the poet's part. When you yourselves look, you will agree: yes, he exists, and so the spirit of the people which created him exists, and the life-force of this spirit exists, and it is immeasurably great. Everywhere in Pushkin one can sense this faith in the Russian character, in its spiritual depths; and once there is faith, then there is hope, a tremendous hope in the Russian people.

> In the hope of glory and goodness
> I can look ahead without fear...

the poet himself said on another occasion; but these words can be directly applied to all his national, creative activity. And there has not been a single Russian writer, either before or since, who was linked so closely and intimately with his own people as Pushkin. Oh yes, we have many connoisseurs of the Russian people amongst our writers who have written with great talent, accuracy and love about the people, but if you compare them with Pushkin, then, with one or at the most two exceptions from his most recent followers, they are really just members of the nobility writing about the people. With the most talented of them, even with these two exceptions I have mentioned, there can be discerned hints of an arrogant approach, arising from a different world and way of life, a desire perhaps to raise the people to their own level and thereby to make them happy. In Pushkin on the other hand the link with the people is an authentic one which approaches the most artless tenderness. Take the tale of *The She-Bear* and of how a peasant killed the bear's mate: or the poem

> Kinsman John, when we start to drink...

and you will understand what I mean.

All these masterpieces of art and artistic insight have been left behind by our great poet as a kind of signpost for future artists and writers. It is possible to say quite definitely: if it had not been for Pushkin there would have been no talents to follow him. Or at least, despite the greatness of their talent, they would not have been able to demonstrate that force and that clarity with which they were subsequently to express themselves even now. But I am talking not merely about poetry or artistic creation: if it had not been for Pushkin, our belief in our Russianness, our now conscious hope in our national strength, and our belief in a specifically Russian destiny as part of the family of European nations would not have been expressed with such irresistible force as it was later, even if only by very few people. This achievement of Pushkin's becomes particularly clear when we take a closer look at what I call the third period of his creative activity.

Let me repeat once more that these periods cannot be rigidly divided. Some works of even this third period could, for example, have appeared at the very beginning of Pushkin's career, for Pushkin was always, so to speak, a whole, integrated organism, bearing within himself all the potentialities for development rather than assimilating them from without. Influences from outside merely awoke what already lay dormant within him. But with the evolution of this organism it is possible to mark off different periods of such an evolution, each one having its own special character and each one growing gradually out of the previous one. And so we can attribute to Pushkin's third period those works in which there is a prevalence of universal ideas, works which reflect the poetical ideas of other nations and which embody their genius. Some of these works appeared posthumously. And it is in this period that Pushkin becomes something almost miraculous, a quite unprecedented phenomenon in literature. Of course European literature has had its tremendous geniuses – its Shakespeares, Cervantes, and Schillers. But show me just one of these great men who possessed to the same degree Pushkin's quality of universal responsiveness. And it is just such a quality, the most important national quality we possess, that Pushkin shared with our people and it is this which, more than anything else, makes him a national poet. The very greatest of European poets could never recreate with such force the genius of another, perhaps neighbouring nation, recreate its spirit, the innermost essence of this spirit and the yearning lying behind its sense of mission, as could Pushkin. Quite the opposite: when they turned to writing about another nation the European poets would, more often than not, recreate it in the image of their own nationality and view it on their own terms. Even Shakespeare's Italians, for example, are Englishmen almost through and through. Pushkin, alone of all the world's great poets, possesses the ability to recreate in its entirety a foreign nationality. Take his *Scene from Faust* or *The Miserly Knight* or the ballad 'There lived on earth a poor knight'. Reread *The

Stone Guest, and if it were not for Pushkin's autograph you would never know that it had not been written by a Spaniard. What profound, incredible images there are in *The Feast in Time of Plague!* But in these images the genius of England can be felt; the magnificent song of the hero about the plague, or Mary's song with the lines,

> The voices of our children rang out
> In the noisy school...

these are English songs, this is the deep melancholy of the British genius, its tears and suffering premonition of its future. Or remember the strange lines,

> Once, wandering through a wild valley...

   This is an almost literal rendering of the first three pages from a strange mystical book, written in prose by an old English religious sectarian – but surely it is more than just a rendering? In the melancholy rhapsodic tones of this poem can be felt the very essence of Northern protestantism, of the English heretic, an unrestrained mystic, with his dull, gloomy and irresistible aspiration, with the impetuous force of his mystical dreams. Reading this strange poetry, you seem to sense the spirit of the Reformation, you begin to understand the martial tones of emerging Protestantism, history itself becomes comprehensible, not just intellectually, but as if you had been there yourself, had passed by the armed encampment of the sectarians, had joined in their hymns, wept with them in their mystical devotions and believed in their beliefs. And then, side by side with this religious mysticism, we find equally religious lines from the Koran – *The Imitation of the Koran;* is this not a Moslem, is this not the very spirit of the Koran and its crescent sword, the simple-hearted majesty of its faith, its terrible, bloody force? And then there is the classical world, there is *Egyptian Nights,* with its terrestial gods ruling over their own people but already despising the people's genius and aspirations, no longer believing in them, but isolated and mad in their isolation and, in their dying agony, consoling themselves with fantastic acts of bestiality, with the horrible sensuality of insects, like a female spider eating its mate. No, I say quite definitely there has not been a poet so universally and supra-nationally conscious as Pushkin and it is not simply this consciousness alone, but its astonishing profundity, the reincarnation of his own spirit in the spirit of other nations, a reincarnation almost perfect, and therefore also miraculous, because such a phenomenon has not occurred anywhere else or in any other poet. It is to be found only in Pushkin; and it is this that makes him a unique phenomenon and for us a prophetic one, because... because it is precisely here that his specifically Russian strength and the national spirit of his poetry finds expression, a national spirit which will develop and become part of our already implicit heritage – and it finds expression prophetically. For what is the strength of the Russian national spirit, if not its ultimate aspiration for universality and the brotherhood of man?

Pushkin, as a completely Russian poet, was able to forsee the potential greatness of the strength of the Russian people, as soon as he tapped its source. And here he is a prophet and a seer.

And indeed, what do the Petrine reforms mean to us, not only in the future but insofar as what has already happened and what we have already witnessed is concerned? What have these reforms meant to us? Surely not merely the adoption of European clothes, habits, inventions and science. Let us look more closely into what happened. Yes, it may well be that Peter originally initiated these reforms merely for this purpose, i.e. a purely utilitarian purpose, but as time went on and as his idea developed, Peter undoubtedly heeded some innermost sixth sense which led him on to long-term goals clearly of a much wider significance than mere short-term expediency. And in just the same way the Russian people accepted these reforms not just for their utilitarian value but undoubtedly because they sensed also almost at once the long-term aim, an aim incomparably higher than short-term expediency – I repeat, of course, that this was not done consciously but nevertheless it was a direct and totally life-giving experience. For it was then that we aspired to that most life-giving reunification, the unity of all mankind. Without hostility (as, it seems, should have been the case) but in a spirit of amity and love we took unto ourselves the genius of every other nation, not concerned with specific racial distinctions, able intinctively almost from the very first to distinguish and remove the contradictions, to excuse and reconcile the differences, and by this we showed our willingness and readiness, after such a short time, for general and universal reunification with all the nations of the great Aryan race. Yes, the destiny of Russians is indisputably a pan-European, universal one. To become a true Russian, to become completely Russian, perhaps simply means (and this should finally be underlined) to become everybody's brother, a *universal man,* if you like. Oh, all this Slavophilism and Westernism of ours has simply been one great misunderstanding, although historically necessary. For the true Russian, Europe and the fate of the great Ayran peoples are as precious as Russia itself, as the fate of his native country, because our destiny is a universality to be won not with the sword but with the strength of brotherhood and our brotherly aspirations for the unification of mankind. If you look more closely into our history after the Petrine reforms you will find signs and indications of this idea, this dream of mine, if you like, in the special nature of our relationship with the European nations, even in our politics. For what has Russia done throughout these two centuries but serve Europe, perhaps much more than herself? I do not think that this was merely because of the incompetence of our politicians. Oh, these peoples of Europe have no idea how dear they are to us! And subsequently, I believe that we, that is of course not we ourselves, but future generations of Russians, will understand to a man precisely what it means to be a true Russian: it is to seek to achieve a final reconciliation of European contradictions, to point out that the solution to the European malaise lies in the universal spirit of Russia, to make room for all our brothers in a spirit of fraternal love, and finally, perhaps to express the final word of a tremendous all-embracing harmony, the ultimate and fraternal unity of all nations according to the law of the gospel of Christ! I know only too well that my words may appear inflated, exaggerated and fantastic. That may be so, but I am not sorry for having expressed them. This needed to be said, especially now, at the moment when we are triumphantly honouring our great genius who used his artistic talent to embody just such an idea. Yes, and this idea has already been expressed more than once; I am saying nothing new at all. But the main thing is that all this will appear presumptuous: 'Is such a destiny for us,' you will say, 'for our poverty-stricken uncultured land? Is it we who are destined to utter this new word?' But am I talking about economic success, or the glories of military victory or science? I am simply talking about the brotherhood of nations and about the fact that it is the Russian nation, above all others, that is most clearly marked out for the universal, all-embracing unification of mankind. I can see the signs for it in our history, in our gifted people, in the artistic genius of Pushkin. It may be that our land is poor but it is this poor land which 'Christ, dressed in serf's clothing, visited and blessed'. Why cannot we receive His final word? Was not He Himself born in a manger? I say again, that at the very least we are able to point to Pushkin, at the universal all-embracing quality of his genius. After all he was able to assimilate the geniuses of other nations and accept them as his own. In his art at least he showed quite indisputably the universal aspect in the aspiration of the Russian spirit, and this alone is a tremendous achievement. If our idea is a fantastic one, then with Pushkin there is at least something on which to base this fantasy. If he had lived longer, perhaps he would have shown the great and immortal aspects of the Russian soul which our European brothers would have understood, he would perhaps have drawn them to us much closer than they are now, he would perhaps have managed to explain to them the whole truth of our ideas, and they would have understood us better than they do now, they would have begun to foresee our motives and aspirations and would have stopped looking at us with such mistrust and arrogance. Had Pushkin lived longer, there would perhaps, amongst ourselves, have been fewer misunderstandings and arguments than exist at present. But God ordained otherwise. Pushkin died at the height of his powers and indisputably carried off some great secret with him to the grave. And now that he is no longer among us, we are seeking to divine this secret.

MEREZHKOVSKY

PUSHKIN

D. S. Merezhkovsky (1885–1941), a prolific poet, novelist and literary critic, was a leading figure in the aesthetic and religious renaissance promoted at the turn of the century in Russian intellectual circles. The writer's political views fluctuated markedly: at first a liberal, his violent attacks on the tsarist regime at the time of the 1905 attempt at revolution compelled him to leave Russia for six years; subsequently, however, his hatred of the bolshevik regime was even more bitter and in 1919 he emigrated again to Western Europe, never to return to his homeland. Much of Merezhkovsky's thought is dominated by his vision of man and history split between opposing impulses which culture should strive to reconcile. In the present extract, for instance, Merezhkovsky argues that Pushkin's work presents a remarkable synthesis between the opposing principles of Christianity and paganism. This essay – drawing unfortunately on the partly fraudulent memoirs of A. O. Smirnova – first appeared in 1896 in an anthology, *Philosophical Currents in Russian Poetry* edited by P. Pertsov, and then again the following year in Merezhkovsky's famous volume of literary studies, *Eternal Companions*.

'I think', remarked Smirnova, 'that Pushkin is a serious believer, but he never speaks about it. Glinka told me that he once came across him with a Bible in his hands and Pushkin said, "This is the only book in the world. Everything is in it".' After one philosophical conversation with Pushkin Barant wrote to Smirnova: 'I had no idea he had such a religious cast of mind and thought so much about the Gospels.'

'Religion,' Pushkin himself remarked, 'created art and literature. Everything which was great, from the most ancient times, has been connected with the religious sense... Without this religious sense there would have been no philosophy, no poetry and no morality'.

Shortly before his death he saw in one of the rooms in The Hermitage two guards standing by Bryullov's painting of *The Crucifixion*. 'I cannot describe the impression made on me by that guard', said Pushkin to Smirnova, 'It reminded me of the Roman soldiers stationed in front of the sepulchre to prevent His true disciples from approaching Him.' He became agitated and began to walk up and down the room, as was his habit. When he left Zhukovsky remarked, 'How Pushkin has matured and how his religious sense has developed! He is much more a believer than I am.' Later the poet wrote one of his best poems about these guards whom he could not get out of his mind.

Tell me, why these custodian guards?
Or is the crucifix official baggage,
And you're afraid of thieves or mice?
Or do you believe you add importance to the King of Kings?

Or are you saving with your powerful patronage
The Lord who was crowned with thorns,
Christ, who meekly gave His flesh
To the scourges of tormentors, nails and spear?

Or do you fear *the rabble* may insult
Him whose death redeemed the race of Adam?
And, so not to crowd the strolling gentlefolk,
Are the *ordinary people* to be kept away from here?

The symbol of divine love turned into official baggage and the guards placed by Benckendorff in front of *The Crucifixion* are, from an aesthetic or religious standpoint, of course, quite monstrous. But is not the age-old structure of civilisation based precisely on this very monstrousness? That is what Pushkin saw, no less clearly than Lev Tolstoy, though the former's indignation was more restrained. Nature is the tree of life, while civilisation is the tree of death, the Upas-tree:

But man sent man
To the Upas-tree with imperious glance.

The entire tower of Babel is erected on this primitive act of violence: 'And the poor slave died at the feet of the invincible sovereign'.

> And in that poison the prince
> Soaked his obedient arrows
> And with them despatched death
> To his neighbours in alien lands.

The terrible power concentrated in these lines was disseminated by Lev Tolstoy, who used it to prepare his huge arsenal of destructive engines, but its original source is in Pushkin.

Out of the air poisoned by the Upas-tree and out of the dungeon built on the debt of blood an eternal voice summons the eternal prisoner, man, to primordial freedom:

> 'We are free birds; it is time, brother, time!
> Thither, where the mountain shows white beyond the cloud,
> Thither, where the sea's expanses are blue,
> Thither, where only the wind roams... and I!'

This feeling possesses a definite historical form. In the primordial Galilean sense of the word, Pushkin is more a Christian than Goethe or Byron. And here we see the original national personality of the Russian poet.

When Goethe contemplates nature he always remains a pagan. If he wants to express the Christian aspect of his soul, he moves away from primitive simplicity and subordinates his inspiration to the finished cultural forms of the Catholic church: Pater Extaticus, Pater Profundus, Doctor Marianus, Maria Aegyptica from *The Lives of the Saints* – the entire world of medieval theology and scholasticism appears in the last scene of *Faust*. A barrier of thousands of years separates him from the naive religious works of the first centuries.

Pushkin's Christianity is different. It is free of all theology and of all external forms. It is natural and unconscious. Pushkin finds an all-forgiving Galilean wisdom in the hearts of wild tribesmen who have never heard the name of Christ. Nature in Pushkin is Russian – tame and 'unfitful', to use Gogol's word. It teaches man tranquility, humility and simplicity. The wild Tazit and the old Gipsy are closer to the original sources of the Christian spirit than the theological Doctor Marianus. That is what is missing in Goethe, and Byron, and Shakespeare, and Dante. To find an equally pure form of the Galilean poetry one must turn back to the seraphic hymns of St. Francis or to the divine legends of the first centuries.

The religion of compassion and chastity as a philosophical principle appears in various historical forms – in the hymns of St. Francis of Assisi, in the Greek dialogues of Plato, in the Indian nihilism of Buddha, and in the Chinese metaphysics of Lao-Tse. It may be defined as an eternal striving on the part of the human spirit for self-abnegation, for fusion with God and for freedom in God from the bounds of our consciousness; it is a striving for Nirvana, or for the disappearance of the Son in the bosom of the Father.

Paganism as a philosophical principle appears in an equal variety of historical forms – in Hellenic polytheism, in the Vedic hymns, in the book of Mana, and in Moses' legislation – and may be defined as an eternal striving on the part of the human personality towards limitless development, self-perfection and the deification of the ego; it is the constant movement of the ego from the invisible to the visible, from the heavenly to the earthly; it is the revolt and the struggle of the tragic will of heroes and gods against fate, the struggle of Jacob against Jehovah, Prometheus against the Olympians, and Ahriman against Ormuzd.

These two irreconcilable or unreconciled principles, these two currents in the world – the one towards God and the other away from God – are constantly at war, but neither is able to gain a final victory over the other. Only at the highest peaks of creativity and wisdom – with Plato and Sophocles, with Goethe and Leonardo da Vinci – do the Titans and the Olympians conclude a truce, and then we sense the possibility of their complete fusion in a harmony which is perhaps unattainable on Earth. Any reconciliation between them achieved by man quickly proves to be incomplete: the two currents flow again in their separate channels and are even further apart; the two principles again dissociate. The one, momentarily victorious, runs to a one-sided extreme, and in so doing produces collapse; it leads to the madness of the ascetics or of Nietzsche – and with new fits and struggles the spirit strives to achieve a fresh harmony and a higher reconciliation.

Pushkin's poetry is a rare example – in Russian literature the only example – of an harmonious synthesis and balance between these two principles; it is a synthesis, moreover, which is unconscious, in comparison, for instance, with Goethe's.

Having examined one side of Pushkin's philosophy, we must now turn to the other. As a Galilean, Pushkin contrasts primitive man with modern civilisation. As a pagan, with this same modern civilisation, which is based on the power of the rabble, the democratic concept of equality and the votes of the majority, he contrasts the autonomous will of the single individual, whether he be creator or destroyer, prophet or hero. The demi-God is the second principal theme in Pushkin's poetry.

There is no point in discussing here those poets who are clearly subject to the spirit of the century (i.e. such natural democrats as Victor Hugo, Schiller and Heine), but even Byron, who is a lord to the core and extols the outcasts and the despised of all centuries, such as Napoleon and Prometheus, Cain and Lucifer, even Byron too often betrays himself by pandering to the spirit of the rabble, by worshipping Jean-Jacques Rousseau, who preached that most blasphemous of all religions, the majority vote, and by lowering himself to the role of political revolutionary, leader of revolt and tribune of the people.

Born in a land which was fated to be particularly strongly influenced by Western-European democracy, Pushkin, as an enemy of the rabble and as a champion of the eternal principle of spiritual aristocracy, is more irreproachable and more fearless than Byron. In this area, as everywhere else, Pushkin, like Goethe, is firm, clear and constantly true to his own nature:

> Be silent, foolish people,
> Labourers, slaves of need and care!
> I cannot hear your insolent murmur.
> You are worms of the earth, not sons of heaven;
> You want a use in everything – you appraise
> The Belvedere statue by its weight.
> You see no use, no use in it,
> But that marble is God! . . So what?
> An oven pot is worth more to you!
> You can cook food for yourselves in it.

The greatest ugliness of the bourgeois era, the concealed spirit of cupidity hidden under the banners of freedom, science and virtue, is here unmasked so boldly that later Russian literature – using all truths and untruths, from the coarse barbarism of

Pisarev to the refined sophistry of Dostoevsky – was to struggle in vain against this side of Pushkin's philosophy. Later Russian literature was to struggle in vain to stretch the joyous raiment of Galilean charity over the naked vulgarity of the rabble.

Are not all Tolstoy's activities based on this democracy of the bourgeois era, though inspired by the poetry of the Gospels and embellished by the wings of Icarus, the waxen wings of mystical anarchism? Lev Tolstoy is nothing but Russian democracy's reply to Pushkin's challenge. Here is how our meek Galilean, the author of *The Kingdom of Heaven,* might have replied to the high priest-poet who was bold enough to say to the rabble's face, '*Procul este profani*':

> No, if you are the elect of Heaven,
> Use your gift, divine envoy,
> For our benefit.
> Correct the hearts of your brothers-in-arms.
> We are faint-hearted, we are perfidious,
> Shameless, evil and ungrateful:
> In our hearts we are cold eunuchs,
> Slanderers, slaves and fools.
> Vices nest in us in flocks.
> If you love your neighbours, you can
> Give us daring lessons,
> And we will listen to you.

The vulgarity of the mass – utilitarianism and the spirit of cupidity – is dangerous because it spreads from the lower to the higher reaches of man's thought, to the spheres of morality, philosophy, religion and poetry, and poisons everything there, reducing everything to its own level and transforming everything into cupidity, into modest and useful virtues, into an oven pot or into the charitable distribution of bread to the hungry in order to assuage the bourgeois conscience. There is nothing to fear when the little are satisfied with little, but when the great sacrifice their greatness to please the little, one fears for the future of the human spirit. Whenever a great artist, in the name of whatever goal – be it cupidity, usefulness, earthly or heavenly benefits – and in the name of whatever ideals alien to art – be they philosophical, moral or religious – finds himself renouncing disinterested and free thought, then by that very act he commits an abomination in a holy place and communes with the spirit of the rabble.

See how a poet who is a true servant of the eternal God judges such composers of useful booklets and popular parables, such correctors of the human heart, such high priests who have taken up a brush to sweep the streets, such traitors to poetry. See how Pushkin judges Lev Tolstoy for his moralistic tales and his disowning of Anna Karenina because she is too beautiful and not useful enough:

> Be gone! What concern
> Of the peaceful poet are you?
> In your cities rubbish is swept
> From the noisy streets – a useful labour!
> But, forgetting their service,
> Their altar and their sacrifice,
> Do priests take a broom from you?
> Not for everyday emotions,
> Nor for profit, nor for battles,
> We are born for inspiration,
> For sweet sounds and prayers.

In all ages – Pushkin remarked in a conversation with Smirnova – there has been an elite, there have been leaders. This goes back to Noah and Abraham. The judicious *will of individuals or of a minority has always guided mankind*. The individual wills of the mass of people are disunited and the man who gains control of the mass fuses these separate wills into a single will. Under all forms of government the people have submitted to a minority or to individuals in such a fateful manner that the word democracy, in its most common sense, seems to me empty and without foundation. Among the Greeks the men of thought were equal and were true rulers. At bottom inequality is a law of nature. Because of the variety of talents, even the variety of physical abilities which exists, there is no uniformity among the mass of mankind; consequently, there is no equality. All changes, for the better or for the worse, have been undertaken by a minority; the crowd have simply followed in their footsteps like Panurge's flock. To kill Caesar, only Brutus and Cassius were needed; to kill Tarquin, Brutus by himself sufficed. The strength of Peter the Great alone was enough to transform Russia, Napoleon, without any help, bridled the remnants of the revolution. All the great deeds of history have been performed by individuals... Their will has created, destroyed and transformed... Nothing can be of greater interest than a history of the saints, i.e. those men possessing an exceptional strength of will... These men were followed and given support, but the first word was always spoken by them. All this is diametrically opposed to the democratic system, which does not recognise this natural aristocracy of superior individuals. I do not believe that the world can have seen the end of that which issues from the depths of human nature and which, moreover, exists also in nature itself – namely *inequality*.

Such was Pushkin's opinion of the modern European ideal. One may disagree with this view, but it is not possible – as certain Russian critics do who want to justify the poet from a liberal-cum-democratic standpoint – to interpret works such as *The Rabble* as a chance mood and as a consequence of Pushkin's lacking a conscious philosophical attitude to the great questions of the age. This theme of spiritual aristocracy in Pushkin's poetry is just as closely connected with the deepest roots of the poet's philosophy as is the other theme of returning to simplicity and to all-forgiving nature. The beauty of the hero who creates the future and the beauty of primitive man who preserves the past are two ideals and two worlds which appeal equally to Pushkin, and which equally distance him from modern civilisation. The latter is hostile both to the hero and to primitive man; modern civilisation is philistine and mediocre, and it lacks the strength to be either aristocratic or of the people, either Christian or pagan.

The poem *The Rabble* was written in 1828. Only two years separate it from the sonnet on the same theme, *Poet, prize not the people's love!* But what a change, what an advance in lucidity! In *The Rabble* one still sees traces of romanticism, the coursing of youthful blood and that hatred which four years earlier had impelled Pushkin to write in a letter to Vyazemsky some immortal words which are no less malevolent and telling than the poem *The Rabble:*

The crowd eagerly reads confessions, memoirs, etc.,

because in its baseness it delights in the humilation of the great and the weaknesses of the strong. It goes into raptures over the revelation of any shortcoming. *'He is little, like us! He is vile, like us!'* You lie, scoundrels: he may be little and vile, but not like you – quite differently!

In this angry outburst one senses an inspiration which may subsequently develop into wisdom, but wisdom is not yet present, any more than it is in *The Rabble*. In both cases we see the bile, venom and pungency of an epigram. The elect of heaven condescends to speak with the crowd, to listen to it and even to debate with it. Only in the last lines,

> Not for everday emotions,
> Nor for profit, nor for battles.
> We are born for inspiration,
> For sweet sounds and prayers

is there a transition to tranquility. But it is a pity that the crowd hears these words. Its animal ears were not created for the candour of geniuses. These things should not be uttered in public squares; the speaker should retire to a holy place:

> Travel along
> The path of freedom, inspired by a free mind,
> Realising the fruits of your heartfelt thoughts,
> And demanding no reward for your noble work.

Reward lies in you yourself. You are your own best judge...

To judge oneself is the prerogative of kings, and kings purchase this prerogative at the cost of loneliness: 'You are king: live alone!' The chosen one does not debate with the rabble. The latter appears in the final three lines of the sonnet, pitiful and dumb:

> Best able to assess what you yourself have done.
> Does it satisfy your rigorous appraisal?
>
> If it satisfies, then let the masses scorn it,

> Let them spit on the altar on which your fire burns,
> Let them rock your tripod in childish play.

This is where the heroic aspect of Pushkin's philosophy reaches full maturity. No longer is there any outburst, any grief, or any passion. Everything is quiet and clear: the words possess the cold firmness of marble.

Before the chosen one emerges from the crowd – while his soul 'partakes of cold sleep' – he seems to be, both to himself and to other people, an ordinary man:

> And among the insignificant children of the world
> He is perhaps the most insignificant of all.

For the prophet or hero to appear, the miracle of rebirth must occur – a miracle which is no less great and terrible than death:

> But no sooner does the divine word
> Touch his keen hearing,
> Than the poet's soul starts
> Like an aroused eagle.

Now he is no longer a man; in him a higher being is born, whom people cannot comprehend. The animals, the leaves, the waters and the rocks are closer to his heart than are his own brothers:

> He flees, wild and austere,
> Full of sounds and consternation,
> To the shores of deserted seas,
> To the broad, echoing, leafy groves.

Christian wisdom is a flight from men into nature; it is seclusion in God. Pagan wisdom is the same flight into nature, but seclusion in oneself, in one's own reborn and deified ego. This miracle of rebirth is expressed with even greater clarity in *The Prophet:*

> And He clove my bosom with a sword,
> And took out my quivering heart,
> And a coal which blazed with fire
> He thrust into my gaping breast.
> Like a corpse I lay in the desert...

Everything human in the man has been torn out and killed. And only now can the prophet rise up out of the dreadful remains:

> And the voice of God called out to me:
> 'Arise, O prophet, see and hear,
> Be filled with My will,
> And, traversing every sea and land,
> Set the hearts of men on fire with your word!'

Thus are the chosen created by an act of divine violence on human nature...

SOLOVYOV

THE SIGNIFICANCE OF POETRY IN PUSHKIN'S VERSE

Vladimir Solovyov (1853–1900), per haps the greatest of the Russian nineteenth-century idealist philosophers, was also a distinguished poet, a publicist, a translator and a literary critic. His mystical doctrine of St. Sophia – the divine wisdom or principle of harmony in the universe – exercised a strong influence on the Russian religious thinkers and the symbolist poets of the early twentieth century. Solovyov's aesthetics, which were set forth in *The General Meaning of Art* (1890) and *Beauty in Nature* (1889), described the task of art as twofold: to transform reality into a cosmos of absolute beauty and to foreshadow a state of positive total unity. The philosopher's preoccupation with aesthetics led him to plan a treatise on Pushkin, but this was never completed. In the present extract from his essay *The Significance of Poetry in Pushkin's Verse* (1897) Solovyov argues that Pushkin, who like all genuine artists was an inspired medium, is the supreme poet of pure beauty.

Pushkin's poetry is poetry in its very essence and *par excellence* and does not admit of any individual or one-sided definition. The very essence of poetry – that which strictly constitutes poetry or which is poetic in itself – has never appeared in a purer form than in Pushkin, although there have been greater poets than he. Indeed, to recognise Pushkin as a poet *par excellence* does not mean that one must recognise him as the very greatest of poets. The power of a work of poetry can issue from many different sources, and the purest and fullest expression of poetry as such is not necessarily the most powerful and most grandiose. Without going so far as to disturb the colossal shades of Homer and Dante, or Shakespeare and Goethe, one might well prefer both Byron and Mickiewicz to Pushkin. From certain standpoints indeed such a preference is not simply a matter of personal taste, but is dictated by an impartial appreciation. And yet Pushkin still remains the poet *par excellence,* a more unalloyed exponent of pure poetry than anyone else...

Byron and Mickiewicz introduced from within themselves a content which, for all its significance, was not essential for poetry as such: the one brought his demonic nature, the other his religious mysticism. Pushkin's personality never held any such dominating central content: his was simply a living, open, extraordinarily receptive and responsive soul – nothing more. The only major and important feature which he recognised in himself was his poetic gift; clearly he could not contribute anything of universal significance to poetry *from within himself;* poetry remained with him *pure poetry,* which acquired its content not from outside but from within itself. The basic distinguishing characteristic of this poetry is its freedom from any preconceived tendency and any affectation. Mickiewicz's dominating tendency was noble and true, but it stands out too obviously and violates the beauty of his poetry. Indeed, *Pan Tadeusz* is justifiably recognised as Mickiewicz's best, if not most characteristic work because in it the poet hardly recoils at all from his purely poetic task and moves closer to Pushkin, the further he draws away from Byron. And as far as the latter 'potentate of thought' is concerned, he was with his whole being like some gigantic affectation addressing itself to the Creator and creation.

In Pushkin we meet no preconceived, conscious and premeditated tendency and no affectation, provided only that we ourselves approach him free of any preconceived tendency and any unjustified determination to discover in the poet that which we especially like and to take from him, not what he offers, i.e. poetic beauty (never mind that!), but what we need from him, i.e. authoritative support for our own notions and concerns. Given a strong desire and using extracts and snippets from his whole corpus, one may of course ascribe to Pushkin every conceivable tendency, some of which are even diametrically opposed to each other – ultra-progressive and ultra-reactionary, religious and free-thinking, westernist and slavophile, ascetic and epicurean. It is difficult to decide which of two varieties of naive pride predominates here in each case – the desire to give Pushkin credit for being numbered among such excellent people as ourselves, or the desire to give ourselves credit for being in agreement with such a superior man as Pushkin.

In fact, all colours are found in Pushkin's opalescent poetry and any attempt to paint it in only one automatically fails because of the obvious strains and contradictions to which it leads. The polychromatic nature of Pushkin's poetry is obvious to everyone, but an external, superficial glance notices only a lack of content, a paucity of ideas and an absence of backbone. A word which here springs to mind is *chameleon* – which is hardly a term of praise. But what rational meaning can such a judgement possess? What content is here demanded of poetry? Any, it would seem, except poetic content. Yet if one were to demand theological propositions of a chemist or chemical experiments of a theologian, one would of course find both deficient; and one has no more logical right to require of a poet a specific cast of mind – whether religious, political, sociological, or whatever. To look unfailingly for any particular content extraneous to poetry itself is to deny poetry's *own content;* and what then is the good of talking about poets? It would be more logical to give them up as hopeless, as empty and useless people.

But poetry has its own content and use. Poetry can and must serve the cause of truth and goodness on earth – but only in its own way, only through its beauty, not through anything else. Now, beauty stands of itself in due relationship with truth and goodness, as their palpable manifestation. Consequently, everything which is truly poetic – that is everything which is beautiful – is by this fact alone rich in content and useful in the best sense of that word.

Genuine poetry requires nothing but beauty. In beauty lies its meaning and its use. The expiring nineteenth century, it is true, has taken shape, towards its end, as an age of counterfeits. Milk and wine are counterfeited. But in these cases, if not shame, then at least fear of the police and of prospective purchasers inspires in the perpetrators a certain moderation and decency; after all, no adulterator would dream of asserting that milk and wine may and must in their very purpose be useless and even harmful. The adulteration of beauty, however, is another matter. There is no law against such 'artistic individuality'. Obvious beauty is declared to be *old-fashioned* beauty, and on its ruins is raised the banner of a *new* beauty, emblazoned by people reminiscent of Shchedrinesque or Dostoevskian characters with such mottos as: 'Be bold!', 'Violate and usurp!' and 'Spit on everything and rejoice!' The difference between the old and the new beauty is that the former used to dwell in a close and natural union with goodness and truth, while the latter has discovered that such a union is not only superfluous but frankly unsuitable and undesirable. But now observe the most curious aspect of all this: at first it is announced that beauty is free from the antitheses of good and evil and of truth and falsehood, that it is above this dualism and indifferent to it, but in the end we suddenly see that this freedom and beauty and this apparently divine impartiality has imperceptibly turned into a hostility towards one side (i.e. towards the right, towards truth and goodness) and into a definite, irresistible attraction towards the other side (i.e. towards the left, towards evil and falsehood) into witchcraft, demonism, satanism and other 'new forms of beauty' which are in fact just as old as 'the devil and his grandmother'.

But why do I speak in this context about counterfeit? Does not real life manifest evil which is beautiful, falsehood which is elegant, and horror which is aesthetic? Of course it does; and if it did not, there would be no point in counterfeiting beauty. But what follows from that? The gleam of lead is by its very nature similar to the gleam of silver, and the natural colour of yellow copper reminds one of gold; but if I am offered a lead shilling or a copper sovereign, I would seem to have the right to call them false. Effective attributes of false beauty are found in nature, but to claim false beauty as genuine is a human act and an act of forgery. Such a deception, like any other, is unmasked by the sterility of its effects. A piece of rotten wood may glisten, but such illumination is of use only to owls; a marsh may throw up little sparks, but even frogs are unable to warm themselves by their heat.

The light and the fire of Pushkin's poetry did not emanate from a rotting marsh. Its genuine beauty was intrinsically inseparable from goodness and truth. Maybe the seven-stemmed flute which the Muse gave him was made from a marsh reed, but:

> The reed was animated by the breath of God
> And filled the soul with a holy charm

– and it said nothing about 'new beauty'. The devotees of the latter must therefore either forcibly graft onto Pushkin their own lusts, which are quite alien to him, or declare his poetry empty of content, uninteresting and unnecessary.

Genuine and pure poetry requires of its priest simply an

infinitely receptive emotional sensitivity which is delicately attuned to higher inspiration. The mind, as the basis of man's willed actions, plays no part at this stage. Pushkin personally was beyond dispute a highly intelligent man; brilliant intellectual flashes are scattered throughout his letters, sketches, essays, epigrams, etc. All this is extremely valuable, but this is not where Pushkin's priceless worth and significance are to be found. We cherish him without reservation not because his works are *intelligent*, but because they are *inspired*. Faced with inspiration, the mind is silent. Pushkin's sharp clear mind, his refined taste, his perfect verbal pitch, and his broad literary education – all these qualities emerged and came into their own when 'the swift chill of inspiration' disappeared and when it was necessary to fashion and shape into its final form, at the behest of the mind, that which was not made by the mind, but created under supreme inspiration. Not everything which Pushkin wrote, even in verse, belongs to Pushkin's poetry – even the man who is supremely open to inspiration does not always experience its influence when he picks up his pen. But when it is a question of true Pushkinian verse, every reader who is sensitive to poetry forgets that Pushkin was intelligent as readily as he forgets that the poet had elegant hand-writing. What mind could have produced the divine inspiration which breathes life into the following most ordinary and everday words? –

> Whom have you not yet counted?
> Who has failed our delightful custom?
> Which of you has the cold world carried off?
> Whose voice is silent at our fraternal roll?
> Who has not come? Who is missing from us?. . .*

The craftsmanship of the human mind can fashion a most beautiful pot out of ordinary clay, but it is not within its power to put into the clay a living soul. And what mind can substantialise in a few words an image which grips the heart like the following?

> Are you sitting in a circle of friends,

---

*Еще кого не досчитались вы?
Кто изменил пленительной привычке?
Кого из вас увлек холодный свет?
Чей глас умолк на братской перекличке?
Кто не пришел? Кого меж нами нет?. . .

Restless devotee of foreign skies?
Or are you again crossing the sultry Tropic,
And the perpetual ice of the midnight ocean?..
You extended your hand to us from over the sea;
You bore but us in your youthful soul
And said again, 'A secret fate perhaps
Has condemned us to long separation...' *

Where is the mind at work here? How could anyone *think up* this simplicity of genius?

---

*Сидишь ли ты в кругу друзей,
Чужих небес любовник беспокойный,
Иль снова ты проходишь тропик знойный,
И вечный лед полуночных морей?
Ты простирал из-за моря к нам руку,
Ты нас одних в младой душе носил
И повторял: на долгую разлуку
Нас тайный рок, быть может, осудил ...

SHESTOV

A. S. PUSHKIN

Lev Shestov (1866-1938), the pseudonym of L.I. Schwarzmann, was a philosopher and critic whose works clearly show the influence of Dostoevsky, Nietzsche and other anti-rationalist thinkers. His rejection of dogmatic and scientific modes of thought and of all abstract systems which ignore the individual human experience led him into a position akin to that of the existentialists; but Shestov's existentialism, like that of Kierkegaard with whom he felt a deep affinity, was based on an ultimate faith, a belief in God. Exiled from Russia in 1919, Shestov settled in Paris where he developed his philosophical views in a whole series of works written in an unmistakably clear and forceful style. The Russian philosopher Berdyaev once wrote of Shestov that he was a man for whom 'philosophy was not an academic pastime, but a matter of life and death'. Shestov's literary criticism can be regarded as a continuation of his philosophy. If in his article on Chekhov, *Creation from the Void,* Shestov was to condemn the writer for his all-pervading hopelessness and lack of belief, in this article on Pushkin, taken from his collection of essays *Speculation and Revelation,* written in 1899 and published posthumously in 1964, Shestov, by contrast, stresses Pushkin's life-giving and liberating force.

A little under a month from now exactly one hundred years will have passed since the birth of Alexander Sergeevich Pushkin; and, sadly, over 60 years since his death. He lived for a mere third of a century; hardly had he achieved the age of greatest maturity, 37 years, when he was plucked from life by death's merciless hand. And what a way to die! It was not illness or accident which put an end to his life: he was killed by a fellow mortal in the heat of affronted pride, by someone who forgot or perhaps, more simply, never even knew, the preciousness of the life he was trampling upon. History has preserved for us the name of Herostratus who destroyed the temple of Diana at Ephesus. No temple has yet been built whose beauty could be compared with Pushkin's great soul. And if the unfortunate D'Anthès had possessed the self-esteem of the Greek madman he might have been totally satisfied. For as long as the Russian people exist, for as long as its memory is preserved in history, new generations, in learning about their great poet, will remember his murderer as well. And no wonder! If Pushkin managed to achieve so much for his people in the course of his short life, what treasures of poetry and beauty he might have left them had he not been cut down at the height of his powers by the meaningless bullet of an empty man. Notice the astonishing, but nonetheless curious coincidence. Pushkin died at the age of 37. In England another great universal genius began, at the age of 38, to create his finest tragedies, tragedies which were to make his name famous and to give him the right to be called a new Homer: William Shakespeare. His *Hamlet* and *Julius Caesar* appeared around the years 1602 and 1603 when he was already past 37. And these two plays were followed by a whole succession of great masterpieces: *Macbeth, Othello, King Lear, Coriolanus, Anthony and Cleopatra,* etc. If Shakespeare had died at the same age as Pushkin, we would never have known *Hamlet* or *King Lear,* and many other inspired works of world literature would have perished as well, works whose authors had been inspired by the immortal genius of the great English poet. But Pushkin died at 37! What *Hamlet,* what *Macbeth* did he take with him to the grave, and how would Russian literature have developed if Pushkin had lived as long as Shakespeare? And this is without mentioning those long-lived geniuses such as Goethe or Victor Hugo who were able to 'take their fill' of earthly life and leave it having achieved everything it was within their power to achieve. Yes, 62 years have passed since Pushkin died and it is now time, it would seem, to reconcile ourselves to the sad fact of his premature end, but whenever we remember this terrible event we are unable to repress an involuntary sigh escaping from our breasts. We are unable to forgive fate and its weapon, D'Anthès, for their cruelty. Who will avenge us this terrible loss? But there is no need to be too ungrateful to fate. Pushkin is no longer with us, he has been taken from us and the priceless pearls of his artistic creations have gone with him for ever into the grave. But Pushkin was with us once, he has left behind a great heritage which no power on earth can take from us now. This heritage is the whole of Russian literature. At one time, not so long ago, at the mention of the word 'literature' our thoughts would automatically turn to the West. There, we thought, is everything in which the creative spirit of man can take pride. There you could find Dante, Shakespeare and Goethe. Now this is no longer so: now people from the West come to us, their constant disciples, with a sense of wonder and awe and listen with eager joy to the new notes resounding throughout Russian literature. Was it so long ago that George Sand and Victor Hugo were the undisputed masters and rulers of the international state of world literature? But listen now: who are the teachers? Count Tolstoy, whose every new work is practically telegraphed to near and distant countries alike; and Dostoevsky, who is imitated so painstakingly but so unsuccessfully by French, German, English and Italian novelists. But Count Tolstoy and Dostoevsky are Pushkin's spiritual heirs; one half of their works is theirs alone: the other half they have inherited from their great predecessor. Dostoevsky says almost as much himself in his famous speech, which, sadly, many people have misunderstood and which has led to fierce and unpleasant arguments. Count Tolstoy, it is true, has renounced Pushkin and in his book *What is Art?* he even expressed surprise at the unveiling of a monument to Pushkin in the 1880s. But this changes nothing at all. Whatever Tolstoy might say, we all know that he is being guided at the present time not by the dispassionate sense of fairness of a historian or a judge, but by secondary considerations, the exigencies of the moment. He is now obsessed with preaching a moral message: anything that can serve the aims of this preaching, he will praise; anything that is hostile to it, he will censure. He has renounced Pushkin, but not *War and Peace* or *Anna Karenina*. And, in both cases, he was quite right. But those who see in Tolstoy's great novels the fullest realisation of Russian creative thought know the initiator of such thought, know the unique, fathomless and most profound source from which all the currents of our literature will for ever spring. Foreigners who now admire Tolstoy and Dostoevsky are in essence paying tribute to Pushkin. Pushkin is inaccessible to them since they do not know Russian, and poetry is completely lost in translation. But Pushkin's successors have expressed no more than the source from which they spring. And they are great precisely because of their ability to keep to the path they were shown.

In what then lay this heritage which the great teacher bequeathed to his numerous pupils? I say numerous, because Tolstoy and Dostoevsky were mentioned earlier simply as the most eminent, gifted and typical manifestations of Pushkin's spirit. After them there is a whole multitude of more or less talented writers. Not only a writer such as Turgenev or such talents as Pisemsky and Goncharov, but almost everyone of any standing in Russian literature bears the imprint of Pushkin's influence. Take as an example Garshin and Nadson, who faded before they had had time really to blossom, and you will see that they too are Pushkin's faithful pupils. All the best Russian writers have a single and eternal inscription on their banners: *ad majorem gloriam* Pushkin, so all-embracing is our great poet's genius.

Belinsky said of Pushkin that he instilled in people the idea of humanity. Coming from Belinsky this is high and very significant praise. When the great critic said this about Pushkin he had in mind the words used by Hamlet about his father: 'He was a man, take him for all in all, I shall not look upon his like again'. And, following Pushkin's example, Russian literature, from the beginning of this century to the present day, has held to a single motto: instil in people the idea of humanity. Such a task is much more complex, far-reaching and difficult than it might at first sight appear. A poet is not a preacher. He cannot merely confine himself to impassioned and fiery phrases which inflame the hearts of his listeners. More is required of him: what is required above all is truthfulness to life, that he should depict life as it really is. But, as we know, life is a very poor teacher of humane ideas. Reality is pitiless and cruel. Its law is the suppression of the weak and the exaltation of the strong. How then can the poet stay faithful to the highest and best impulses of his heart and at the same time depict reality? Apparently there is no possibility of choice; it is clearly impossible to serve two masters; one must either describe reality or one must depict the realm of unrealisable fantasy. This question has not been resolved in recent Western European literature. The great writers of Western Europe have been unable to resolve such a terrible dilemma. Either you have great idealists, such as Victor Hugo or George Sand, or avowed realists such as Flaubert, the Goncourts, Zola and many others. The greatest European writers have not been able to find those elements of life which would reconcile the manifest injustices of reality with those invisible but universally esteemed ideals, which each person, even the most insignificant, preserves for ever in his innermost being. Proudly we can say that this question has been resolved by Russian literature and we can point to Pushkin with a sense of astonishment and awe: for he was the first to stand his ground when confronted by the terrible sphinx who had already devoured more than one great standard-bearer for humanity. The sphinx asked him: How is it possible to look at life and still believe in truth and goodness? Pushkin replied: Yes, it is indeed possible, and the mocking and terrible monster disappeared. The great poet's whole life and creative activity exemplified this. He showed the way for future Russian writers and the Russian people saw Pushkin followed by Gogol, Lermontov, Turgenev, Goncharov, Ostrovsky, Pisemsky, Dostoevsky and Tolstoy; and those very Europeans, at whose feet we not so long ago once timidly sat, came to us seeking words of consolation and hope.

These words might perhaps seem exaggerated to some people. It might perhaps be thought that this question of realism and idealism was not such a terrible one after all, so that to introduce the idea of the sphinx was going too far, and secondly that it was not Pushkin who resolved it. As an answer to these points we propose on the one hand to take a rather more detailed look at Pushkin's works and, on the other, to remind ourselves about two other great Russian writers, Gogol and Lermontov. They were both contemporaries of Pushkin but it was neither they nor their works which determined the future development or brilliance of Russian literature. Of course they exerted a tremendous influence on the views of later generations. But, fortunately, it was not they who were destined to stand at the head of our intellectual life. Everybody knows Gogol's terrible fate. A realist, he described all the horrors of reality with its Khlestakovs, Skvoznik-Dmukhanovskys, Sobakeviches, Manilovs etc., but he himself was unable to withstand these horrors and became the victim of his own creations. He was unable to solve the sphinx's riddle and the monster devoured him. We know now that his words 'through visible laughter and invisible tears' were not used allegorically or metaphorically, but were actually true. We saw him laugh and did not believe that he was weeping; only when his correspondence with friends appeared did we realise just how tormenting these questions were to him. So too with Lermontov. We were not destined to see the atrophying of his tremendous talent; a bullet obligingly saved him from Gogol's fate. But from what he wrote we know what torments he had to suffer. At the age of 25 he wrote: 'And life, as you coldly look around you, is such a stupid empty jest!' Who has the strength to master the sense of horror and revulsion induced by reality when confronted by the images which pursued Lermontov? One such person did exist: Pushkin. How strange it is that Lermontov, who faced just the same problems as Pushkin, would invariably let himself be overcome by these problems. You have only to compare *Evgenii Onegin* with *A Hero of Our Time*. Onegin and Pechorin are blood brothers, twins, suckled, if you like, by the same breast. Whereas, however, Pushkin triumphed over Onegin, Lermontov totally surrendered to the figure of Pechorin. Think of these two novels. Wherever Pechorin appears he brings with him grief, unhappiness and destruction, like the angel of death. Nobody is able to withstand his mighty strength. It is as if Lermontov is saying to us: this is all that there is and can be in life. You cannot like Pechorin: he is nasty, vindictive and pitiless. And yet he is superior to everyone else; all the rest are nothing compared to him. The men are petty, cowardly, stupid and commonplace. And as for the women – Pechorin has merely to nod at them and they are ready to surrender themselves utterly. The unsophisticated Bela, the charming Princess Mary and the unhappy Vera Ligovskaya – all of them are his slaves, grovelling at his feet. There is nobody on earth who is stronger or more powerful than Pechorin. This, in other words, is what life is like: brute, pitiless strength prevails over all else. This is the message of *A Hero of Our Time;* it is the apotheosis of heartless egoism. Lermontov is unable to overcome Pechorin and, in his desire to remain truthful, openly acknowledges him as his victor and sings him a hymn of praise, which is the due of every conqueror. And then after this came his poem 'And life...' Pechorin stifles all faith and all hope.

In Pushkin we see, with a sense of joy, the exact opposite. His Onegin too appears as a conqueror at first. Everywhere he too is superior, both in society salons and in the country. Even towards Lensky his attitude is one of supercilious disdain which, in essence, is more insulting than any scorn. With the women too it is the same. Not only society ladies, but even Tanya, with her profound, sensitive nature which expresses the essence of the countryside, are taken in by this social lion who hides the total vacuum within himself under a mask of disillusionment and who substitutes fashionable phrases for genuine emotions. He murders Lensky for no reason at all, and then leaves the countryside to look for new opportunities of conquering the hearts of other women, experienced and inexperienced: for it is by such conquests that he lives. As he follows the novel's climactic moments and sees everywhere a triumphant Onegin, the reader asks himself in alarm: will he really triumph? Was Pushkin really unable to find in Russia and in Russian life anybody or anything which could halt the triumphant procession of this heartless character? Are we once again destined to see him as an object of universal envy, and to see him expressing merely a somewhat dubious envy for an assessor from Tula stricken by palsy?

But now Tatyana reappears on the scene. Dostoevsky rightly remarked that the novel should have been called after Tatyana rather than Onegin, for she is the real hero. This is an extraordinarily profound remark which, it seems to me, should become the *profession de foi* of all Russian writers – not merely of novelists and poets, but of critics, journalists and even economists. Our heroes are not the Onegins, but the Tatyanas; this is the essential idea of Russian literature. It is not brute, self-assured egoism or heartless cruelty which conquer, but a profound, if quiet and unspoken, belief in one's own worth and in the worth of every individual. Tatyana rejected Onegin! The concluding lines of her final speech to Onegin have evoked many arguments among us:

> But I am pledged to someone else;
> To him I will remain faithful unto death.

Such arguments are a tribute to the critical sensitivity of Russian writers. Everybody understands that these two short lines contain the idea of the entire novel, that they throw light not only on all the characters in it but also, much more importantly, on Pushkin himself. Tatyana, now older, could easily have failed a second time to see through Onegin, she could have responded to his call. But Pushkin could never have made this mistake. He directed all his energies to finding that element in life before which the presumptuous but empty opportunism of the Onegins of this world would crumble to dust. Pushkin needed to show us that ideals really do exist, that truth does not always walk abroad in rags and that falsehood, vested in brocade, really does bow its proud head before the higher ideal of good, and not merely in dreams. Pushkin took Tatyana from Russian life, and Onegin, utterly disgraced and annihilated in his attitude of senseless denial, left her. He knows now that he needs to raise himself to Tanya's level rather than lower himself to her. In this lies his salvation – and the source of our joy.

Tatyana's moral victory over Onegin symbolises, as we have said, the victory of the ideal over reality. And this is the heritage which Pushkin left to his successors, to all Russian writers; it is a heritage which the best representatives of Russian literature still hold sacred. And the main point is that this is not an imaginary victory – a fact which we shall never tire of repeating. In introducing idealism into our literature, Pushkin at the same time introduced realism. There was nothing more hateful to his innate sense of truth and honesty than falsehood. He did not contrive this victory, but merely recorded what in actual fact existed, what he himself had seen. The magnitude and difficulty of the achievement can be seen from the futile efforts of Gogol to create a 'positive character'. Despite all his frantic searchings these efforts bore no success. Even his mighty talent failed to live up to the unequal task. 'It's tedious on this earth, gentlemen' – he exclaimed, worn out by his vain quest. Is it then astonishing that he should view Pushkin with such awe? You will remember his words 'Pushkin is a great, an extraordinary phenomenon'? Pushkin took his positive characters from life. And do not think that he achieved this by turning his back on reality so as not to see its horrors. On the contrary, his attention was captured by all life's most depressing aspects and he examined them tirelessly and patiently until he had found an explanation for them. After all, Pushkin is the author of *Mozart and Salieri, The Feast in Time of Plague, Boris Godunov, The Captain's Daughter* and *The Water Nymph*. One horror after another passed before his spiritual gaze, and yet he was not dismayed. Everywhere, in everything, he was able to find an inner and profound significance, as if life had decided to reveal all its most precious secrets to its chosen favourite. The most striking example of this is his *Feast in Time of Plague*. Even the gloomiest fantasy could not conjure up a more horrible picture. The human mind must apparently retreat in fear and trembling before the omnipotent spectre of all-conquering death. Who will dare to look such an all-powerful phenomenon directly in the face, to look at something which plucks everything which is most precious from use? Pushkin dared to do this because he knew that a great secret would be revealed to him. Do you remember those magnificent lines spoken by the toastmaster?

> There is an exaltation in battle,
> Or on the lip of an abyss,

On the storm-tossed ocean,
'Midst angry waves and tempestuous dark,
In an Arabian sandstorm,
Or in the breath of plague.
Everything that threatens disaster
Contains inexpressible delight
For mortal hearts – a pledge,
Perhaps, of immortality.

These lines appear to us like a revelation from on high. They contain a call to courage, to arms and to hope, just at the very moment when people have usually given up all hope and lower their hands in impotent despair. Pushkin is inspired, when everybody else would be paralysed. He is audacious and firm just at those moments when we normally hasten to hide in confusion and fear from life's threatening aspect and, failing anything better, simply close our eyes like an ostrich hiding its head under its wing when it sees that disaster is inevitable. The whole purpose and calling of the poet lies in this courage in the face of reality: this is the source of his inspiration and the secret of his creativity which we ordinary people rightly call divine; he is so far removed from us, so inaccessible. It is when we start sobbing and giving ourselves up to despair that the poet remains calm and firm in the everlasting hope that the door shall be opened to those who knock, and that those who seek shall find.

No less striking than *The Feast in Time of Plague* is the little tragedy *Mozart and Salieri*. This is a genuinely Shakespearian piece – both in depth of conception and in content. Before us we have the most horrible type of criminal: a person who, out of jealousy, murders a genius, someone who far outshines him in creative talent. Salieri himself delights in Mozart's music and calls his victim an angel descended from heaven to bring us some of the songs of paradise. And yet he pitilessly kills his great rival. This is clearly a thankless theme for an artist. A preacher seems to be needed – someone who can rise up in anger and call down the wrath of heaven onto the head of this worst of all murderers, who has taken from mankind its finest source of joy, a great musical genius. But even here Pushkin did not yield. With the majestic calm of omniscience he goes up to Salieri, looks with profound insight into his tortured soul and pronounces a verdict of not guilty. And the rest of us, unable in everyday life to restrain our indignation at the sight of the humblest and most pathetic of criminals, now follow Pushkin's example, and, chastened and disarmed, we all begin to feel, not anger against the murderer, but compassion and pity. We cannot refrain from recalling just one extract from the famous opening passage of *Mozart and Salieri*. Salieri, in deep solitary reflection, says:

> People say there is no justice on earth,
> But neither is there justice in heaven.

In this monologue Pushkin reveals such a profound understanding of the human heart and such superhuman insight into life's awesome secret. Salieri opens with this terrible sentence. He has come to the conviction, that there is no justice, not simply on earth but in heaven as well, and it is this which impels him to commit the terrible crime. Where is the person whose anger would not be stilled by the unfortunate Salieri's simple and terrible words? Where is the judge who, hearing the monologue Pushkin puts in Salieri's mouth, would not relent and would be so cruel as to condemn the tormented murderer? Here lies the solution to the awful question which Salieri himself puts. There *is* justice on earth, if people are able to understand and forgive the man who takes Mozart from them, if they are able to look on this tremendous crime with tears in their eyes and compassion in their hearts. And throughout *Mozart and Salieri* we all have the same feeling: the anger aroused in us by the murderer gives way to a tremendous compassion for him; the executioner's hand is silently lowered. It may be that in everyday life we still need all these terrible methods in order to safeguard public law and order; it may be that we still need to keep 'the lash, the prison and the axe' to ensure the harmony of ever more strained human relationships; it may be that 'in practice', as they say, it is impossible to forgive the 'guilty' and that the principle of justice must be the harsh law of retribution. This may all be true; but, alone with our conscience and guided by the great poet's example, we now know something else: we know that crime arises not out of evil passions but out of man's inability to solve the riddle of life. Salieri killed Mozart because he found justice neither on earth, nor in heaven.

Such was Pushkin's insight into the criminal and into everybody. All those whom he touched – the weak, the sorrowful, the broken, the downcast and the guilty – went away strengthened, consoled and acquitted. If time permitted, we would be able to point to clear signs of Pushkin's philosophy in every one of his works. He remains true to himself at all times and in everything he does. He always looks for and finds those elements in life on which belief in a better future for humanity can be based. And, curiously, in order to strengthen this belief he does not need to go back into history or examine any stratum of society with which he is not linked by the immediate ties of everyday relationships. His faith, in other words, does not need to rely on illusion, for which, in turn, perspective is a necessary condition. He has no need either to turn away from reality or to distance himself from it. He stands constantly at the centre of reality without losing the ability to comprehend it. Whenever Lermontov needs to rest from the harrowing immediacy of everyday life, he goes back into history; he abandons his own class and looks for raw material for his works from the lower classes which were quite unfamiliar to him. There he finds, if only momentarily, faith and hope. He is able to contrast the merchant Kalashnikov's unyielding and noble courage with the insolence of the *oprichnik* Kiribeevich, with his broom and dog's-head insignia – someone who lived many centuries before his time. Remember these inspired lines:

> I have not come to you to joke
> Or for amusement, heathen,
> But for the last and awful battle.

Lermontov needs perspective so that he can find the truth. He found nobody to counter his latter-day Kiribeevich-Pechorin with his handsome uniform and white gloves. Pushkin on the other hand, while able to depict with consummate skill the life of simple people – we need only mention *The Captain's Daughter* here – was equally at home depicting the complex life and behaviour of the intelligentsia. His work had no need of illusion. He was on familiar ground wherever he turned – a striking ability which he passed on to his successors. Turgenev, Dostoevsky and Tolstoy are, I repeat, in Pushkin's debt for everything that is the best in their work. There is the same detailed, conscientious and honest view of reality, the same truthful realism. And this detailed and conscientious analysis of reality not only does not destroy their faith and courage, but, on the contrary, strengthens their conviction of life's profound meaningfulness. Look at Turgenev's work, look at how many priceless pearls of spiritual beauty he created. But all his women – as has long since been pointed out – have Pushkin's Tatyana as their prototype; like her, they appear as moral arbiters, as lamps to light the way. Dostoevsky and Tolstoy have even more memorable examples. It would be scarcely possible to cite any other modern European writer who sought for the solution to life's most oppressive mysteries with such strange and obdurate persistence as Dostoevsky. Together with his heroes, the Raskolnikovs, the Karamazovs and others, he descended into such abysses of human torment that it seemed there could be no way out, and yet he was not destroyed by these psychological experiences, nor by the awful trials he was forced to undergo in the course of his tormented life. The reader who accompanies him into the kingdom of eternal darkness is always able to make his way back to the light under his guidance, bearing within him a profound belief in life and in the power of good. Dostoevsky fears no opponent, however destructive; he looks the most extreme scepticism boldly in the face, utterly convinced that, when confronted, it will yield to belief in life. It is the same with Tolstoy; his artistic aims were not shaped purely by the aesthetic impulses of the heart either. He put pen to paper only when, after long and anxious reflection, he felt able to illuminate for himself and for others life's riddle. That great epic of Russian life, *War and Peace,* which has been justly compared with Homer's *Iliad,* was the result of just such a process. What a catalogue of countless horrors must have met the great writer's eyes as he read the chronicles for 1812. That awesome and terrible movement of peoples from west to east, accompanied by mass murders and the destruction of whole nations, by robberies and mob violence – such a picture of pointless and futile devastation must present to the ordinary reader a terrible condemnation of life. How is it possible to look for good in a world which had been held for fifteen years in the thrall of Napoleon? Surely, to take the war of 1812 as the theme of a novel would mean that the author intended to destroy all hope and belief in people. This terrible episode in our history would seem to be a factual justification not only of Pechorin's gloomy philosophy, but also of Ivan Karamazov's – Ivan Karamazov who in an outburst of despair cried eternal damnation on good and evil. And yet Tolstoy emerges as the victor. I know of no novel which has such a healing and uplifting effect as *War and Peace.* In every line, over everything that happens in this tremendous work, you can sense life's mighty and profound spirit. The more tragic and terrible the circumstance, the bolder and firmer the writer's viewpoint. He is not afraid of tragedy and looks it squarely in the face. A great pupil is being guided, you feel, by a great teacher, Pushkin, and you hear the poet's words, which have already been quoted:

> There is an exaltation in battle...

Dangers, disasters and misfortunes, far from undermining the Russian writer's creative spirit, strengthen it. He emerges from each new trial with renewed faith. Europeans listen to the strange new themes of our poetry with a sense of astonishment and awe. Not so long ago, in connection with Tolstoy's works, the famous French critic Jules Lemaître exclaimed: 'What is the secret of the Russian writers' art? How are they able to make us believe in the improbable, how can they dare to seek for belief in reality, a reality which justifies only non-belief?' And strangely enough the French sceptic is himself forced to acknowledge that he is unable to break free from the power of Russian literature. This is of great significance: to conquer the mind of a Frenchman means to conquer the whole world. Perhaps Dostoevsky's prophecy is destined to come true: he called Pushkin 'a universal man'. Perhaps — we trust it will be so — the message of this universal man is destined to prevail throughout the world. And that will be the happiest of victories; not merely because the national pride of the Russian people will be satisfied, but because the conquered will rejoice at such a victory even more than the conqueror. It is the victory of a doctor over a patient and his disease. And where is the patient who will not bless the name of his healer, our great poet Pushkin?

AIKHENVALD

PUSHKIN

Yu. I. Aikhenvald (1872–1928) was sceptical of attempts to theorise about the nature of literature – in 1914 he published an essay attacking Belinsky – and the bulk of his own criticism consists of brilliantly composed, personal, impressionistic reflections. Most of his best-known work appeared during the first decade of the twentieth century: a translation of the complete works of Schopenhauer (1901–10), *Studies of Western Writers* (1910) and the famous *Silhouettes of Russian Writers* in three volumes (1908–1910). His chapter on Pushkin in this last work was issued in 1908 as a separate booklet. Our present extract, in which Aikhenvald stresses Pushkin's universal responsiveness, form the opening pages of this study. Aikhenvald was among the group of almost two hundred intellectuals deported by the Soviet government in 1922. He settled in Berlin where until his death in a street accident six years later he contributed regularly to the Russian *émigré* paper, *The Helm*.

In Chapter 8 of *Evgenii Onegin* Pushkin relates his poetic autobiography. His muse seems to grow before our eyes, and his inexhaustible spirit unfolds in ever-increasing depth and variety. In his schoolboy's cell and in the Lycée gardens his early muse, a divine visitant, composes her first verses. She and Pushkin are listened to graciously and admiringly. And then:

Old Derzhavin noticed us
And blessed us as he sank into the grave.

This celebrated scene at the Lyćee examination is highly symbolic: it was an historic moment, a mountain-pass on the high-road of Russian literature. The old man, a personification of the eighteenth century, giving his blessing to this curly-headed boy, this young eaglet, was an apotheosis staged by life, a triumphal changing of the centuries. Then, as the companion of turbulent youth, the muse assumes the form of a Bacchante. As a loving maiden, she accompanies her poet into exile, and remaining herself invisible, with the magic of a tale heard only by him, she gladdens his silent and solitary path. As a romantic Leonora, she gallops with him in the moonlight over the crags of the Caucasus, or, now pious, she leads him to the shores of the Crimea to listen to the eternal prayer of the sea, to the mysterious chorus of the billows as they sing hymns of praise to the father of the universe. As an untamed muse, the muse of a girl from the Steppe, Zemfira, she wanders with the gipsies in the depths of sad Moldavia. Then the scene changes again ('The wind blew, the thunder crashed') and she appears as a young country gentlewoman, the lovely Tatyana, with a melancholy pensiveness in her eyes and a French novel in her hands. And it is she again at the society ball, the muse now an aristocratic lady, a born princess.

As varied as this are the metempsychoses of Pushkin, the universal poet.

It is impossible to characterise him better than he did himself (though he had more than just himself in mind) in his celebrated poem *Echo:*

> If a beast roars in the dense forest,
> If a horn sounds, or thunder rolls,
> If a maiden sings beyond the hill,
> To every sound
> You bring forth at once
> Your reply in the empty air.
>
> You hearken to the rumble of thunder,
> And the voice of the storm and the waves,
> And the cry of country shepherds –
> And send an answer;
> But to you comes no response ... Such
> Are you too, o poet!

He is truly an echo of the world, a faithful and melodious echo, borne from land to land to respond passionately to all things, so that no single valuable sound in the life of the universe should die away without trace. This sensitivity and this gift for a full-throated response to all living voices contain something supremely human, since no-one has to limit himself to a specific sphere of impressions, and for every man the world should exist as a whole.

That is why, in creating, Pushkin recreated. He took over and imitated a great deal – even other poets, shedding tears over the creative fantasies of others, for artistic creations themselves also become a part of nature, primary material, and return to take their place in the general totality of things; they too evoke a response in the empty air. As a general rule, Pushkin did not express any original, singular or striking thoughts; he responded rather than called – and this was precisely because he was a true poet. He was very intelligent and highly cultured, but all that treasure-house which might have comprised the full happiness and wealth of another man was for him only an appendage. All these gifts were for him only something secondary which did not penetrate to the very kernel of his art and did not define it. Free in spirit and royally unconcerned, he revealed as an artist no trace of intellectuality; he is a poet of 'simple' verse. His strength lies not in the intermediate work of thought, not even, on the other hand, in making sudden, purely intellectual discoveries, but rather in his immediate intuition, in his inspired ability to grasp the essential beauty of every object; his strength lies, in other words, in his comprehension of beauty. And in his own soul there was so much of this beauty that it was able to find fulfilment, harmony and inner rhythm only in the entire diversity of nature and in the entire boundlessness of human existence. His universally responsive nature was like a many-stringed instrument, and the world played on this Aeolian harp, extracting wonderful songs from it. The sensitive ear of this great Pan of poetry heard heaven, earth and the beating of hearts – and that is why we listen to him today.

But being an echo of the universe is not something passive and mechanical: in order to answer, one must first hear. And this listening to the world reflects a deeper philosophy of life, since in listening free choices are made. After all, Pushkin reproduced not those things which are dispersed in time and space and doomed to oblivion, like the sorrowful wave breaking on a distant shore. No, his artistic instinct unhesitatingly brushed aside everything fortuitous and corruptible; instead he always caught the very ground and fascination of reality, the eternal grain within transitory events and objects. He sang for amusement, without any far-reaching purpose, but the result was depth and seriousness. What he repeated and what he retained from the current chaos of life's hollow roar was precisely that which deserves immortality; it was precisely those things which should remain in the world, it was precisely those pure responses which form the thought and the music of the world.

In his wide responsiveness as an echo of the soul and of deeds, of events internal and external, of the past and the present, Pushkin appears to lose his individual face. But divinity also has no face. Definite features, or a physiognomy, inhere only in that which is limited. The universe as a totality does not possess them. And Pushkin, in the very process of dissolving in the sounds which reproduce everything and respond to everything, finds himself and his own great microcosm.

From play to prayer, from joke to hymn, runs the spectrum of life, and this spectrum is reflected in Pushkin's poetry. It accomplishes the whole human cycle and unfolds the living scroll of a natural individuality which breathes with the fullness and the power of the breath of life. We see before us no shallow silence of apathy and indifference to the burning lures of the earth, no mediocre nature at peace in its drab sinlessness: on the contrary we see passionate youth, fighting and throbbing in temptation, and the wine foaming at the celebrations of Bacchus and Aphrodite; we hear the luxurious sounds of frenzy, idleness and passion; 'under the sky of my Africa' seethe the agitating desires of a sensual nature – and all this ends with the Madonna, that purest model of the purest charm. The serious hymns, inspired by the Gods, and the peaceful songs of the Phrygian shepherds, Apuleius and the desert fathers and virtuous women, the pagan element and the Christian element, all dispositions, the chiaroscuro of diverse feelings and thoughts – all these found in him a sympathetic response in the continuously bubbling song of his never-silent lyre.

A hundred-armed knight of the spirit, Pushkin in his burning curiosity, full of sounds and consternation, embraces everything; he sees and hears everyone and responds to every man. He said that the soul was indivisible and eternal, and he proved the truth of this in himself. Everything interested him. Seeming not to recognise any boundaries or limits, nor to sense that anything was distant or past, being eternally present and existing everywhere, always the contemporary of all, he moves in this supra-spatial and supra-temporal capacity from country to country and from age to age, and for him nothing is foreign or alien. Ovid lived and suffered long ago, but Pushkin shares his sufferings now, resurrects in himself Ovid's yearning image and sends him a fraternal greeting along the chain of the centuries. That panorama of life which unfolds before us so vividly and splendidly in the incomparable message to Yusupov passed through the poet's imagination in an even greater diversity of pictures and colours. And what Pushkin lacked in external perceptions (and to his chagrin he never saw those foreign climes where the sky glistens indescribably blue, he never saw the Brenta and the waves of the Adriatic) he filled out through the titanic power of his inner vision and relived in himself other ages, other lands and other cultures – the Trianon, the French Revolution, the tales of Beaumarchais and every vicissitude of human fate. He transformed Ariosto into a fable with the spirit and the atmosphere of old Russia; he transmuted the Koran, and the Russian words in which he reincarnated it rang out with an Eastern melody and an Eastern philosophy and were tinged with the colours of mosque and muezzin; he reproduced Shakespeare and Goethe; in the ideal journey of his creative dreams he visited Europe and the East; he comprehended Don Juan, the Miserly Knight and that other poor knight who had one vision beyond the grasp of the mind; he comprehended Salieri's envy, and the Empress Cleopatra, and the wise Oleg, and the sage Pimen, whose image shone through to him across the darkness of time. He understood and felt close to Anacreon, and the Song of Songs, and the songs of of André Chénier whose muse accompanied him to the guillotine, and Hafiz, and Horace, and everything which ever stirred and delighted men.

This triumph over the restrictions imposed by the modest share of human strength allotted to any one man, over the limited capacity of even the most highly gifted individual spirit, this poetic ubiquitousness, is of course far more than that richness of themes and subjects which has long been noted by all students of Pushkin; it is far more than a superficial virtuosity and a highly flexible artistic technique; it is not even simply an astonishing talent's powerful wings which do not flag even on the most distant flights – rather is it a manifestation of the *unity of life* which Pushkin bore within him and which made rightful and possible his bold entreaty that he should be assumed into the celestial ark, into the vicinity of God. It is an inner, organic communion with every psychology, an empathy with the whole of creation. In the most diverse spheres, through the veil of foreign peoples and tongues, over the course of many ages, always and everywhere, Pushkin recognises with profound empathy the single universal human heart and indivisibly experiences its joys and sorrows, like Mahadeva, who assumed human form in order to experience for himself the manifold life of mankind. As Schopenhauer remarks, reiterating Indian wisdom, to everything external to his own personality, to everything which is not he, the egoist squeamishly responds with, 'That is not me, that is not me!' The compassionate man, on the other hand, hears in all nature the thousandfold repeated invocation, '*Tat twam asi* – That is you, that is also you.' From Pushkin's works it is indeed this latter cry which calls to us and, thanks to Pushkin, we too send back a welcoming response to every breath – particularly of course to every human breath. And his aesthetic universalism is at the same time a supreme ethic. To the centre of his spirit stretched living threads from every living thing...

BLOK

THE POET'S ROLE

Alexander Blok (1880–1921), the most gifted of the symbolists, was one of Russia's greatest poets. His verses reflect his development from an early ecstatic worshipper of the mystical Beautiful Lady, through despair at the modern world and his own inadequacies, to an enthusiastic supporter of the Bolshevik revolution, which, however, quickly induced a fresh state of despair from which the poet never recovered. In his reflections *The Poet's Role,* which were delivered as an oration in February 1921 on the eighty-fourth anniversary of Pushkin's death, Blok draws on Pushkin's life and work to illustrate some of his own thoughts about the essence of poetry and the poet's mission. When he goes on to attack those who impede the poet in his task of transmitting to the world his inspired visions of harmony Blok has in mind the new Soviet regime as much as the bureaucrats of Nicholas I.

From early childhood our memories preserve a happy name – Pushkin. This name, its very sound, fills many days of our lives. The names of emperors, generals, inventors of weapons of slaughter, torturers and martyrs are forbidding. But next to them stands this light and elegant name – Pushkin.

Pushkin managed to bear his creative burden very lightly and happily even though the poet's role is neither light nor happy, but tragic; Pushkin played his role with a broad, assured and free sweep, like a great master, and yet at the thought of Pushkin our hearts are often wrung: the festive, triumphal progress of the poet, who could not influence external affairs, since his sphere is an inner concern, namely culture – this progress was all too frequently interrupted by the dark interference of people who valued an oven pot higher than God.

We know Pushkin the man, we know Pushkin the friend of the monarchy, and we know Pushkin the friend of the Decembrists, but all this pales before Pushkin the poet.

A poet is an immutable value. His language and his devices may become obsolete, but the essence of his concern does not. People can turn away from the poet and his concern. Today they raise monuments to him, tomorrow they want to 'throw him overboard from the ship of modernity'. Both actions define only such people, but not the poet himself. The essence of poetry, like the essence of all art, is immutable. Both these attitudes of people to poetry are in the end of no importance.

Today we honour the memory of the greatest Russian poet. It seems to me appropriate to speak on this occasion about *the poet's role* and to reinforce my words with some of Pushkin's thoughts.

What is a poet? A man who writes in verse? Of course not. A man is not called a poet because he writes in verse; rather, a man writes in verse – that is, he brings words and sounds into harmony – because he is a child of harmony, because he is a poet.

What is harmony? Harmony is a concord of the forces ruling the world, an order in the life of the world. Order is Cosmos, the opposite of disorder, or Chaos. The Ancients taught that Cosmos, or the world, is born out of Chaos. Cosmos is related to Chaos as the dancing waves of the sea are related to the massive surging of the ocean. A son may be different from his father in all but one hidden feature, but that feature is the one which makes them similar.

Chaos is the primeval, elemental anarchy; Cosmos is a harmony which has been built, a culture. Cosmos is born out of Chaos. The element conceals within itself the seeds of culture; out of anarchy is created harmony.

The life of the world comprises the continuous creation of new breeds and new species. They are cradled in anarchic Chaos, but tended and selected by culture; harmony gives them shapes and forms, which again dissolve in the anarchic fog. The meaning of this process we do not understand, and its essence is unclear; we console ourselves with the thought that the new species is better than the old, but the wind soon extinguishes this little candle with which we attempt to illuminate the darkness of the world. The order of the world is uncertain; it is the native child of disorder and may well not coincide with our notions of what is good and what is bad.

We know one thing: the species which replaces another is new, and that which is replaced is old. In the world we observe perpetual change, and we ourselves participate in the evolution of species. Our part is largely inactive: we degenerate, we grow old and we die. Sometimes it is active: we may occupy a position in the culture of the world and promote the formation of new species.

The poet is a child of harmony, and this gives him a role in the culture of the world. Three concerns are incumbent upon him: first, to liberate sounds from the native anarchic element in which they reside; secondly, to bring these sounds into harmony, or to give then form; and thirdly, to transmit this harmony into the external world.

Once these sounds, captured from the element and brought into harmony, are transmitted into the world, they begin their own work automatically. 'A poet's words are already his deeds'. They manifest an unexpected power: they test human hearts and produce a certain selection from the heaps of human clinker. They may collect certain parts of the old species bearing the name 'man' – those parts which are of use in the creation of new species, for the old is clearly declining quickly, degenerating and dying.

There is no opposing the power of harmony transmitted into the world by the poet. The struggle against it is beyond both individual and combined human strength. 'If only all felt thus the power of harmony', yearns the lonely Salieri. But everyone does feel it, though mortals in a different way from God or from Mozart. No-one can evade the sign which poetry makes in flight or the name which it gives when necessary, any more than he can evade death. The name is given unerringly.

Thus, for instance, those who are simple fragments of the element, those to whom it is not given to understand, never earn a bad name from the poet. He does not give the name 'rabble' to those people who are like the earth which they plough, the wisp of fog from which they have emerged, or the beast which they hunt. On the other hand, those who refuse to understand, though they ought to understand much because they too serve culture, are branded with the shameful name 'the rabble'. Even death does not rescue them from this appellation; the name remains even after death, as it has with Count Benckendorff, Timkovsky or Bulgarin, and with all those who impeded the poet's fulfilment of his mission.

in the bottomless depths of the spirit, where man ceases to be man, in depths inaccessible to the states and societies created by civilisation, roll waves of sound like the waves of the ether which fill the universe; in those depths proceed rhythmic tremors similar to the processes which create the mountains, the winds and the floods, the vegetable and the animal kingdoms.

This depth of the spirit is screened by the phantasms of the external world. Pushkin says that it is screened from the poet perhaps more than from other people: 'Among the insignificant children of this world he is perhaps the most insignificant of all'.

The first concern which the poet's ministry demands is that he should reject 'the cares of the vain world', in order to raise the external veils and reveal the depth. This demand separates the poet from the ranks of 'the insignificant children of this world':

> He flees, wild and austere,
> Full of sounds and consternation,
> To the shores of deserted seas,
> To the broad, echoing, leafy groves.

Wild, austere and full of consternation, because the dissection of spiritual depths is as difficult as the act of giving birth. To the sea and into the forest because only there, in solitude, is it possible to gather all his strength and commune with 'native chaos', the anarchic element which produces the waves of sound.

The mystery is performed – the veil is raised, the depth is revealed, and the sound is received into the soul. Then the second demand of Apollo is that this sound, raised from the depth and alien to the external world, should be confined within the firm and palpable form of a word. Sounds and words must form a single harmony. This is the sphere of craftsmanship, and craftsmanship demands inspiration just as does communion with 'native chaos'. 'Inspiration', said Pushkin, 'is that state of the soul when it is most vitally disposed to receive impressions and consider concepts and so to explain them'. Consequently, it is impossible to draw a sharp line between the first of the poet's concerns and the second. The one is totally linked with the other: the more veils are raised, the more intense the communion with Chaos and the more difficult the birth of sound, the clearer the form which it strives to assume, the more insistent and harmonious it is, and the more urgently it pursues human hearing.

The time has come for the poet's third concern. The sounds

which have been received into the soul and brought into harmony must be transmitted to the world. And this is where the poet's celebrated clash with the rabble occurs.

There can hardly ever have been a time when the common people were called the rabble. Only those who themselves deserved this appellation applied it to the common people. Pushkin collected folk songs and wrote in the common vein, and his peasant nurse was very close to his heart. Hence, one would have to be stupid or wicked to think that by 'the rabble' Pushkin could have meant the common people. A dictionary of Pushkin's language will clarify this – if Russian culture revives.

By the rabble Pushkin meant more or less the same as we do. He often accompanied this noun by the adjective 'society', giving a collective name to that hereditary court nobility who had nothing left except their titles. But even before Pushkin's own eyes the position of the hereditary nobility was being quickly taken over by the bureaucracy. These officials are in fact our rabble, the rabble of yesterday and today – not nobility, not common people, not animals, not lumps of earth, not wisps of fog, not fragments of the planets, not demons and not angels. Without the addition of the 'not' only one thing can be said of them – that they are people. And that is not especially flattering, for *people* are men of business and vulgarians whose spiritual depth has been hopelessly and solidly screened off by 'the cares of the vain world'.

The rabble demands of the poet that he should serve what they serve – the external world: as Pushkin says simply, they demand from him 'a use'; they demand that the poet should 'sweep rubbish from the streets', 'illumine the hearts of his brothers-in-arms', and so on.

From their own point of view, the rabble are right in their demands. In the first place, they will never be able to enjoy the fruits of that concern demanded of the poet which is somewhat greater than the sweeping of rubbish from the streets. In the second place, they instinctively feel that this concern, somehow, sooner or later, works to their detriment. The testing of hearts by harmony is not a calm pursuit, guaranteeing that smooth course of events in the external world which the rabble desires.

The rabble class, like other classes of humanity incidentally, progresses extremely slowly; thus, for instance, in spite of the fact that during the course of recent centuries the human brain has developed at the expense of all the other functions of the organism, men have come to the idea of isolating from the state only one organ, the censorship, to protect that order in their world which is expressed in the forms of the state. In this way they have placed an obstacle only on the third path of the poet – on the path of transmitting harmony into the world. One would imagine that they might think of placing obstacles on the first and second paths as well, that is they might try to find means to muddy the many sources of harmony. What restrains them – slowness of wit, timidity or conscience – we do not know. But perhaps they are already seeking such means?

However, the poet's concern, as we have seen, is quite incommensurable with the order of the external world. The poet's tasks are, in the conventional phrase, universally cultural. His task is a historical one. Therefore, the poet has the right to repeat after Pushkin:

> And it is little worry to me whether the press
> Freely deceives blockheads, or whether a tactful censorship
> Restricts the jester in his journalistic schemes.

In saying this, Pushkin ratified the rabble's right to establish a censorship, since he assumes that the number of blockheads would not diminish.

The poet's concern is by no means to get through unfailingly to all blockheads. Rather, the harmony he has extracted carries out a process of selection among them with the aim of extracting from the heaps of human clinker something more interesting than average humanity. This aim will of course sooner or later be achieved by true harmony. No censorship in the world can impede this basic concern of poetry.

On this day, a day dedicated to Pushkin's memory, let us not argue whether Pushkin correctly or incorrectly distinguished the freedom which we call personal from that which we call political. We know that he demanded 'another', 'secret' freedom. In our view it is 'personal', but for the poet it was not only personal freedom:

> ... To no-one
> To render account; to serve and please
> Oneself alone; for authority and livery
> Not to bend conscience, thoughts or neck;

> According to *whim* to gallop here and there,
> Wondering at the divine beauties of nature,
> And before works of art and inspiration
> To revel silently in raptures of tenderness.
> That is happiness. That is one's right!

This he said just before his death. In his youth Pushkin spoke about the same thing:

> Love and secret freedom
> Instilled in the heart a simple hymn.

This *secret freedom*, this *whim* (a word which was subsequently repeated loudest of all by Fet: 'the bard of mad whims!') is by no means simply personal freedom, but a much greater one: it is closely linked with the first two concerns imposed on the poet by Apollo. Every item enumerated in Pushkin's poem is a necessary condition for the liberation of harmony. Permitting interference in the matter of testing people with harmony, i.e. in the third concern, Pushkin could not permit interference in the first two concerns. Even these concerns are not individual.

Meanwhile, Pushkin's life, as it moved towards its close, became increasingly frustrated by the obstacles placed upon his path. Pushkin weakened, and with him weakened the culture of his time, the only cultural age in nineteenth-century Russia. The fateful forties were approaching. Over Pushkin's deathbed Belinsky's infantile prattle was heard. This prattle seemed to be completely opposed and completely hostile to the courteous voice of Count Benckendorff. It still seems so to us today. It would be too painful for all of us if that proved not to be the case. And even if it is not quite the case, let us nevertheless think that it is. After all, for the time being:

> Dearer to us than ten thousand base truths
> Is the deception which ennobles us.

But in the second half of the century, that which could only just be heard in Belinsky's infantile prattle Pisarev shouted at the top of his voice.

I will refrain from any further juxtapositions, for it is still impossible to make the picture completely clear. Perhaps beyond the web of time something will be revealed quite different from that which flashes in my impudent thoughts and quite different from that which is firmly fixed in thoughts opposed to mine. Further events must be lived through; the verdict in this case lies in the hands of future historians of Russia.

Pushkin is dead. But 'for the young the Posas never die', said Schiller. And Pushkin was not killed by d'Anthès' bullet. He was killed by lack of air. And with him died his culture.

> It is time, my friend, it is time! The heart begs for peace.

These are Pushkin's dying sighs and also the sighs of the culture of Pushkin's time.

> There is no happiness on earth, but there are peace and freedom.

Peace and freedom. They are essential to the poet if he is to liberate harmony. But peace and freedom can also be taken away. Not external peace, but creative peace. Not childish freedom, not the freedom to play the liberal, but creative freedom – secret freedom. And the poet dies, because there is no air for him to breathe, because life has lost its meaning.

The amiable officials who impeded the poet's testing of men's hearts with harmony have retained for ever the sobriquet of rabble. But they impeded the poet only in his third concern. The testing of hearts by the poetry of Pushkin in its full compass has been pursued in spite of them.

Let then those civil servants who are now preparing to direct poetry along certain channels of their own, encroaching upon its secret freedom and preventing it from fulfilling its secret mission, beware of earning a worse appellation.

We die, but art lives on. Its ultimate ends are not known to us and cannot be known. Art is consubstantial and indivisible.

I should like, simply for amusement, to proclaim three simple truths:– There are no particular arts. One should not give the name of art to that which is really something else. In order to create works of art, one must have the ability to do so.

To these happy truths of common sense, which we all sin against, we may swear by the happy name of Pushkin.

EIKHENBAUM

PROBLEMS OF PUSHKIN'S POETICS

B. M. Eikhenbaum (1886–1959) was a talented, provocative and influential Soviet critic whose numerous works on Russian literature and literary theory invariably stimulated discussion and controversy. Together with Shklovsky, Eikhenbaum was a leading member of the Formalist school of criticism which eschewed all critical approaches to literature other than an analysis of the purely literary and linguistic devices of the author concerned. Such an approach can be seen most clearly in Eikhenbaum's famous article *How Gogol's Overcoat was Made*, written in 1918. Subsequently, in the 1930s and 1940s, Eikhenbaum was to dilute these strictly formalist views and in his critical works, particularly on Leskov and Tolstoy, he acknowledged the value of placing the author in his historical context. This historicism can be seen to a certain extent in the present extract from *Problems of Pushkin's Poetics* (1921), but Eikhenbaum makes it quite clear that his primary interest lies in an examination of form, rhythm and metre, in the devices which Pushkin uses to achieve his effect, and in the syntactical relationship between his poetry and his prose.

Those admirers of Pushkin who, in trying to elevate him to even greater heights, assert that he is an unexpected phenomenon in Russian poetry, do so in vain. Pushkin is not a beginning, but the end of the long road traversed by eighteenth-century Russian poetry. And it is to this that he is beholden for his position in Russian poetry. 'Only of a totally disorded and confused poet can one say that everything he writes is his own; of a real poet – this is impossible' (Goethe). Pushkin ends, rather than initiates a line. Having assimilated all the poetical traditions of the eighteenth century – the century which was truly to mould and shape

Russian art – Pushkin created a canon, which was classical in its sense of balance and apparent lightness of touch. He had no followers, nor could he have, since art cannot live by canons. Art creates a canon so as to supersede it. Russian poetry after Pushkin looked for new ways to supplant him – it fought against him, rather than learnt from him. The young Lermontov follows in his footsteps but only to gather sufficient strength to fight him. He takes over the figure of Byron, abandoned by Pushkin, in order to use just the same weapon. He searches in English and Russian poetry for new models for Russian verse, so that he might free himself from the Pushkinian iambic tetrameter. But Russian verse was fated to change to a branch line in order to prepare for a new blossoming, independent of Pushkin. This 'side-track' of Russian poetry goes from Tyutchev and Fet to the Symbolists. Only the poetry of Nekrasov stayed on the main line – but this was precisely because he did not struggle against Pushkin and acted as if Pushkin had not existed. The Symbolists started to talk about Pushkin only when they had become conquerors and masters – his equals. And from the heart of symbolism there arose a new classicism; in the poetry of Kuzmin, Akhmatova and Mandelshtam we find a new sense of Pushkin's classicism, underlined by Mandelshtam's attractively paradoxical aphorism: 'Classical poetry is revolutionary poetry.'

Against this living background we have sensed Pushkin anew and seen him in a new light. We have seen all the complex and refined nature of Pushkin's genius, as it brings to a close that dazzling era of Russian poetry begun by Lomonosov and Tredyakovsky. We have understood Pushkin's historical mission – to set Russian poetical language on an even keel, to create on the basis of experience an integrated, stable and complete artistic system. With Pushkin, words lost their heavy quality, just as a skilful architect will make the most massive material seem as weightless as lace. The reactionary tendencies of Derzhavin's imitators were superseded, whereas all the positive achievements of the old poetry were assimilated into the system. For this reason Pushkin is not revolutionary at all; far from rejecting his teachers, he is constantly in their debt. Derzhavin, it is true, is for him 'a bad, free translation from some magnificent original', but his immediate teacher is Zhukovsky; someone for whom he has profound respect:

I agree with Bestuzhev about Pletnyov's article, but not with his condemnation of Zhukovsky. Why bite the breast that suckled us, just because we have cut our teeth? Whatever you say, Zhukovsky has had a crucial influence on the spirit of our literature; and his style in translating will always remain a model one. Oh, this republic of letters! For what does it condemn? For what does it crown? I am not just a follower of his but a pupil. But all I can do is to wander along a country track, rather than dare to venture along his road.

Pushkin's country track proved to be the main road of Russian poetry, but for a long time after Pushkin any movement along it became impossible. Zhukovsky's road led off to one side, and along it Tyutchev and Fet wended their solitary ways. Zhukovsky went away from the eighteenth century, whereas Pushkin returned to it. To form a theoretical framework for Pushkin's poetry we need to study the poetry of the eighteenth century. It is only when seen against this background that his system of artistic devices is sharply contoured. Pushkin exhausted all the possibilities of Russian verse, both literary and rhythmical, insofar as earlier poetry had prepared the way for them. A sophisticated system of epithet, metonymy and periphrasis constituted the chief attraction of his style, which appeared simple and light, because he had achieved mutual proportionality of the parts and taken heed of their relationships; *he found the correct forms*. A classical 'prototype' was discovered which was unknown to Derzhavin. The old elegies, epistles and odes appeared in a new guise. There was even a link between these and Pushkin's long narrative poems. It was no accident that in *Prisoner of the Caucasus* so much prominence was given to the opening description of the Caucasus and the Circassians, a description deriving from Derzhavin and Zhukovsky. The romantic subject remained undeveloped: The Circassian who captured my Russian could have become the lover of the girl who freed him; her parents and brothers could all have had their own parts to play and their own individual characters; but I scorned all this'. The romantic hero became just a part of an evolving landscape, whose source is not Byron but Zhukovsky (*Ode to A. F. Voeikov*, 1814). The epilogue embodies the still living tradition of the ode:

> But from the East comes a heartfelt cry!...
> Humble, O Caucasus, thy snow-capped peaks,
> For Ermolov approaches!

From here the road leads to the historical poems, to *Poltava* and *The Bronze Horseman*.

In the 1830s Pushkin's lyrical activity declined, and there is a slow movement away from poetry and towards prose. *Evgenii Onegin* paved the way for this. Here we have a lyrical anthology, but here too we have the beginning of an approach to subjects for which verse is no longer necessary:

> My friends, what's the point?
> By God's will, perhaps,
> I shall abandon verse.
> Inspired by a new demon,
> Scorning Phoebus' threats,
> I'll turn to humble prose;
> In old age's happy years
> I'll write an old-style novel –
> Not some awesome story
> Of evil's secret torments,
> But a simple, homely tale
> Of Russian family customs,
> Of love's entrancing dreams,
> And of how we used to live. (Chapter 3, stanza 13)

> ... It's true
> I love my hero deeply,
> And will return to him of course;
> But now I have no time for him.
> The years direct my thoughts
> Towards austere prose,
> Away from playful verse,
> Which, sadly, I'll pursue
> With e'er decreasing zest... (Chapter 6, stanza 43)

Pushkin's presentiment came true: not only he but all Russian literature after the 1820s went along the path of 'austere prose'. This was a fundamental change and not just a transition. Verse and prose are practically different art forms – 'phenomena which are hostile and almost opposite' (de Musset). In Pushkin, as the culminating peak of a whole line of poetry, such a change is very characteristic. Prose begins to interest him as early as the the 1820s: 'Prose demands a great deal of thought; brilliant phrases are useless; poetry is another matter' *(On Style)*. He agrees that Russian poetry has become 'highly enlightened', but – 'the Russian language cannot yet be sufficiently attractive for anybody, apart from poets; we have neither a literature, nor books'. On *Roslavlev* he repeats: 'Our literature, of course, possesses a number of excellent poets, but we cannot demand that all our readers have an exclusive love for poetry. All we have in prose is Karamzin's *History*'. And the readers themselves, through Marlinsky, were already loudly clamouring for prose:

> Children are more interested in rattles than compasses: poetry, like flattery, is tolerable to the ears of even the most mediocre people; but prose style demands a knowledge not only of the grammar of language but also of the grammar of reason, it demands variation of style and smoothness of transition, and it cannot tolerate repetition. This is why we have so many poets and practically no prose-writers. The poets, it is true, can still be heard chirping away under every stone but everybody stopped listening to poetry as soon as it became so universal. And now, at last, the confused mumbling has grown into a general demand for the pure water of prose.

And Russian literature responded to such a demand. In Lermontov's works both elements are equal, but there is an interesting distinction between his poetic style and the style of his mature prose. His early prose is rich in metaphors, rhythmic syntactical parallelisms and periods – the heritage of poetry *(Vadim)*; later it becomes simple and clear. In the prose of Gogol and Turgenev, who themselves began by writing verse, a stylistic affinity with poetry can be sensed. The prose of Tolstoy, Leskov and Dostoevsky develops along lines which are quite separate from poetry, inherently hostile to it, in fact. This is not just chance, but some sort of law. A typical example of this in French literature is the difference between the prose of Chateaubriand and Hugo and that of Stendhal and Mérimée. The distinction between prose and verse forms is not a superficial or a typographical one, but organic and fundamental, no less so perhaps than the distinction between ornamental and naturalistic art. An unceasing war is waged between them. Prose gathers up the outworn feathers which have fallen from the wings of poetry and takes on a musical, stylistically refined form, rich in alliterations and rhythmical cadences. (As, for example, in the prose of Marlinsky or of Andrei Bely). The borderline between prose and poetry virtually disappears, but only until triumphant prose casts off its magnificent clothing and appears in its rightful form. There are interesting examples of this: 'In order to write good poetry of whatever kind', says Batyushkov, writing in 1817, 'in order to write in a vigorous, varied and pleasant style, with feeling and originality, one must write prose a great deal, not for publication but simply for oneself. I have frequently found this method to be successful; sooner or later what one has written in prose becomes useful.' 'Prose is the mother of poetry', Alfieri once said, if my memory serves me. The young Tolstoy observes in his diary: 'Have been reading and writing poetry; it's going fairly easily. I think this will be very useful for the development of my style'. The same idea can be found in Rousseau's *Confession:* 'I occasionally used to write mediocre poetry; it is quite good practice for developing elegant inversions and improving one's prose style'. Characteristic too is Batyushkov's attitude to Chateaubriand's prose, in which he rightly sensed a threat to poetry: 'He ... has ruined both my head and my style: I was even prepared to write a long prose poem, a prose tragedy, a prose epigram, in poetical prose. Don't read Chateaubriand!' (Letter to Gnedich, 1811).

> The years direct my thoughts...
> Away from playful verse...

– this is not simply a joke. In his *Thoughts of a Traveller* (1833–35) Pushkin says:

> I think that, in time, we shall turn to blank verse. The Russian language has too little rhythm. One thing leads to another; the flame of passion is always followed by the cold iron of reason, and behind emotions art is inevitably lurking. Who has not become bored by strange and complex stories of love and murder, by themes of truth and artificiality etc?

It was not chance that led Pushkin to publish, in Volume I of

The Contemporary (1836), an article by Baron Rozen entitled *On Rhythm,* in which it is suggested that poets should forego using such an empty plaything, so unworthy of poetry. Pushkin felt strongly that the development of Russian poetry should stop. He himself saw the tremendous difference between his poetic idiom and his prose idiom; the former had achieved its full blossoming, within the limits of the classical canon, whereas the latter was still totally disordered.

> I have appeared in print now for sixteen years and my critics have (quite correctly) noticed five grammatical errors in my poetry; I was always sincerely grateful to them and each time I corrected the error. But when I write prose I make many more mistakes, and my dialogue is even worse – almost as bad as Gogol's.

All this confirms that Pushkin's prose appeared not as a supplement to his verse but as something new, something which replaced his poetry. During the years 1828, 1829 and 1830, for example, Pushkin wrote at least 30 poems a year, among which can be found such poems as: 'When, for mortal man, day's clamour has ceased'; *The Upas-tree; The Rabble; The Avalanche;* 'On Georgia's hills'; 'When I stroll along the noisy streets'; 'Frost and sun – heavenly day'; *To the Poet; Devils; Autumn; Invocation;* and others. In 1831 he wrote seven, in 1832 – nine, and in 1833 – eight, of which only one is lyrical ('God grant that I not lose my mind') and in 1834 – only three. Prose is clearly beginning to prevail.

What do we mean when we talk of Pushkin's prose? It had apparently no antecedents – the Russian short story was practically non-existent then. Neither Karamzin, nor Marlinsky, nor Narezhny had anything to offer Pushkin. The simple brief phrase without rhythmical form or stylistic figures; the compressed short story with the emphasis on the denouement and a sophisticated narrative technique – where are the models for this? In 1825 Pushkin wrote to Marlinsky:

> You should stop writing tales with romantic episodes – these are all right for Byronic-type poems. A novel demands simple conversation; relate everything simply ... take an entire novel and write it with all the freedom of normal conversation or of a letter.

Marlinsky uses his prose to declaim, Pushkin to narrate. Even Belinsky, who did not understand *The Tales of Belkin* at all, sensed Pushkin's narrative skill.

Pushkin created his prose on the basis of his verse. It is precisely this which explains why it is so far removed from his verse. This is not the 'poetical prose' of Marlinsky or Gogol. A slight plot develops into an absorbing theme, told in a freely conversational manner. These are not stories which have been quickly dashed off. Just the opposite: by using subtle artistic devices Pushkin holds back the story's onward rush, forcing the reader to assimilate every step. A complex thematic structure is built upon the foundations of a simple plot. *The Shot* can be extended into a single straight line – the story of the duel between Silvio and the Count. But, in the first place, Pushkin introduces a narrator, who creates the division of the story into two parts with an interlude between them (the beginning of Chapter 2); and, in the second place, the novel has two other narrators, apart from the author – Silvio and the Count. Hence the note of unexpectedness when the interlude abruptly leads onto the interrupted narrative. Silvio plays a secondary role; significant here is the casual manner in which his subsequent destiny is related at the end. Characteristic of the story is its tempo of narration, its emphasis on the thematic structure. This can be seen in *The Snowstorm* as well. Of especial interest is the way in which the story is weighted towards its conclusion. This device is totally unmotivated: the thematic device has been laid bare. Instead of one straight line, there are two parallel ones which meet abruptly at the end. A piece of the narrative, the marriage of Marya Gavrilovna with the unknown officer, is taken out and placed at the end. It is as if the reader is making up a picture from separate blocks – something which he finally succeeds in doing only at the end of the story. Marya Gavrilovna's exclamation: 'So it was you!', with which the story ends, brings all the disparate pieces of the picture together in a single movement. In *The Undertaker* the plot is manipulated in a deceptive way: the denouement brings us back to the point at which the story begins and destroys it, turning the story into a parody. As M. Gershenzon has pointed out, there is a hidden parody of the thematic scheme in *The Stationmaster* as well: the conclusion does not coincide with the story of the Prodigal Son whose picture hangs in the station-master's room. And finally, in *Lady into Peasant*, Pushkin parodies the idea of the extended theme of two lovers, belonging to two mutually hostile families *(Romeo and Juliet)*. It is not fortuitous that Aleksei and Akulina together read *Natalya, the Boyar's Daughter,* which uses this same idea. But, in Pushkin's story, Liza does not wish to be either Juliet or Natalya, and the parents' sudden reconciliation distorts the usual idea, turning the situation into a comic one.

This is how Pushkin's prose began: from *Evgenii Onegin, Count Nulin* and *The Little House at Kolomna* to *The Tales of Belkin*. It was an interest in thematic structure which led Pushkin to prose and it was his extensive poetical experience which gave it simplicity and conciseness. It was born out of poetry, not to challenge it, as with Marlinsky, but to achieve a balance. This is why Pushkin the poet can be seen in it despite the absence of specific poetical devices. In 1834 Senkovsky wrote to Pushkin: 'C'est le langage de vos poésies ... que vous transportez dans votre prose de conteur; je reconnais ici la même langue et le même goût, le même charme'. It is interesting that, although Pushkin starts the development of Russian prose he does not create a tradition. Pushkin has no followers in prose either. Pushkin's successors clearly built their prose on the ruins of verse, whereas, with Pushkin, prose emerges from verse itself, from a balancing of all its parts. It is important to bear in mind here that Pushkin's classical poetry, his iambic tetrameter, develops not on a basis of music (such as the 'musical' verse of the romantics) but on the basis of common speech, as it were. This opens a way to prose which would have been impossible, for example, for Tyutchev or Fet, Balmont or Blok. It would be extraordinarily interesting to examine the architectonics of Pushkin's prose style and his poetic style — there exists between them a kind of affinity, as a result of which Pushkin's prose creates a special effect, quite unlike the prose of prose-writers. Between the parts of a phrase there seems to exist a mathematical relationship, a heritage from poetry. I shall take as my example the opening of *The Shot*:

1 Мы стояли в местечке ***.
2 Жизнь армейского офицера известна.
3 Утром – ученье, манеж;
4 обед у полкового командира
5 или в жидовском трактире,
6 вечером – пунш и карты.
7 В *** не было ни одного открытого дома,
8 ни одной невесты;
9 мы собирались друг у друга,
10 где кроме своих мундиров
11 не видали ничего.

The number of syllables in these 11 *articula,* as the Romans might have said, varies from 6 to 14, but with a characteristic predominance of 7, 8 or 9 syllabled phrases, and with the balancing effect of longer phrases being succeeded by shorter ones. Is there not a link here with the eight-or-nine-syllabled line of the iambic tetrameter, within whose limits the *articula* of Pushkin's speech are customarily placed? It is also characteristic that each such *articulum* has, in the vast majority of cases, three or four stresses. And, finally, if we take complete phrases, excluding the first as introductory, we see that *articula* 2-6 make one whole and *articula* 7-11, another; a symmetry which seems deliberate, seems to arise from an innate poetical sense – all the more so since in each of these two wholes we find 4 syntactical members: 1) жизнь армейского офицера известна, 2) утром – ученье, манеж, 3) обед у полкового командира или в жидовском трактире, 4) вечером – пунш и карты. Here too, it seems, the hidden influence of the verse-form is revealed.

I shall choose one more extract:

1 Цесарь путешествовал;
2 мы с Титом Петронием
3 следовали за ними издали . . .
4 По захождении солнца
5 нам разбивали шатер,
6 расставляли постели –
7 мы ложились пировать
8 и весело беседовали.
9 На заре
10 снова пускались в дорогу
11 и сладко засыпали
12 каждый в лектике своей,
13 утомленные жаром
14 и ночными наслажденьями.

Here the syllabic structure of the *articula* is even more striking: the variation is merely between 7 and 9 syllables, with 7 syllables being especially persistent. If we take the *articula* «Цесарь путешествовал»,«мы ложились пировать»,«каждый в лектике своей», is there not a link with the trochaic tetrameter? And once again there is a symmetry: the first three *articula* are introductory and the ninth is limiting; between them are two groups of five (4-8, 10-14) corresponding to each other and analogous to stanzas.

But these are all questions which are as yet unexplored. I simply think that with these passing observations I am confirming those immediate feelings which arise from reading Pushkin's prose. Somewhere Pushkin calls prose 'chaff'. His own prose, however, is a long way from chaff. because it arose directly from his verse...

GERSHENZON

READING PUSHKIN

M. O. Gershenzon (1869–1925) was a literary historian, publicist and translator whose principal interest lay in the development of Russian thought in the nineteenth century. Opposed to the radical materialists, he contributed an essay to the celebrated volume *Landmarks* (1909) which was an indictment of the main tenets of the Russian intelligentsia. Unlike the other members of the *Landmarks* group, however, Gershenzon remained in Russia after the Bolshevik revolution. Gershenzon tended to view works of literature as psychological documents and through the method of slow reading which he invented he attempted to uncover the mainsprings of writers' inner lives. One of his most famous books on these lines was *Pushkin's Wisdom* (1919), but in the present volume Gershenzon is represented by a later, less esoteric essay, *Reading Pushkin,* which appeared in 1923. Here the critic analyses in detail various lines of Pushkin's verse to illustrate his thesis that slow reading brings a rich harvest.

In the old days a child used to be taught to read first by syllables — which forced him to take an intelligent note of the individual letters and their various combinations in the syllables — and only through this process would he be brought to the ability to read by words and phrases, i.e. fluently. The result of such training was highly beneficial: all his life, even in rapid reading, a man would preserve the habit of articulate attention, he would see every word and follow the disposition of the words in each sentence. Nowadays the child is straight away taught to read fluently, or intuitively. Almost before he has learnt the shape of the letters he is taught to guess, at a glance, a whole word, and then immediately the next one, and the next one, and thus to race to the end of the sentence over the words which he is supposed to recognise in a flash, without looking carefully at any of them, almost, as it were, without seeing them. The modern reader does not *see* words because he does not look at them; he appears not to read the wise and beautiful body of each word: racing at full speed, he glimpses the words' shadows and unconsciously fuses them into some airy meaning which is no more substantial than the shadows of which it is composed.

In the old days, then, people used to read comparatively slowly and reflectively, like a pedestrian, who sees everything in detail as he goes along, enjoying what he sees and recognising what is new. Modern reading, however, is like a fast bicycle race, where the roadside scenes flash past, merging together and then disappearing in a motley blurred line. Pursuing speed above all else, we have forgotten how to walk. Nowadays only a very few people can read on foot; almost everyone reads in the saddle at 30 or 40 versts – I mean, pages – per hour. One wonders what they have seen in the pages which have flashed past, whether indeed they have managed to observe and discern anything at all.

Any book which is rich in content must be read slowly; poets must be read particularly slowly, and among Russian writers Pushkin must be read the most slowly of all, because his short lines are richer in content than any others written in Russian. This rich content can be discerned only by a leisurely walker who moves slowly and keeps an attentive eye open. Pushkin's deep thoughts are faced with such deceptive clarity, his charmingly neat points are levelled off so smoothly, and his precision is so natural and unforced, that in rapid reading they may not be noticed at all. But wander on foot through Pushkin – and what marvellous flowers are to be seen at the roadside! And more than flowers: here a silvery brook sparkles in the sunlight, or a laughing beam of light is suddenly darkened by an encroaching cloud; over there mountains, wreathed in perpetual snow, tower up and fill the whole horizon. One sees the smile and the tears of a child, the playful trick of a lover, the divinely free play of spiritual powers and continual reflections on faith, on the mystery of life and on death.

I am not going to speak about the philosophical depth of Pushkin's poetry which only the penetrating gaze can plumb, nor about the extraordinary compactness of his works which, strange to relate, has caused many of them, apparently so open and clear, to remain closed to this day. But, even in a simple reading, what a rich harvest the slow approach can reap, and what marvellous details escape the hasty glance! In rapid reading one wouldn't notice how Tatyana awaits an answer to her letter;

> But a day passed with no reply.
> The next dawned; still nothing at all.
> Pale as a shade and *dressed since morning*,
> Tatyana waits. When will it come?

That charming, so lightly uttered *'dressed since morning'* speaks volumes. It says, first of all, that Tatyana was confidently expecting, not an answering letter from Onegin, but Onegin himself (in which her sensitive feminine instinct was not mistaken); it shows her to us during this time properly coiffured, laced and dressed from early morning – and at the same time it obliquely depicts her normal everyday appearance, when she would be by no means 'dressed since morning', but would perhaps spend the whole morning unkempt, in her house-jacket and slippers and revelling in a novel. So much is contained in three short words!

After their defeat at Poltava, Charles and Mazeppa flee south. They are galloping over the Ukrainian steppes, when suddenly a small farmstead appears near the road. It is Kochubei's. With a shudder Mazeppa sees

> ..... the desolate yard,
> The house, and the secluded garden,
> And a door open to the countryside.

It is impossible to portray more completely the abrupt desertion of a farm, from which all the inhabitants have suddenly flown in panic-stricken terror, abandoning it to the whim of fate. The poet has achieved this effect with one stroke – the door leading to the open country stands open.

Even the following detail is worth pausing over briefly: in *Evgenii Onegin* the maidservants sing as they pick berries,

> We will gather cherries,
> Cherries and raspberries,
> And red currants.

These three berries are not enumerated by chance: they do in fact ripen at the same time in central Russia, and the girls name them because they are actually picking them at that moment. Moreover, the naming of these berries together determines the date of Onegin's meeting with Tatyana, because in central Russia these particular berries all ripen in late July and early August. In rapid reading it is even easier to miss those *single* significant words which abound in Pushkin. After her many days of waiting, when Tatyana eventually sees Onegin driving into the courtyard, up to the porch, she ran through the *other* entrance (i.e. the servants' entrance) and thence through the back yard and into the garden, which was situated, as one would expect, behind the house.

In *Arion* we read:

> Only I, *mysterious* singer,
> Was thrown to the shore by the storm.

That is, his escape from the shipwreck is connected with his special *mysterious* nature; everyone else in the boat perishes, he alone is saved – and *not by chance:* he is saved because he is a bard. That was in fact Pushkin's idea and he hints at it with the word 'mysterious'. Much earlier, in his poem *To Delvig,* he expressed the idea directly:

> The Gods' confidant fears not the angry storms:
> Over him is their high and holy providence.

In *The Gipsies* Aleko, after listening to the old gipsy's tale of Mariula, who had run away from him to another encampment, furiously exclaims:

> But why did you not run
> Straight after *the ungrateful girl*
> And plunge a dagger into the kidnappers
> And into her treacherous heart?

Everything he feels is expressed in the one word 'ungrateful'. A woman should be *grateful* to a man for his love! And the man is *justified* in punishing her if she ceases to love him! Thus Aleko's slave-owning attitude to love, which has been concealed until that moment, suddenly flares up in this one word; a large element of his nature is sketched by a single word which bursts forth accidently. What a delight to note and understand this word – but could one possibly note it in a rapid reading of *The Gipsies?*

Or, among niceties of a different order, is it not a pity when some stylistic subtlety is lost without trace by the reader's inattention? The second verse of the poem *The Poet* begins:

> But no sooner does the divine word
> Touch his keen hearing...

Scarcely one in a thousand readers of *The Poet* realises what these two lines mean. But they simply continue the image with which the poem opened six lines earlier:

> Until Apollo summons
> The poet to holy sacrifice...

'The divine word' is precisely the call of Apollo, summoning the poet to holy sacrifice.

In the poem *The Field Marshal* the concluding lines, 'O men! Pitiful stock, deserving tears and laughter', do not by any means constitute a moral pendant to a descriptive piece, as everybody thinks. Pushkin is describing George Dawe's portrait of Barclay de Tolly, which inspired him to write the poem:

> He is painted full length...
> ... Calm and morose.
> He gazes, it seems, *in contemptuous meditation*.
> Perhaps the artist exposed his own thoughts
> When he depicted him thus,
> Or perhaps it was involuntary inspiration –
> But Dawe gave him this expression.

And Pushkin does no more than set out in his poem this thought of Dawe's, i.e. the thought which is contained in the portrait itself. From this point in the poem to the very end he is simply elucidating the 'contemptuous meditation', expressed in Barclay's face by the painter. Now the portrait itself speaks, now Dawe speaks through his portrait, but not Pushkin himself. And the whole poem, grasped in this way, acquires an air of integrity, inner unity and *modesty* which is a great joy to behold. Pushkin conveys to us in words what Dawe expressed through his portrait; of himself he contributes only his agreement with the painter. Consequently, in the concluding lines of the poem,

> But whose lofty image in a future generation
> Will inspire a poet to rapture and tender emotion!

he is not speaking about himself ('a poet'), but about himself and Dawe together, and also more generally, about any poetic soul...

TOMASHEVSKY

INTERPRETING PUSHKIN

B. V. Tomashevsky (1890–1957) was an outstanding and intellectually wide-ranging Soviet philologist and literary critic. After graduating as an electrical engineer at Liège University he went on to study French literature at the Sorbonne. In 1925 Tomashevsky published his *Theory of Literature: Poetics* and also *Pushkin – Modern Problems of Historico-literary Study* which did much to set Soviet Pushkin scholarship on a sound footing. Tomashevsky was one of the editors of the monumental *Complete Works of Pushkin* (Academic Edition, 1937–49) and towards the end of his life he issued the first volume of a planned general monograph, *Pushkin 1813–24,* for which he was posthumously awarded the Belinsky Prize of the Academy of Sciences. 1960 saw the posthumous publication of *Pushkin and France.* In *Interpreting Pushkin,* which is a chapter from *Pushkin – Modern Problems of Historico-literary Study,* Tomashevsky assails Gershenzon's idiosyncratic exegesis of the poet and at the same time argues convincingly that it is impossible to establish Pushkin's personal views from an examination of his poetic works.

In Pushkin's works we find very few expressions of opinion.

From whomsoever I might have been descended, my way of thinking would not have depended on that to the slightest degree. I have no intention of renouncing this way of thinking, *though to this day I have not revealed it anywhere and it is no-one else's business.*

Thus Pushkin wrote about himself. Although he is speaking here about his social and political views in a narrow sense, the same remarks apply to the poet's 'philosophy' and 'attitude to life'.

Pushkin did not reveal his views and considered them to be no-one else's business. His contemporaries, infected with philosophical aspirations, were the first to count this as a defect in Pushkin and they emphasised his lack of 'thought'. The elusiveness of Pushkin's thought remained a sad fact to be assimilated by later generations for whom everything in literature revolved round 'thought'. Russian literature was rich in every sort of problem and every sort of philosophy. It seemed unthinkable that Russia's greatest poet should be weak precisely in this area. In order to master and assimilate Pushkin it was essential to interpret him and to ascribe to Pushkin some 'philosophy' which would serve as his passport for entry into literature and as his patent of the title of a Russian classic. The elusiveness of his thought served merely to intrigue investigators: the more difficult the task, the more tempting it became. Pushkin's poetry appeared as a sort of rebus which had to be deciphered and as an object for 'analysis in depth'.

This analysis in depth began long ago: traces of it can be found even in Pushkin's lifetime in articles by the Pogodin circle. But there one sees only modest hints. The classical attempt at a deep interpretation of Pushkin is Dostoevsky's brilliant speech. This speech is typical of Dostoevsky – and completely misses Pushkin. Later, understandably enough, imitators of Dostoevsky appeared. Merezhkovsky's *Eternal Companions* provided us with a new image of Pushkin. But the method of analysis in depth was definitely established in the works of M.O. Gershenzon. (At the present time the Russian Freudian school – Ermakov in Moscow and Kharazov in Baku – taking their point of departure from Gershenzon, are subjecting Pushkin to depth analysis after their own fashion, but so far Russian Freudianism has produced only caricature works in this field and I shall, therefore, not touch on the movement).

It is quite natural that those who have analysed Pushkin in depth have always found in him, to their great satisfaction, a complete correspondence with their own philosophy. In the majority of works of this type we observe typical self-confessions of the authors themselves in the quotations they give from Pushkin. A highly characteristic example of this is, for instance, V. Gippius' brochure *Pushkin and Christianity* (where, incidentally, almost nothing at all is said about Christianity).

P.E. Shchegolev remarked in one of his reviews that the blunders which led people to accept Zhukovsky's obscure and idealistic meditations as works by Pushkin were organically linked with a method of research in which the exact meaning of the object of study disappears and Pushkin's works are regarded as mysterious hieroglyphs. The more an investigator loses his grip on the objective aspect of the works and allows an intuitively revealed inner meaning to come to light, the more on the whole the object becomes unimportant, since it is very easy to underpin any work with any foundation if that foundation is not determined by the work itself but attached to it by means of simple sophisms.

Such a system of interpretation through a selection of arbitrary arguments and speculations deriving solely from the author's wit rather than from a rigorous and methodologically sound study was often to be seen in expositions of Pushkin's social and political views. Each author would appropriate Pushkin to his own party and support this by random quotations out of which he would reconstruct his personal system. (The most recent example of such an attempt is N. Fatov's book depicting Pushkin as an anarchist).

But these works share in common with the philosophical and psychological analyses of Pushkin in depth perhaps only their arbitrary method of argument (everyone recalls the system of argument in Merezhkovsky's critical articles) and their striving to appropriate the poet to themselves. In other respects works of this type possess their own peculiar methods, their own logic and methodology.

The basic method in Gershenzon's works is the method of 'slow reading' which he invented. This method, which has seduced many followers of Gershenzon, is extremely enticing and its conclusions seem to be incontrovertible.

Gershenzon first applied the principle of slow reading to his biographical researches. He proceeded from the assumption that Pushkin's poetry possesses an 'elementary truthfulness' (indeed truly elementary if Gershenzon denies the possibility that Pushkin might write a poem about winter in another season and suggests in the said instance that the winter must be understood more deeply as a metaphor or even a symbol, basing his argument solely on the dating of the poem). This 'truthfulness' enabled Gershenzon to detect in the poems the biographical declarations with which he constructed his system.

Here we are not concerned with Gershenzon's biographical devices since they have already been discussed elsewhere. But the transition from biography to a philosophical analysis in depth, following the same method of research, is typical. At the root of this gradual and imperceptible transition lies the assumption of an integrated system of knowledge. Or, putting it more simply, the sought-for depth of Pushkin's 'attitude to life' is equated with the *facts* of his life which are inseparably linked with his behaviour. Just as in the biographical researches a hypothetical system was found to interpret the external behaviour of the poet, so here too a system is found for the inner, spiritual behaviour of Pushkin as an individual.

Slow reading is employed in order to decipher the mysterious hieroglyphs, to pinpoint 'concealed' hints and to recreate a spiritual edifice which could explain the logic of these hints. Slow reading passes the text through a filter in order to catch such hints.

I will permit myself a few elementary objections to the system of slow reading. The first point is that literary diction, especially poetic, rhythmical diction, possesses its own inherent aesthetic tempo. Accelerating or decelerating it destroys the aesthetic principle of its construction, removes its structural principle. This is a feature of considerable importance. We all know that it is impossible to transpose verse into prose: it comes out 'not quite the same'. A serious aphorism expressed in verse becomes flat in prose. The reverse is also possible: a light metaphor in verse becomes heavy in prose and acquires meanings which are not inherent in the verse.

This factor alone suggests the danger of applying a method which alters the tempo of literary diction. But there are other no less important objections. Meaning resides not in words, but in phrases. A phrase possesses a certain unity as an intonational sequence, and one of the components of intonation is tempo. In decelerating our reading we, as it were, reaccentuate the discourse (at the level of meaning and logic), breaking it up into smaller phrases (since willy-nilly we impose on it pauses, logical stresses and meaningful cadences). Meanings begin to creep in where none existed before; every word begins to jump out of its context and create for itself a surrogate phraseological environment.

But in a tightly constructed work of literature the meaning of a word is determined exclusively by the context which excises every superfluous association. The existence of such superfluous associations, unless they are consciously intended (puns, deliberate ambiguities, etc.) is a defect in a work of literature. On the other hand, if we separate each word from its phrase as we read, we destroy the context and thereby give the superfluous associations full freedom to indulge themselves. In slow reading the question automatically arises, 'What does this word mean?' And quite inevitably the question is resolved not from the minimum number of possibilities defined by the context but from the maximum number of associations which may be connected with the given isolated word. These associations are inevitably subjective since they arise in the mind of the reader and not as a result of the interaction between author and reader. They are subjective in the sense that they characterise not the work itself in its unique meaning but the spontaneous thoughts of the reader which are determined by his individual psyche. Hence it is clear why slow reading always leads to a touching harmony of soul between reader and author. It is simply that for the objective meaning the reader substitutes his own and is then delighted when in his own associations he recognises himself.

By its very nature the mechanism of slow reading discredits a similar approach made to a text with the aim of understanding it. (I accept slow reading as a means of noting grammatical forms, orthography, etc; I welcome it in proof-reading because the proof-reader must apprehend the words out of their contextual meaning in order to spot misprints in individual letters, but I protest against slow reading as a means of *understanding* a work and of discovering its meaning).

In any work there is a mass of verbal 'padding', to use L.B. Shcherba's expression. A phrase needs its verbal filling, a certain intonational rounding. Words which are sufficient in terms of meaning can be insufficient in terms of complete phrasing. "Neutral" words appear – fixed epithets, dead metaphors, etc. In normal reading these padding words are not interpreted, but slow reading brings the padding into the foreground and forces one to interpret it in this way or that – whether one wants to or not. The upshot is a revaluation of words and a re-weighing of meanings.

Thus, when the word *l'amour* grew stale, the French replaced it by *les feux*. In poetic language the latter word lost its metaphorical nuance and was transformed into a poetic term meaning simply 'love'. Naturally Russian poets copied the term and in every bosom 'a flame was ignited' without any connection with the primary meaning of 'ignition' or 'flame'. At best the words possessed a hyperbolical nuance. But the slow reader will naturally be set alight by every flame and will reach the point of creating 'a thermodynamic theory of psychic processes'. And so, Pushkin is saddled with the philosophy of one of the Greek sages who saw fire as the original source. But the slow reader need only glance at another poet, at Batyushkov for instance, to discover that the same Greek sage sits there too. And from this the computation is made – by the calendar – that Batyushkov 'influenced' Pushkin and instilled in him precisely this spiritual principle of thermodynamics.

It is a good thing that with the present example we have to hand real facts which refute this type of argument. But the result is much worse when slow reading operates with ethereal 'emanations' which deepen the poet's wisdom. In biographical and historical literary studies the principle is quite innocent – since it can be opposed by scientific methods and any conclusions can easily be verified. But in dealing with more elusive matters it is positively dangerous...

Let us turn to the 'positive' results of these investigators. The most modest of them (among whom I include in the first place M. Gofman as the author of *Pushkin's Benediction of Life*, a work imbued with the spirit of Gershenzon, in spite of the polemics the author directs against the latter) outline a rather thin and flat 'philosophy' for Pushkin: *joie de vivre*, a capacity for responding to everything, a whole-hearted love of life in all its aspects, an infinite patience and an acceptance of 'good and evil'. But this type of passivity is in reality the worst charge against Pushkin. The characterisation is essentially negative, and objectively – since every 'philosophy' pre-supposes some choice, some demarcation between 'good and evil' – in effect a denial of evil. A sugary acceptance of everything is by no means typical of Pushkin (that particular basic attitude is better associated with Zhukovsky). And in any case such a pitiful 'philosophy' is hardly one with which to parade publicly, let alone to aspire to a place among the classics. 'Pushkin's wisdom' is clearly not to be found here.

The said wisdom has been doggedly and painstakingly revealed by Gershenzon. It must be admitted that in his most recent works the wisdom has become somewhat shallow. Pushkin's 'dreams' and 'shadows' and 'flame' turn out to be very flat and ornamental. Therefore I will refer to Gershenzon's most 'profound' book, *The Wisdom of Pushkin*, and take from there the essay of the same title (the first essay in the book and the second according to the table of contents). Gershenzon accompanies his work with the following remarks:

> This was Pushkin's teaching. But he was a poet, not a philosopher. The wisdom which I disclose here in his poetry was of course not perceived by him as a system of ideas, but it lived in him and it is our legitimate right to formulate his speculations in the same way as one can outline on paper the plan of a finished building... I am formulating Pushkin's immanent philosophy, and my exposition refers to his poetry in the same way as a geographical map refers to an existing country.

One could object here to these figurative comparisons. The relationship of a map to a country, a portrait to a man, or a letter to a word is indisputably rather different from the relationship between Gershenzon's wisdom and Pushkin's poetry.

Pushkin once wrote to Delvig, 'You reproach me for *The Moscow Messenger* and for German metaphysics. God knows how much I hate and despise the latter'. Pushkin would hardly have expressed a more favourable opinion of the wisdom formulated by Gershenzon. Indeed:

> Pushkin's most general and fundamental dogma which conditions his entire outlook is the conviction that being appears in two aspects, as completeness and deficiency... completeness, since it is internally full, abides in a state of imperturbable calm, whereas everything deficient is constantly searching and ranging.

The proof of all this is that Pushkin's angel (in the poem with that title) does not move or look but simply 'stands radiant with lowered head', whereas the demon 'flies, looks and speaks'. From this is derived the generalisation. It turns out that Mozart too stands radiant with lowered head, while Salieri flies, looks and speaks; and the same thing happens to Tatyana (completeness) and Onegin (incompleteness). 'Well then,' asks Gershenzon, 'does this mean that the ancient Eastern dualism was resurrected in Pushkin and that he too divides men into the children of Ormuzd and the children of Ahriman?' In answer to this question one can reply quite simply that it is somewhat early to reach for Ormuzd and Ahriman, that in all the literature of the eighteenth century a clear demarcation line was drawn between positive and negative heroes, between 'the radiant' and 'the flying', that Pushkin protested resolutely against this demarcation and in his own work overcame the morally evaluative lines between virtue and vice and that his individual endeavour moved in this direction rather than towards any 'two principles' which have a very simple root in the composition of a novel which demands that the heroes be given a strong emotional colouring. But Gershenzon contents himself with a declaration of the fundamental dogma and proceeds to develop it as follows:

> According to Pushkin, that which is deficient is powerless to cure itself spontaneously. Every desire and action stems from a deficient nature; therefore, in longing for perfection and seeking after it, you sink with this new desire and action even deeper into deficiency... Pushkin's entire philosophy preaches the opposite – quietism: remain in a state of sinfulness, do not add to your desires another, that most impassioned of all desires – the desire to free yourself from desires, which is a state of saintliness.

After this revelation, this time unsubstantiated (obviously it is a logical inference from the first premise and requires no verification in Pushkin's texts) Gershenzon goes on to 'unvoiced revelations': 'That which is deficient possesses a potential completeness, it is of the same nature as perfection'. This unvoiced principle of relationship entails further inferences:

> Deficiency appears to Pushkin as a disease when a contradiction seems to be created within a personality. But sometimes it happens that an element will suddenly fill the soul like a volcanic explosion. Nothing moves Pushkin more than the sight of these tremendous eruptions.

However, the author does not pause to study Pushkin's eruptions; he simply declares that, 'Pushkin never tried to define perfection, but from the whole structure of his depositions one must conclude that he saw it as a state where the elemental force is distributed evenly throughout the personality and circulates, as it were, harmoniously through it.' After classifying perfections,

Gershenzon again returns to the theme of wisdom in general: 'Poetry is cunning – it stretches over the surface of its depths a rational icy film which delights and absorbs the gaze; but under this film deep-water monsters swim wide and free'. The greatest of the deep-water monsters, swimming completely freely, is naturally 'wisdom'. But poetry is of course not as cunning as this. Gershenzon has outwitted poetry.

Here is not the place to speak about the essential nature of this wisdom. Perhaps it is indeed really wise; it is in any event abstruse. But how does this wisdom stand in relationship to Pushkin? By now it is quite clear that Pushkin and the said wisdom are two different things, since the latter develops as a chain of syllogisms from a first premise and the author does not even have recourse to the normal method of interpreters – that of expressing their own thoughts via quotations from Pushkin. For the said wisdom suitable quotations were not to be found in Pushkin.

At the root of this type of interpretation lies the false concept of an 'integrated system of knowledge', which controls literary facts as if they were facts of another, non-literary order. The modern habit of forcing ideological stuffing into literature compels people to look for it in Pushkin too, whereas for Pushkin himself every thought was to be judged as an artistic theme, from the point of view of its aesthetic potential. It is impossible to paraphrase Pushkin and even more impossible to make logical computations on the basis of a metaphorical paraphrase.

Gershenzon is of course an individual phenomenon, but he is a seductive phenomenon and one which has seduced. Indeed, what a joy it is, 'what a striking discovery', to find a philosophical code in Pushkin. With the same degree of success people look in him for ideological codes of another order, including even a legal code (cf. researches into Pushkin's views on jurisprudence). As long as we continue to treat Pushkin's works as allegories, we shall inevitably get bogged down in various wisdoms, both of the Gershenzon type and of varieties diametrically opposed to him.

Without raising the broad question of the appropriateness of such an approach to any work of literature (since life has forced all sorts of literature to indulge in allegory), I would like simply to emphasise that in the case of Pushkin, who is a representative of a quite definite literary tradition, in the case of a poet who does not conceal his thought, but quite the reverse, strives for exceptional clarity, such approaches are completely unsuitable.

Pushkin should be read without any intricate philosophising.

MIRSKY

THE PROBLEM OF PUSHKIN

Prince D.P. Svyatopolk-Mirsky was the son of Prince P.D. Svyatopolk-Mirsky, one of Nicholas II's Ministers of the Interior. In 1911 he published a book of verse, but his first serious critical works appeared in England where he spent the years 1922 to 1932. Mirsky published articles in T.S. Eliot's *Criterion*, an excellent study, *Pushkin* (1926), and his well-known *History of Russian Literature* which was issued in two volumes (1926 and 1927). During this period in England he also produced *Lenin* (1931) and *Russia, A Social History* (1931). In 1932 Mirsky returned to the Soviet Union where he took an active part in literary life, writing on English affairs, contemporary Soviet literature and the Russian classics. His bold and at times paradoxical opinions, which had been well received in England, led Mirsky into difficulties in his homeland: during the Great Purge he was arrested and in 1939 he died in Siberia. Mirsky's article *The Problem of Pushkin*, from which we give an extract, appeared in 1934 in the *Literary Heritage* volume, No. 16-18, which was devoted entirely to Pushkin. Mirsky classifies Pushkin, in Marxian terms, both as a spokesman for the progressive nobility of his day and as a poet of the bourgeois cultural revolution and argues that Pushkin's split class loyalties are most strikingly reflected in *The Bronze Horseman*.

Pushkin's life and work pass through two stages. During the first stage the only vehicle of political and cultural progress was that social group to which he himself belonged and with whom he felt naturally united — the progressive nobility. He was its indisputable and direct spokesman. Pushkin was not a Decembrist, but he was the leader of a cultural revolution which ran parallel to the political revolution of the Decembrists. The advanced section of the nobility 'was climbing into the third estate', and for this section of the nobility Pushkin created on Russian soil a poetry which had absorbed the entire artistic heritage of European early-bourgeois culture. Nicholas I's triumph and the agrarian crisis which had brought the landowner-based economy to a standstill upset everyone's calculations.

As Pokrovsky demonstrated some years ago, this period of the blackest political reaction was not a period of either economic or cultural stagnation. The slow but steady expansion of capitalist industry and the long drawn-out agrarian crisis combined to accelerate the growth of capital's share of the economy. At the same time, the advanced groups of the Russian intelligentsia took only fifteen years to travel the long road from a superficial acceptance of eighteenth-century 'enlightenment' to left-Hegelianism and Saint-Simonism – for which Germany had needed almost three quarters of a century. But this apparently clear path of gentry free-thinking gave way to dark and hidden corridors. The nobleman and free-thinker with republican or constitutionalist leanings ceased to be the chief vehicle of bourgeois progress. Pushkin's social group, deprived of its leaders and dispersed, found itself forced from the main path of history. The tsarist regime arrayed itself in old Petrine garments and fostered the industrial bourgeoisie, who, satisfied by Nicholas' economic policy, became in return his completely loyal subjects. The new enlightened class, now taking its bearings not from France or England but from Germany, also renounced active political opposition. The middle landowners returned to the old *corvée* system, but this furnished them only poor support. In the cities the new bourgeoisie flourished, establishing everywhere and in every action the buy-sell principle; it was full of bourgeois effrontery, but completely lacking in class dignity.

In this situation Pushkin went astray. The second stage of Pushkin's work is distinctive in that this period of social confusion and blindness was for him a time of immense artistic development. This combination of circumstances ultimately deprived his art of that quality of 'normality' which Marx saw in the Greeks and which can still be seen both in the Italians and in Shakespeare. But in this extremely complex and 'abnormal' stage Pushkin still remains, in the last analysis, a poet of the bourgeois cultural revolution and an ideological exponent of enlightenment and genius.

The fact that Pushkin capitulated to the autocracy does not in itself in any way invalidate his role as a pioneer of the bourgeois cultural revolution. Whereas the political leaders of the bourgeois revolution might often display a genuine loyalty to principle and whereas participation in the revolutionary cause gave an air of heroic staunchness even to such socially typical noblemen as Lunin and Yakushkin, for bourgeois ideologists and poets a certain baseness and a certain sycophancy towards the powers that be was no rare occurence. Hegel glorified the Prussian state as the highest incarnation of the absolute. Goethe 'with ceremonial seriousness occupied himself with the most petty businesses and *menus plaisirs* of the most petty German court' (Engels). Even Diderot fawned on Catherine II. But although the servility of Goethe and Hegel distorted and disfigured the basic line of their work, it did not make them deviate from it. Pushkin's sycophancy went deeper, to the very heart of his work, and inspired poems which are equal in power to his greatest achievements (e.g. *Poltava*); it clouded his historical vision to such an extent that at one time he saw Nicholas I as the repository of historical progress, while the poet's revolt against his own sycophancy was painted in the fantastical colours of a 'six-hundred-year-old nobility'. In these depths of Pushkin's servility, just as in that inordinate social snobbery which in his private life was the chief cause of his death, one sees of course more than mere individual chance. The roots of these phenomena are to be found in Pushkin's being still very close to the feudal, serf-owning soil of the gentry – much closer than were Goethe or Hegel. The growth of bourgeois culture in Russia was faster precisely because fast growth did not allow the vestiges of the old order to disappear in time. Even in the following generation the most progressive representatives of the gentry intelligentsia, who advanced immeasurably further than Pushkin and who were closely linked with the international revolutionary movement, were not by any means free of these birthmarks – one need only recall for instance Bakunin's *Confession*.

With Pushkin all this was much deeper and more organic, and in the works of his final years it is impossible to separate the 'already moribund' nobleman from the great poet of bourgeois liberation. They live together, locked in indecisive combat, 'embracing each other more tightly than two friends'.

The struggle was waged within the poet and within individual works. We have a particularly striking example of this indecisive combat in *The Bronze Horseman,* where the struggle is waged over every image. Not a single one can be ultimately interpreted from one point of view. Every interpretation opens the door to another, and no single interpretation can be accepted as final. The poem remains ambiguous to the end. At first glance it is a glorification of Peter I. The least complex part of the poem is the opening section, where 'Peter's creation' is glorified as the capital of Russian tsardom. Further on, however, from behind the image of Peter the autocrat, Peter-cum-Nicholas I, emerges the image of Peter the revolutionary, 'who jerked Russia up onto its hind legs' – an image which gives him a much greater affinity with Napoleon than with Nicholas. (Incidentally, as far as I know, *The Bronze Horseman* has never been compared with Barbier's *L'Idole*, written only a year earlier; the images of the two poems show an unmistakable resemblance). At the same time Petersburg is transformed from a symbol of triumphant autocracy into a symbol of culture, into a symbol of bourgeois construction – a sort of Holland reclaimed from the sea.

On the other hand Petersburg, the tsarist capital, is contrasted with 'the Finnic waves'. The image of the flood as a symbol of revolution was widely current in Russian poetry of the 1830s (e.g. Pecherin's mystery-play or Lermontov's poem 'And the day came'). Pushkin mobilises all his poetic resources to convey the impression of the enormous strength of the waves, and when he depicts the mechanics of the flood his verses achieve the ultimate in power and effectiveness. At the same time, Petersburg's helplessness in the struggle against the waves is underlined. The opening section of the poem concludes with an invocation, appealing to the good will of the waves, in which, although their 'anger' is called 'vain', the epithet sounds highly unconvincing. Highly convincing, on the other hand, is the scene where 'the late Tsar' helplessly looks upon the 'dire disaster with sorrowful eyes'. The Tsar is powerless to save his capital from 'the divine element', and his only hope is that God will eventually withdraw His element; he is also powerless to save his subjects, and 'the generals' ('Count Miloradovich and Adjutant-General Benckendorff', Pushkin's footnote efficiently explains), 'embarking on their dangerous journey' to save 'the people drowning in their homes', are set in a comic key. The comic element is muffled here, but it emerges quite distinctly when the scene is subsequently echoed in the appearance of another titled personnage, Count Khvostov, with his 'immortal verses'. Thus, the poem is ambiguous and equivocal even apart from the basic conflict between Peter and Evgenii.

Here again at first sight Peter seems to overcome Evgenii: Peter is grandiose, while Evgenii is pitiful. But the Evgenii theme is consistently sustained, without the slightest hint of irony, in the key of 'bourgeois drama'. Evgenii is spoken of – and quite correctly – as the ancestor of Akakii Akakievich, Makar Devushkin and all the 'philanthropic' literature of bourgeois realism. But, in comparison with Evgenii, Akakii Akakievich and even Makar Devushkin are almost clowns. If one holds that a yardstick of the democratisation of art is the extent to which authors are free from the obligation to depict lower-class characters in a comic light, then *The Bronze Horseman* travels much further along this road than Gogol and Dostoevsky. The conflict between the pitiful mad tatterdemalion and the master of half the world provided ready material for comedy. Quite determinedly avoiding the slightest hint of comedy meant recognising the equality of Evgenii and Peter; it meant recognising the former's defeat as fortuitous and provisional. In spite of his externally pitiful appearance Evgenii grows into a tragic hero, and his downfall evokes not contemptuous pity, but 'horror and sympathy'. And Pushkin's semi-deification of Peter, which endowed him less with the characteristics of a god than with those of a demon, promotes Evgenii's elevation to the level of a sort of theomachist, while transforming Peter into an external power of evil, hostile to man, in the albeit hopeless struggle against which the combatant is ennobled.

The Bronze Horseman is rightly recognised as one of the high points in Pushkin's entire work. Only a supreme poet could have taken the chaos and confusion of his historical views and of his turbid doubts and hesitations, in which a false motive is substituted for every real one, and transformed them into an harmonious system of images linked with the profound and complex image of a struggle with no decisive outcome.

At the same time, however, *The Bronze Horseman* also reveals the narrowly national character of Pushkin. In his entire cast of mind Pushkin is much more cosmopolitan and European than Gogol or Tolstoy, and yet he remains a narrowly national poet – in the sense of being a classic only among his fellow-countrymen, whereas Gogol and Tolstoy have a place in the common literary treasure-house of all mankind. Pushkin acted as a sort of focus: he absorbed into himself the enormous artistic experience of the entire previous development of bourgeois humanity and reproduced it for the new Russian bourgeois culture. This is the meaning of that notorious 'universal humanity' which Dostoevsky saw in him. It follows, however, that one sees in Pushkin's work nothing which is new in principle compared with the early-bourgeois literature of the West. On the scale of world history Pushkin does not mark a new step forward.

However, in attempting to cope with this broad and generalised task of recreating for Russia that which had been created in older countries, Pushkin responded extremely sensitively to every concrete development in the Russian history of his day. There are many among us who regard such a responsiveness to the topics of the day as a self-evidently significant quality. If encoded hints at the struggle between the Prussian and the Austrian factions at the court of Elizabeth can be found in the ostensibly innocent verses of Sumarokov, our literary specialist unhesitatingly counts this to Sumarokov's credit. This attitude is of course an extremely crude distortion of the basic Marxian thesis that the artist is inevitably a child of his age. There is more than one way of responding to topics of the day.

Pushkin's responsiveness to the history of his time was deeply subjective: he interpreted it first and foremost from the standpoint of his personal adaptation to it. This is true both in a crudely biographical and in an ideological sense. Pushkin apprehended events in this way or that according to their effect on his own position and interpreted them from this point of view. Pushkin's theories of history are deeply subjective and 'topical': they are always called upon to answer the question of Pushkin's place in contemporary society. This is an approach highly characteristic of a nobleman with something to lose and reluctant to lose it.

Thus, *The Bronze Horseman* too is a lyrical account of Pushkin's reflections on what the state of affairs under Nicholas I held in store for him. It is a lyrical expression of his own confusion in the face of a narrowly concrete and (as Pushkin failed to realise) relatively ephemeral situation. For the Russian reader this 'situation' is a part of his 'historical memory'(or, less figuratively speaking, a part of his 'general education'): we know what Pushkin faced in agonising confusion and what his reflections were about. The non-Russian reader does not know this. For him the unifying meaning is absent from the poem. He sees only a magnificent series of pictures and a most enigmatically formulated conflict between figures whose substance is unclear to him.

Quite different are the works of Gogol which appeared at almost the same time. *The Inspector General* and *Dead Souls* do not suffer from any narrowly national character because Gogol, while depicting the conditions of Russia under serfdom with a far greater degree of concrete realism than Pushkin, at the same time depicted them in a more generalised manner, selecting those details which were typical on a broad historical scale and providing simultaneously both a portrait ('crooked mug') and a generalised image of those conditions of serfdom, the struggle against which led to the Russian revolution. Pushkin was never able, and indeed never strove to provide such a generalised image. Gogol provides general knowledge about Russia under serfdom: Pushkin presupposes such knowledge in his readers. This is what makes Pushkin narrowly national, in a way in which Gogol is not.

All these are complicating factors in Pushkin's work, but they are not the most important point. The most important point is that Pushkin created for Russia what had been created for the older bourgeois nations by their classical writers from the Renaissance to the beginning of the nineteenth century...

# VINOGRADOV

PUSHKIN'S STYLE

V.V. Vinogradov (1895-1969) was a highly distinguished Soviet philologist who during a long and successful intellectual career published many important studies devoted to Russian grammar, the history of the Russian language and Russian literature. Among his works on the classical Russian writers were *Pushkin's Language* (1935) and *Pushkin's Style* (1941). In 1947 Vinogradov succeeded G.O. Vinokur as the chief editor of the four-volumed *Dictionary of Pushkin's Language* (1956-61). The extract below is taken, however, from an earlier essay, *On Pushkin's Style* which, like Mirsky's essay in the present collection, was a contribution to the impressive *Literary Heritage* volume 16-18 (1934) devoted to Pushkin. Discussing the question of poetic quotation, Vinogradov cites the phrase spirit of pure beauty' which appears in celebrated poems by both Zhukovsky and Pushkin and considers the various associations it possessed for the two writers.

A poetic quotation can bring into one of Pushkin's compositions not only the context of the literary work from which it was taken, but also a wider range of images and ideas from the entire work of another writer. It is therefore essential for the investigator of Pushkin's style to know not only the meaning and application of the other writer's phrase in its 'homeland', in the context of a particular work, but also its structural weight in the other writer's whole literary system. He must survey all the ideological and symbolic associations of the phrase. Only then can he fully determine to what extent the 'borrowing' exhausts the meanings of the original and the nature of its influence on the symbolism of the work by Pushkin.

A graphic illustration of the importance of this type of semantic investigation is provided by a stylistic analysis of Zhukovsky's phrase *spirit of pure beauty [genii chistoi krasoty]* which appears in Pushkin's lyric 'I remember a wonderful moment' (1825). N.I. Chernyaev was the first to establish that the phrase *spirit of pure beauty* was taken from Zhukovsky's poem *Lalla-Rookh* (1821) and he noted in general terms the points of correspondence between the two poems. This comparison was not entirely convincing however, and N.F. Sumtsov was prepared to consider the repetition of the phrase a product of common contemporary tendencies in phrase-construction and a consequence of similar work on the same lexical material. But that is not the case. In the mass of familiar poetic cliches of the 1820s any fresh poetic phrase used to stand out very sharply and was soon assigned to its inventor. For instance, in his article *Two anthological poems* P.A. Pletnyov, analysing Vyazemsky's poem *To a solitary beauty*, took the lines

> Thus orphaned here in a lonely land
> A goddess of beauty without sacrifices and altars

and wrote:

> *Thus orphaned here* – a new and very accurate expression. It vividly depicts the state of a soul which is full of fine sentiments but lonely, and which shares its existence with no-one. *A goddess of beauty* – a phrase repeated more than once by many poets – has a certain freshness here because it is followed by words which explain why the poet employed it: *without sacrifices and altars.*

Against this transparent linguistic background Zhukovsky would not have tried to assert any individual rights over the phrase *spirit of pure beauty* which was of such significance for him. For Zhukovsky this phrase was connected with a personal, precise and strictly delineated complex of images of a heavenly vision, 'fleeting as a dream', with symbols of hope and sleep, with the theme of 'pure moments of existence' and the liberation of the heart from 'the dark earthly domain' and with the theme of inspiration and emotional revelations:

> So that the heart should know about Heaven
> In this dark earthly realm,

> Heaven permits us through a veil
> To steal a glimpse from time to time.

The spirit of beauty manifests itself in everything which is beautiful on this earth and:

> ... when it departs from us,
> As a gift of love, while still in sight,
> It ignites in our sky
> A farewell star.

The cluster of images clinging to the phrase *spirit of pure beauty* embraces also the symbol of poetry, 'the first flame of inspiration' (cf. the poem *The Appearance of Poetry in the form of Lalla-Rookh*). Moreover, for Zhukovsky the idea of poetry is inseparably connected with the themes of other worlds and of moral perfection:

> Divine harmony itself –
> We sensed her existence
> And, as she absolved the soul, we sensed
> Her beckoning it into paradise.

All these images, which are symbolically concentrated in the phrase *spirit of pure beauty,* appear again, after *Lalla-Rookh,* in the poem 'I would meet the young muse' (1823) in a different emotional context, a mood of expectant longing for the 'giver of songs' and for this spirit of pure beauty; it is the mood in which the poet contemplates the latter's star:

> O spirit of pure beauty! ..
> But you are familiar to me, pure spirit,
> And your star shines for me.

It is known that Zhukovsky supplied his own commentary to the symbolism associated with 'the spirit of pure beauty.' Fundamental to this is his conception of 'the beautiful':

> The beautiful has neither name nor form; it visits us in the best moments of existence... it appears to us only momentarily, uniquely in order to proclaim itself, to animate us and to ennoble our souls... only that is beautiful which does not exist...

The beautiful is attended by sadness and by a striving 'towards something better, something mysterious and remote which is associated with it and which exists for you somewhere. And this striving is one of the most inexpressible proofs of the immortality of the soul':

> The beautiful is the fleeting herald of a better world... it is an entrancing longing for man's real home; it affects the soul not through present reality, but through a dim memory, compressed into a single moment, of everything that was beautiful in the past and through a mysterious longing for something in the future.

The mystical complexion of the symbolism attached to the image of the spirit of pure beauty appears again in Zhukovsky's fragment *The Raphael Madonna*...
But the moral-cum-mystical basis of all this symbolism was quite alien to Pushkin, and the disagreement between him and Zhukovsky over the matter was very sharp. It centred on different concepts of the essential nature of poetry, and for Zhukovsky the image of poetry stood in the middle of this circle of poetic symbols. Zhukovsky tried to convert Pushkin to his faith. Jokingly he wrote to him:

> You have been created to join the gods. Forwards! The soul has wings. It does not fear heights, for that is its true element. Give freedom to those wings and heaven is yours... Farewell, little devil, be an angel!

A few months later Zhukovsky wrote again, this time more seriously and sternly:

> To everything which has happened to you I have a single answer: poetry. You possess not talent, but genius. You were born to be a great poet. Be worthy of it. Your entire code of morals is contained in that phrase. By the authority given to me I offer you the premier place in the Russian Parnassus. And what a place, if you will combine a sublimity of aim with the

sublimity of genius. Dear brother in Apollo, this is within your power. And with this you will be unaffected by everything in life which noises around you.

Concerning *The Gipsies* Zhukovsky wrote, in late May, 1825:

I know nothing more perfect in style than your *Gipsies*. But, my dear friend, what is its aim? Tell me, what do you want of your genius? What remembrance of yourself do you want to leave to your country which is in such need of the sublime? What a pity we disagree.

Pushkin replied:

I am sorry that I do not have your advice – nor even just your presence, which is itself an inspiration... You ask what the aim of *The Gipsies* is. What about this? – 'The aim of poetry is poetry', as Delvig says (if he didn't steal the remark). Ryleev's thoughts have an aim, but they never hit the target.

In his poem 'I recall a wonderful moment' Pushkin exploited Zhukovsky's symbolism, but brought it down to earth and eliminated its religious and mystical basis. Characteristically, from all Zhukovsky's poems Pushkin singles out as 'lovely' *To the fleeting familiar spirit* (1819) and seems to contrast the romantic reverie of this poem with the other-worldly, mystical and ethical symbols of *Lalla-Rookh*.

In *To the fleeting familiar spirit* the poet begs the spirit to stay:

O my spirit, abide with me a while...
Stay, be my earthly life,
Be the guardian angel of my soul.

Here too the image of the spirit is fused with poetry and inspiration:

Was it not you who bore aloft the soul
Through the divine inspiration of poetry,
Shone before it like a divine vision
And revealed to it the beauty of life?

In 'I remember a wonderful moment' Pushkin fuses the image of poetry with that of his mistress and preserves a substantial number of Zhukovsky's symbols, except for the religious and mystical ones. (Note in Pushkin the erotically metaphorical 'Erench' significance of the words 'heavenly' and 'divinity': *heavenly* = beautiful; *divinity,* according to Tatishchev's lexicon, in poetic diction refers to a beautiful woman – '*c'est une divinité que j'adore'*).

> And I forgot your tender voice
> And your heavenly features...
> My days dragged quietly by
> Without divinity, without inspiration...
> And for it were born again
> Divinity and inspiration.

With this material Pushkin builds a work which possesses not only a fresh rhythmical and figurative structure but also a different resolved meaning, quite remote from Zhukovsky's ideological and symbolic conception. And only this other semantic scheme, the external token of which is the line

> Like a spirit of pure beauty

can aid the complete elucidation of the structure of meaning in Pushkin's poem...

LEZHNEV

PUSHKIN'S PROSE

A.Z. Lezhnev (1893-1938) began his career as a literary critic and an historian of literature in the 1920s. He produced a book on Gorky, one on Heine and Tyutchev and another on art in general, as well as a series of articles on contemporary Soviet writers. In 1937 Lezhnev, like Mirsky, was arrested and, in the euphemistic Soviet phrase, 'illegally repressed.' His book *Pushkin's Prose* with its sub-title *An Experiment in Stylistic Investigation* was first published in the year of the author's arrest and then reissued in 1966, eleven years after his 'posthumous rehabilitation'. In the present extract Lezhnev discusses the aphoristic style of Pushkin's critical articles.

Many years ago Annenkov pointed out the special character of the prose style in Pushkin's articles. He did not regard these as criticism in the true sense – an opinion which was also held by Chernyshevsky. They had in mind more than simply the brevity and the sketchy nature of Pushkin's 'notes'.(Chernyshevsky called Pushkin's critical articles 'remarks': 'We say "remarks" because his reviews are all very slight and written apparently in haste under the influence of first impressions'). They also had in mind Pushkin's method of exposition.

The aphoristic nature of Pushkin's articles is manifested in two ways. Firstly, it is seen in their structure, comprising usually no more than a concise exposition of various ideas which are not developed in any detail or supported by detailed arguments. (Annenkov wrote that their content 'simply sets out an idea without any digressions and without examining it from different sides, as would a true critical analysis'). Secondly – and this follows from the peculiarities of the structure – it appears in the very character of the sentences, which acquire an aphoristic pointedness from being so condensed and rich. The centre of gravity is clearly transferred from elaborating an idea to expressing it vividly, comprehensively and memorably. The nucleus of the idea is contained within a tight casing where it is compressed to the limit, but it has wings, like downy plant-seeds to be borne away by the wind.

In accordance with Pushkin's generally laconic style, aphorisms are also found in his narrative prose, when the author introduces his own comments or footnotes. Sometimes aphorisms are introduced into the dialogue, e.g. 'He has the profile of Napoleon and the soul of Mephistopheles'; or: 'For amatory adventures our winter nights are too cold and our summer ones too light', etc. Pushkin's footnotes may in fact be regarded as interpolated publicistic material. However, because of their limited role in the text of the stories the significance of such aphorisms is small. But it is quite another matter with Pushkin's articles: here aphorisms become the basic means of expression.

In many cases they appear as such directly, as isolated and finished *dicta,* enjoying an independent existence. This is the case in his notes – a genre which was widely cultivated by Pushkin. With him a note consists of either a plain aphorism or an aphorism which has been rendered somewhat more complex by a brief development of its idea.

Characteristic examples of the plain aphorism are:

> A scholar without talent is like the poor Mullah who cut up and ate the Koran, thinking this would fill him with the spirit of Mahomet.

> Uniformity in a writer betokens a one-sided, even if perhaps deep intellect.

> Envy is the sister of competition, and hence of good family.

> Grammar does not prescribe rules for language, but elucidates and confirms its usages.

> No-one has feelings in his ideas and taste in his feelings more than Baratynsky.

> You have to try to get the majority of votes on your side – so don't insult fools!

The following are examples of the more complex and more extended aphoristic note:

> Some people have no concern for the glory or the tribulations of their motherland. They know its history only from the days of Prince Potemkin and they have some grasp of the statistics only of that province where their estates are situated; but with all that they consider themselves patriots because they love fish-and-vegetable soup and their children run about in red shirts.
>
> The colder, the more calculating and the more cautious we are, the less we are subjected to onslaughts of ridicule. Egoism can be repulsive, but not ridiculous, since it is eminently reasonable. However, there are people who love themselves with such tenderness, gaze upon their own brilliance with such rapture and think of their own well-being with such emotion and of their displeasures with such compassion that in them even egoism has all the ridiculous side of enthusiasm and sentimentality.
>
> By his nature man is more disposed to censure than to praise (says Machiavelli, that great connoisseur of human nature). Foolish censure is less obvious than foolish praise; if a fool sees no merit in Shakespeare, that is ascribed to his fastidiousness, eccentricity, etc. If the same fool enthuses over a novel by Ducray-Duminil or Polevoi's *History,* everyone regards him with contempt — though to a thinking man his foolishness is more obvious in the first case.

Pushkin's notes are usually grouped in cycles and are often interspersed with anecdotes and various other jottings. The alternation of short aphorisms with more extended notes, of notes with anecdotes and of anecdotes with reminiscences of this or that event reduces somewhat the sharp pointedness of the aphorisms which, if unrelieved, would have produced a too uniform and too highly spiced impression. Pushkin's style, with its insistence on naturalness, finds a solution here too: through the variety of his selection he imbues the whole cycle with the softness and the richness of chiaroscuro.

An article by Pushkin may be defined as a series of aphorisms connected by a common idea. A note like the short comment on censure and praise quoted above may serve as the prototype for an article and as a transitional link between a simple, independent aphorism and an article. The first maxim is: *man is more disposed to censure than to praise*. The second maxim, which constitutes a consequence of the first, is: *foolishness of censure is less obvious than foolishness of praise*. The third maxim is: *but for a thinking man foolishness manifests itself even more clearly when it consists of censure*. A caustic and topical literary example gives the note a polemical tone. This is almost a set pattern for articles by Pushkin.

But in Pushkin there is a substantial difference between the note and the article. Isolated aphorisms or (to a lesser extent) the aphorisms in the short note are sharp and bald, and must be so since they represent the muscles of an idea without any skin, fat, or connective tissue. The article does not permit a continuous accumulation of maxims, particularly within the framework of Pushkin's style. Such an article would become either pretentious or difficult to read. In collecting his notes in cycles Pushkin employed complex and varied arrangements in order to avoid this undesirable side-effect, but in an article he has to use other techniques. In the first place, the aphorisms themselves are turned more modestly. In the second place, he inserts between the aphorisms a stylistically neutral connective tissue – normal uncondensed sentences without any pointedness. The pattern of the article will be as follows: individual aphorisms are scattered singly or in groups throughout its entire length, but in such a way that they are situated at key points, where they, as it were, crystallise the meaning; they are connected by a common idea. The muscular system of the article is not laid bare, but concealed, yet the train of thought is very precise.

An example of this structure is provided by Pushkin's article *M.E. Lobanov's View of Literature, both Foreign and Russian,* which was directed against an obscurantist lecture by an academic writer calling for further censorship measures against literature. (Lobanov had come close to branding literature as 'immoral' and 'stupid' in its entirety). Every basic step in Pushkin's argument is expressed aphoristically, so that its entire course is marked by aphorisms, interspersed with extracts from the lecture and with

Pushkin's own comments. Firstly, Pushkin protests (very circumspectly, for obvious reasons) against Lobanov's abuse of his academic chair:

> There are heights from which satirical reproaches should not fall; there are titles which impose upon one an obligation to moderation and decency, independent of any censor's surveillance, *sponte sua, sine lege*.

Secondly, Pushkin tries to prove that one connot unreservedly demand of literature elegance and moral admonitions:

> The moral sense, like talent, is not given to all..... Thoughts, like actions, can be divided into the criminal and those for which one is not answerable..... To demand from all works of literature elegance or a moral aim is like demanding that every citizen lead an irreproachable life and reach a high level of education..... The law strikes only at crimes, while leaving weaknesses and vices to the conscience of the individual.

Thirdly, Pushkin defines the task of art: 'The goal of art is *the ideal,* and not *moralising.*' Fourthly, he speaks about the shortcomings of the phrenetic French school, and if his language does not become directly aphoristic it certainly acquires an extraordinary sharpness and expressiveness: 'The literature of shocks, prison, punch, blood, cigars, etc.' Fifthly, he questions Lobanov's view that the censorship must 'penetrate all the contrivances of those who write':

> Absurdity, like stupidity, is subject to the ridicule of society and does not provoke legal action.

The aphorisms in Pushkin's articles are rarely dressed elaborately. They prefer to do without metaphorical vestments. Their pointedness derives purely from their meaning. They are built for the most part on opposition, contrast and clash of meanings. For instance:

> Often one disagrees with his thoughts, but they make

one think. [On Vyazemsky]

To write only colloquial language means to be ignorant of the language.

Yakovlev... sober would remind us of Talma drunk.

Bryansky never stirred anyone in tragedy or made anyone laugh in comedy.

Karamzin is our first historian and our last chronicler.

There is no truth where there is no love.

Where there is no love of art there is no criticism.

Our critics' judgements usually amount to: 'This is good because it is beautiful, and this is bad because it is nasty'.

Drama was born in the public square.

Laughter, pity and horror are the three strings of our imagination plucked by the magic of drama.

The truth about the passions and a verisimilitude in the feelings experienced in given situations – that is what our intelligence demands of a dramatist.

Criticism is the science which reveals the beauty and the shortcomings of works of art and literature.

It is easy to see that the last few examples lack pointedness of expression. They are aphorisms of accurate formulation, condensations of thought in a pure form. This type of aphorism is very common in Pushkin. Close to it are aphorisms of the type, 'Drama was born in the public square', which are more striking and metaphorical in appearance, but which still carry concealed in them the function of formulation. In their seriousness and the business-like tone of their ideas Pushkin's aphorisms are reminiscent of the calm, unseasoned inner profundity of Goethe's, while their sharp outlines indicate a kinship with the aphorisms of the French school from which they are indeed clearly descended. An example will show how a Pushkinian aphorism, for all its typical sharpness, grows into the organic train of thought of an article:

> Baratynsky belongs among our finest Russian poets. He is original in this country because he thinks. He would be original anywhere because he thinks for himself, soundly and independently, while feeling strongly and deeply. The harmony of his verses, the freshness of his style and the liveliness and precision of his enunciation must strike anyone endowed with the slightest taste and feeling. Besides the charming elegies and the short lyrics which everyone knows by heart and which are continually imitated so unsuccessfully, Baratynsky has written two short novels which in Europe would have brought him fame but which in Russia were noticed only by connoisseurs. Baratynsky's first youthful poems were once greeted with rapture. His latest ones – which are more mature and closer to perfection – have enjoyed a lesser public success.

A series of sentences is pointed aphoristically. Even if an aphorism is paradoxical ('He is original in our country because he thinks'), it is fitted into the whole and set in the generally firm but restrained intonation (behind what is said one senses much that is left unsaid; behind the text there is a sub-text) in such a way that there is not the slightest hint of artificiality or pretentiousness.

Pushkin the critic and publicist is remarkable for the wide variety of forms in which the prose of his articles is cast. Excluding the intermediate literary genre of notes, it might seem as though in essence he knew only two modes – the short declaratory article and the polemical article. (He presents the rather unusual combination of a master of both aphorism and polemic). The polemical article, however, is not a genre, but a combination of genres, which allows a wide variety of formulations – and Pushkin made wide use of all them. In his writings we find dialogues, sometimes with a sharp satirical tendency, caricature-tales in the style of the fable, lampoons, and a special kind of concealed polemical lampoon where the argument is ostensibly about subjects which are somewhat remote from contemporary Russian literature and so academic that the article's sharp tone is incomprehensible, but where really some quite different, though not directly mentioned topical issue is at stake (e.g. the article *On The Memoirs of Vidocq* which is aimed at Bulgarin). Generally speaking, almost every one of Pushkin's articles is polemical, but the polemics in them are either a secondary feature (at least on the surface) or half hidden, or when they are more obvious they are expressed in a fairly restrained manner. A specimen of this is provided by the conclusion of the article *On Mme. de Staël and Mr.A. Mukhanov,* with its magnificent tone of restrained indignation:

> One should speak of this *lady* in the polite language of the educated. This *lady* was favoured by Napoleon with persecution, by monarchs with trust, by Byron with his friendship and by Mr. A.M. with a journalistic article which was not particularly intelligent and most unseemly.

Consequently, Pushkin's polemical lampoons stand out very sharply in his critical and publicistic legacy. This is almost another Pushkin with a different voice, in whom one senses new, unsuspected possibilities...

The artistic code which emerges from Pushkin's critical articles is very consistent and highly organic and coincides in all essentials with Pushkin's own practice. This is something which is by no means necessarily true. Tchaikovsky, for instance, pointed out that a man's artistic sympathies do not necessarily coincide with the trend of his own work. He himself was an example of this, with his own subjective and tragic art contrasting with his cult of the clear, harmonious Mozart. But if Pushkin's articles had come down to us on their own, without a single one of his creative works, we would still be able to reconstruct with a large measure of certainty the general characteristics of his artistic spirit. That is no idle boast. Indeed, take such tenets of Pushkin's as the primacy of essential points and thought and the law of simplicity; take his aversion to fame and to that conventional poetry which is raised in the lobby and progressess no further than the drawing-room; take his preference for folk drama which is presented in the public square over the artificial drama of polite society and his demand for a free, wide-ranging portrayal of characters; take his rejection of the unnatural, inflated and stilted aesthetics of the French romantics and the 'shortsighted pettiness' of the French realists. All these features, in one way or another, directly or indirectly, are embodied in his creative work...

SHKLOVSKY

NOTES ON PUSHKIN'S PROSE

Viktor Shklovsky (b. 1893) has left his mark on Soviet literature not only as a gifted and immensely influential critic but also as a writer of great originality. A leading theoretician of the futurist movement and founder of Russian formalism, he made an indelible impression on his generation. In the period 1913-1930, a period of improvisation, experimentation and tremendous energy in all aspects of Russian culture, Shklovsky led the fight for the restoration of a genuinely original and truly creative Russian literature. His insistence, as a formalist critic, that literature should be seen primarily as a means of expression, a 'device' free from social, historical or political connotations brought him, from 1930 onwards, increasingly into conflict with orthodox Soviet criticism; although he was forced to modify his views, Shklovsky never completely surrendered his adherence to the primacy of form in literature. This extract on *The Queen of Spades*, taken from *Notes on Pushkin's Prose (1937)*, and written in a typically simple, disjointed style, shows quite clearly Shklovsky's commitment to his view of literature as language.

The story is based on card-playing principles, on the significance of number and suit. It has a swift, impetuous opening:

'Once they were playing cards at Guards-Officer Narumov's'. This is one of the most famous of Pushkin's openings, indicating the setting and place of the action.

Lev Tolstoy started work on *Anna Karenina* after reading the extract beginning: 'The guests were arriving at the dacha...'

'The guests were arriving at the dacha.' 'That's the way you should begin,' said Lev Nikolaevich out aloud. 'Pushkin is our teacher; he involves the reader in the action of the story straight away. Another writer would have begun by describing the guests and then the rooms, but Pushkin launches straight into the narrative'. Lev Nikolaevich retired to his room and at once began to rough out the opening of *Anna Karenina,* which, in its first draft, started with the following sentence:'Everything was in confusion in the Oblonsky household' (P. Biryukov).

Pushkin's opening leads us straight into the middle of events. The end of the card game, morning, supper and conversation. 'The long winter night passed imperceptibly; they sat down to supper between 4 and 5 in the morning'.

In a similar setting Marlinsky would have given us a whole series of stories: first of all a humorous anecdote, then something rather more serious, finishing up finally with some heart-rending tale.

Pushkin has a conversation containing the entire exposition:

'How about Hermann?' said one of the guests, indicating the young engineer. 'Not once in his life has he picked up a card or doubled a stake, and yet he sits with us until five o'clock watching us play!'

'Card-playing fascinates me', said Hermann, 'but I am not in a position to sacrifice what is essential in the hope of obtaining something extra'.

'Hermann is a German: he's thrifty, that's all there is to it', Tomsky remarked. 'But if there is somebody I don't understand, it's my grandmother, the Countess Anna Fedotovna'.

'What?' shouted the guests.

'I can't understand,' Tomsky went on, 'why my grandmother never gambles!'

'What's so astonishing about the fact that an old woman in her eighties doesn't gamble?' said Narumov.

'You don't know about her then?'

'No we don't, nothing at all!...'

'In that case, listen...'

Here we have a characterisation of the main characters – a young man and an old woman who does not play cards – which prepares us for their fatal meeting.

After the heroes have been introduced, Tomsky tells the story of how the Countess, as a young woman, obtained the secret of the three winning cards from Saint-Germain, and how she passed on this secret to Chaplitsky, now deceased.

And so the story begins with an ancedote, containing the plot, with a description of young men carried away by card-playing and with a characterisation of Hermann, linked with the characterisation of the Countess...

The theme of the poor young man seeking a position in life was already a familiar one. Very often this poor young man was depicted as an artist or a poet. He was beset by horrible circumstances which forced him to crime. The culmination of such a type in Russian literature is the figure of Raskolnikov.

In *Crime and Punishment* Dostoevsky links the future of Dunya, who has to marry somebody she does not love, with that of the prostitute Sonya. Dunya is getting married in order to secure the means to support her brother. Raskolnikov commits the crime motivated by the desire to support his mother and save his sister.

This is very traditional and can be seen in many writers before this, including Nekrasov the prose-writer, and Panaev. It is the theme of the poor young man who, motivated by considerations of sentiment, seeks to acquire wealth.

Pushkin, in giving Hermann a small income, changes the sentimental motivation for the 'young man's' actions. He is someone seeking a position in life.

Pushkin indirectly vulgarises this image by linking it with a virtuous German, a German bourgeois. Of all the people linked with the name of Napoleon this is the most unromantic...

Pushkin's attitude to Hermann is cold. Hermann is at one and the same time Napoleon and the hero of some trite novel. Pushkin is not carried away by his hero in the same way as Stendhal is carried away by Julien Sorel's career in *Le Rouge et le Noir*.

The hero's downfall has the following parodying epigraph:

'Attendez.'
'How dare you say *attendez* to me!'
'I said *attendez* sir, your excellency!'

This epigraph is followed by a description and precise characterisation of Hermann's mania.

It is as impossible for two fixed ideas to coexist in the spiritual world as it is for two bodies to occupy the same place in the physical world. In Hermann's imagination the image of the dead countess was quickly replaced by the three, seven and ace, which were constantly on his mind and his lips. On catching sight of a young girl he would say: 'What a slim girl! ... A veritable three of hearts'. When asked the time he would reply: 'Five to seven of clubs'. Every stout gentleman would remind him of an ace. The three, seven and ace would haunt his dreams and take on all kinds of forms. The three would blossom out in the shape of a magnificent magnolia, the seven would appear as a gothic gate, and the ace as a huge spider.

This is a somewhat unusual passage for Pushkin, containing perhaps certain features of Gogolian prose style.
The card game itself is portrayed by Pushkin laconically.
He uses a minimal number of features to characterise the important players; he is clearly only concerned with the process of the game itself.

Some generals and privy councillors were playing whist; the young people were sitting sprawled on the damask settees, eating ice-creams and smoking pipes. The host was sitting at a long table in the drawing-room and acting as banker; around the table a group of about twenty players had gathered. The host was a man of about sixty with a very respectable appearance; he had a fine head of silver-grey hair; his full fresh face bore a good-natured expression; his eyes shone with a smile that never disappeared.

Hermann plays, wins, doubles his stake, places his cards for a third time and loses.

He loses because he makes a mistake and places the wrong card. He leaves the table. The epigraph comes true: fate tells him '*Attendez,* sir'.

In Tchaikovsky's opera Lizaveta Ivanovna throws herself into the Winter Canal. The opera has a much simpler story-line than the tale, in which the link between Lizaveta Ivanovna and Hermann is more complex. Lizaveta Ivanovna replaces the old countess; she is the means by which Hermann can achieve his aim.

Pushkin arranges Lizaveta Ivanovna's fate so that he rewards her with happiness, as if the blessing of the dead countess has transferred itself to her.

In Liza's position there is a very definite symmetry.

> Lizaveta Ivanovna married a fine young man; he has some government post or other and a reasonable income: he is the son of the old countess' former bailiff.
> Liza is bringing up a poor young relative in her house.

The figure of Liza is not fully developed by Pushkin, but the introduction of the theme of an impoverished aristocratic girl, deceived by a man 'of his time' is of tremendous significance and shows Pushkin's secret dislike for Hermann. Liza is closer to his heart than Hermann.

Liza herself is like some epigraph from an unrealised novel...

The Queen of Spades had an enthusiastic reception from its readers and was twice mentioned in the *The Library for Reading*. After he had read the first two chapters Senkovsky wrote Pushkin a long letter.

Senkovsky praised the story's style and good taste. He said that this was exactly how Russian should be written, and how everybody, even merchants, should speak; Senkovsky did not go any further down the social order...

Senkovsky compared the story's style to 'several pages' of one of Pogorelsky's stories, *The Nun*.

Belinsky spoke about *The Queen of Spades* with rather less fervour.

> *The Queen of Spades* is not strictly a story but a consummate tale. The characterisation of the old countess and her ward, their relationship and the strong but

demonic and egoistical Hermann are portrayed with astonishing truthfulness. Strictly speaking, it is not a story but an anecdote: for a story the content of *The Queen of Spades* is too exceptional and fortuitous. But as an anecdote, we repeat, it is a work of consummate skill.

The story was very well received by society. It was perhaps the only late work of Pushkin which was successful.

Pushkin wrote:
My *Queen of Spades* is in great vogue. Everywhere people are gambling on the three, seven and ace. At the court they have seen a similarity between the old countess and Princess Natalya Petrovna but apparently nobody is angry.

Society could well have seen the story as an anecdote about the failure of an upstart, a parvenu, who brings cold calculation and prudence into his card-playing.

It is a story about Hermann's downfall.

For Pushkin Hermann is not a heroic figure, but he knows that Hermann, although no hero, is a man of the future.

Let us now turn our attention to the style of the story. For Pushkin form was not merely the external appearance of the work.

Smoothness of style, which writers have sought to attain by various dramatic devices, was achieved internally. Pushkin's language is rich, precise and idiomatic; but it would be wrong to think that Pushkin wrote only in a conversational style. In the third number of *The Contemporary* in 1836 Pushkin, in an anonymous letter, wrote:

The richer a language's expressiveness and phraseology, the better it is for a skilful writer. The literary language is continually being enlivened by colloquial expressions but it should not renounce what it has acquired over many centuries. To write only colloquial language means to be ignorant of the language.

It has become customary to hold the view that it is Pushkin's letters which are the source of his prose style. Such a view is hardly correct. Pushkin's first letters are in traditional style with long complex sentences.

The letters have their own thematic construction and are full of superb descriptions. In his early letters Pushkin seems still to be under the influence of Karamzin and his *Letters of a Russian Traveller*. This is how he describes the Caucasus in 1820, in a letter to his brother:

> I regret, my friend, that you were unable to share with me the sight of this magnificent mountain range, with its ice-covered summits which from a distance seemed immovable and iridescent against the setting sun.

This is still written rhythmically; a little further on there is the phrase: 'I am sorry you did not climb with me the sharp summit of Mt. Besh-tau.' Pushkin is still using complex phrases but he is aiming for the idea, the picture, rather than the style.

Many years later he is to find different words for a description of clouds, words which are precise and as if freed from the pressure of grammar.

This is how Pushkin describes the clouds of the Caucasus in his *Journey to Erzerum*:

> This morning, while travelling past Kazbek, I saw a marvellous sight. White clumps of cloud straggled out across the mountain top, and an isolated monastery, lit up by the sun's rays, seemed to be floating in the air on top of the clouds.

This is just how the clouds of the Caucasus appear.

But a great deal of work was still needed in order to be able to describe them in such a way. We know of two drafts of a letter he wrote to Delvig from Mikhailovskoe. It is a literary letter and begins by mentioning a book by Muravyov, *A Journey through Tauris*. Sentimentality is still present, although Pushkin underlines the difference between his impressions and those of Muravyov. But Pushkin is constantly returning to reality. Here is an extract from the letter:

> We crossed over from Asia to Europe (from Taman to Kerch) by boat. I set off at once for the so-called tomb of Mithridates (the ruins of some tower or

other), picked a flower there as a memento of the place and lost it the next day without any regret. The ruins of Panticapaeum did not make any more impression on me. I saw traces of streets, an overgrown ditch, some old stones and that was all. I travelled all over the south coast and M's journey awakened many memories in me; but the terrible walk along the cliffs of Kykeneis have not left the least trace in my memory.

By the time Pushkin came to write *The Queen of Spades* he had achieved supreme simplicity of language.

He writes in very short sentences, almost without resorting to adjectives. This is how one of Pushkin's contemporaries describes his manner of writing at this time:

His style is brief and precise, avoiding all superfluities, anything that might embellish it. He rarely uses metaphors but when he does they are relevant and sharp. His art lies in his choice of words, which are always to the point. You always feel that it would be impossible to express his thoughts differently. Take the description of Hermann's arrival at the countess' house. Here the adjectives are so simple: 'the weather was terrible, the wind howled.'

Liza's portrayal is simple too. We learn that she is dressed in a 'light cloak', while her head is 'decked with flowers'. The flowers are for the ball, and the cloak is for herself. This little detail says a great deal. The setting is conveyed by the words 'faded' 'ancient', 'sad'. The most unexpected epithet here is 'sad' – unexpected because it qualifies the word 'symmetry'.

Now read the entire extract and see how short the phrases are. Their brevity is slightly modified by the fact that Pushkin uses semi-colons instead of full-stops. This punctuation gives a more even intonation. But the brevity of phrase is even more striking in the drafts. In one them Pushkin notes a phrase from the historian Golikov: '... threatened him with force, but Shipov replied that he was capable of defending himself.' This is the Pushkin transcription: 'Shipov was unyielding. He was threatened. He stayed firm.'

Pushkin's style is brief, his phrases direct. Here is the extract from *The Queen of Spades*:

The weather was terrible; the wind howled, the snow fell in large wet flakes; the lamps shone dimly; the streets were empty. From time to time the cabby dragged along the street with his emaciated nag, looking out for a late fare. Hermann stood there without his coat, feeling neither wind nor snow. At last the countess' carriage drove up. Hermann watched as the servants carried out the bent old woman, wrapped in her sable coat, followed swiftly by her ward dressed in a light cloak, her head decked with flowers. The doors slammed. The carriage rolled away heavily through the soft snow. The doorman shut the doors. The windows went dark. Hermann began to pace up and down outside the empty house; he went up to a lamp and looked at his watch: it was 11.20. He stayed under the lamp, gazing intently at the hour hand, waiting out the remaining minutes. At precisely half past eleven Hermann stepped on to the countess' porch and entered the brightly lit entrance-hall. The doorman was not there. Hermann ran up the stairs, opened the doors of the anteroom and saw a servant sitting asleep under a lamp in a dirty, old-fashioned armchair. With a light and firm step Hermann walked past him. The large hall and drawing-room were dark. They were feebly lit by the lamp from the anteroom. Hermann went into the bedroom. In front of a little shelf filled with old icons a gold sanctuary-lamp glimmered. Faded damask chairs and settees with down cushions and with their gilt worn away stood in sad symmetry around the walls decorated with Chinese wallpaper.

Pushkin's new fluency of style has been achieved, despite the abrupt sentences, by an unbroken train of thought.
It has been organically conceived.

VINOKUR

PUSHKIN AS A PLAYWRIGHT

G. O. Vinokur (1896–1947) was a leading Soviet specialist in the study of both language and literature. He wrote works on the history of the Russian language, was one of the editors of Ushakov's four-volumed Dictionary and published critical essays on a number of literary figures. At the same time Pushkin's work always remained one of Vinokur's chief interests. A member of the Pushkin Commission of the Academy of Sciences from 1933, he was one of the editors of the monumental *Complete Works of Pushkin* (Academic Edition, 1937-49) and from 1938 until his death he served as the chief editor of the *Dictionary of Pushkin's Language* (1956-61). The present essay, *Pushkin as a Playwright,* which provides a general outline of Pushkin's achievements in the field of drama, appeared in a volume of fifteen articles which was published in English in 1939 by VOKS (the All-Union Society for Cultural Relations with Foreign Countries).

Throughout his life, Pushkin was attracted to dramatic writing. Unfortunately, none of the dramatic attempts made by the poet in his childhood and youth have been preserved. We have learned of them only from memoirs of his contemporaries.

It is known that Pushkin closely followed Russian dramatic literature even as a schoolboy at the Lycée in Tsarskoe Selo (1811-1817). In 1815 Pushkin jotted down a note, *What I think of Shakhovskoy* in which he subjected the then great celebrity of Russian comedy to bold and severe criticism. In the course of the three years spent in Petersburg after he graduated from the Lycée and before he was exiled to the south of Russia (1817-1820), Pushkin frequented the theatre and contracted friendships with a few prominent playwrights of those days. The theatrical impressions of these three years left a distinct mark on Pushkin's works and were of great importance in furthering his development as a playwright and in stimulating his appreciation of the art of the drama.

Russian dramatic literature of that time was at a low level. This applied particularly to tragedy which, at the beginning of the nineteenth century, suffered from the severe decline that had set in after the hackneyed Russian imitations of Racine, of which there was a large repertory produced in the second half of the eighteenth century, had ceased to answer the needs of the time. In the first decades of the nineteenth century very few new Russian tragedies were produced. The most prolific writer of tragedies in those days was Ozerov who, by innovations after the manner of the sentimentalists, attempted to put some life into the dying traditions of classicism. His efforts, however, led to no significant results.

For some time Ozerov enjoyed notable success among his contemporaries, but Pushkin was always critical of this mediocrity. He considered, and rightly too, that Ozerov failed to rid Russian drama of its main defect – imitation. Pushkin regarded with more favour the comedy of those years, among the founders of which was the young Griboedov who later immortalized himself by his famous comedy *Woe from Wit*.

Pushkin's first attempt at play-writing, traces of which have been found among his papers, was in the field of comedy. Pushkin worked on his first play in 1821 when he was in exile at Kishinyov. It was, however, soon abandoned by him. About thirty lines of introductory verse and a detailed plan is all that has reached us of this comedy. The chief character of the comedy was to be a worldly young man whose passion for cards led him to stake his old devoted servant – a serf. It is evident that the comedy was conceived as a play to expose the evils of society. Here, social motives were to play a great part, which is quite in keeping with the whole political biography of Pushkin. It is known that in the first years of his exile to the South, Pushkin professed views similar to those of the left Decembrists.

The radical political ideas shared by Pushkin in those years found a still more remarkable reflection in another dramatic attempt of his – the unfinished tragedy *Vadim* (1822). The subject of the tragedy is the legendary Novgorod uprising led by Vadim, the champion of national-republican ideas, against the foreign conqueror Rurik in the ninth century. The choice of the subject itself shows the great influence which the ideas of the Decembrists had on Pushkin. For the Decembrists, Vadim was a historical symbol of the struggle for political freedom. The text of this dramatic essay shows that Pushkin conceived his tragedy as an agitational production since it is full of transparent allusions to the political situation of his time. The text speaks of the universal hatred of the population for the government and of 'young citizens' who are seething with indignation. On the other hand it is worth noting that in these fragments Pushkin still clung to tradition as far as dramatic technique is concerned. The two manuscripts of this piece are written in classical iambic hexameters.

Pushkin's very first completed dramatic work, the famous tragedy *Boris Godunov*, revealed the poet as a mature and original playwright. *Boris Godunov* was written in 1825 at the village of Mikhailovskoe where Pushkin was in exile from 1824. However, on account of censorship difficulties which dragged on for years, *Boris Godunov* was published only in 1831 in an expurgated form and with alterations that were forced upon the author by the censor.

Pushkin never saw his tragedy staged. It was not until 1870 that permission was given by the tsarist censorship to stage an expurgated version of this classical Russian drama. Many parts had been suppressed and certain alterations had arbitrarily been made in the text.

Boris Godunov is a work to which Pushkin attached great literary and social significance. The drama was dear to the heart of its author for two reasons: first, as a fully-formed answer to the important problems of history and politics that agitated him; and second, as the product of a deliberate and well-thought-out decision to overturn Russian dramatic traditions and effect a thorough reform of Russian dramatic literature.

This historical aspect of *Boris Godunov* is closely associated with Pushkin's studies of Russian history, in the materials of which Pushkin sought an answer to the question of the historical meaning of his own time and of his own fate. The historical theme of *Boris Godunov* has nothing in common with the historical convention of the tragedies of the classical school, for whom history was important because of its decorativeness and the traditional nature of its subjects.

The study of Shakespeare was a real revelation to Pushkin and in *Boris Godunov* he continued Shakespeare's methods. 'What a man this Shakespeare was!' Pushkin exclaimed, 'I cannot overcome my amazement! How small Byron, the tragedian, looks in comparison to him!' Shakespeare's full-blooded realism, the living sense of historical concreteness permeating his historical dramas, helped Pushkin finally to rid himself of the 'Byronic' ideas of his youth and at the same time suggested to him the methods of struggle against the traditions of French classicism in Russian drama.

While retaining all his respect for the poetic genius of Racine, Pushkin nevertheless definitely turns to Shakespeare. The latter influences not only the literary ideals of Pushkin but the poet's entire outlook. In February 1826 after the defeat of the movement of the Decembrists, Pushkin while waiting in great agitation for news concerning the fate of his friends, whose ideas he shared, wrote to Delvig: 'Let us not be like the French tragedians, either superstitious or one-sided, let us look upon the tragedy with the eyes of Shakespeare.'

This Shakespearean view of history, the endeavour to regard history as an objective process subject to natural laws, and of which the content is 'the fate of man, the fate of the people,' was typical of Pushkin. Similar feelings pervaded Pushkin when at the end of 1824 he was perusing the tenth and eleventh volumes of Karamzin's *History of the Russian State* which had then just appeared. These volumes dealt with the tensely dramatic events which took place in Russia in the sixteenth and seventeenth centuries. Pushkin availed himself of this very interesting material and wrote one of his monumental works revolving upon the momentous question of the fate of Russia. It is this question that Pushkin attempts to answer in the form of a dramatic story of Tsar Boris.

The tsar, the aristocracy and the people are depicted by Pushkin in a state of inevitable antagonism. And in this historical conflict it is the movement of the people that plays the decisive part. The people, the masses, in Pushkin's drama are not introduced for mere stage effect; they take an active part in the events and have a direct influence on the issue of the conflict. The mass- or crowd-scenes in *Boris Godunov* are the most original to be found in any dramas in the world. There is no doubt that in these scenes Pushkin went further than Shakespeare.

The reform of Russian dramatic style which Pushkin set as his object in *Boris Godunov* is closely linked with the historical conceptions which Pushkin embodied with such great poetic skill in the remarkable characters of this drama. Following Shakespeare, Pushkin renounced the three classical rules of unity and used blank verse in pentameter instead of the traditional Alexandrine verse. Pushkin also introduced a few prosaic scenes into his drama, and enriched its language by many forms of popular speech. However, these changes had a greater significance for Pushkin than the mere change of form. The various styles of dramaturgy and of theatrical presentations meant for Pushkin various outlooks and various solutions of the question as to the relation between art and life.

Pushkin gave expression to these ideas in the following remarkable words: 'I am firmly convinced that the popular rules of the Shakespearean drama, not the court usage of the Racine tragedy, are suitable for our stage.' Thus Pushkin associates the question of dramatic style with the character of the audience for whom the dramatic performance is intended. Pushkin set before himself the question of whether a popular tragedy was possible in Russia. He was inclined to answer this question in the negative. The unfavourable reception accorded *Boris Godunov* by the majority of Pushkin's contemporaries shows that indeed Russia at that time was uncongenial to the development of genuinely democratic dramatic art, and that Pushkin towered high above his readers and critics.

Pushkin had a premonition that his tragedies would not be understood by his contemporaries. He expressed the fear that the failure of his *Boris Godunov* might delay the reform of Russian drama. In this respect Pushkin's fears proved ungrounded – there was no returning to the past. But for a long time Russian drama produced nothing that could be compared to Pushkin's *Boris Godunov*. However, Pushkin had begun to look for new paths in the dramatic genre even before *Boris Godunov* was first published.

In the autumn of 1830, within a short space of time, Pushkin wrote a cycle of little tragedies. They vary in length from 200 to 500 lines of verse and the number of scenes from one to four. The cycle consists of the following four pieces: *The Miserly Knight, Mozart and Salieri, The Stone Guest,* and *The Feast in Time of Plague.* These little tragedies, the most peculiar creations of Pushkin's genius, constitute a special stage in Pushkin's evolution as a dramatist.

The distinguishing feature of these little tragedies is, above all, the fact that their subjects have been borrowed from Western European life and literature. Pushkin took special care to lend his little tragedies a Western European appearance. The first of them is provided with a subtitle: *Scenes from Chenston's Tragi-comedy,* 'The Miserly Knight'. Pushkin evidently had in mind Shenstone, but there is nothing in the works of the latter even suggestive of *The Miserly Knight*.

The leading characters in this tragedy are a medieval baron by the name of Philip (who is obsessed by a passion for hoarding) and his son Albert. The cupidity of the baron leads to a sharp dramatic conflict between him and his son.

Pushkin's second little tragedy is based on the legend that Mozart was poisoned by Salieri, who envied the former's genius. At one time Pushkin had an idea of calling this play *Envy* and intended to present it as a translation from the German...

The Stone Guest is Pushkin's version of the undying theme of Don Juan.

The subject of the fourth little tragedy is given in its title. It is a translation or rather a dramatic adaptation of part of John Wilson's tragedy, *The City of the Plague*.

To a certain extent Pushkin's little tragedies are in contrast to *Boris Godunov*. In the former, the broad historical theme of the popular theatre gives way to the poetical treatment of a particular moral and psychological problem. They form a series of very fine, masterly studies of cupidity, envy, love and death.

In choosing West-European material for his themes, Pushkin was no doubt guided by the wish to raise his works to the level of world tradition and free them from the imprint of national exclusiveness. If it is true that the whole of Pushkin's work represents the highest synthesis of the national and European elements in Russian culture, then his little tragedies should be regarded as the most graphic and brilliant demonstration of this synthesis.

From the point of view of literary and dramatic technique the little tragedies represent but a development of particular scenes in the style of *Boris Godunov*. The rapidly changing scenes of *Boris Godunov* (the action is set in Russia, then in Poland, now in the tsar's chambers, the public squares, at the monastery, then in the battle-field) in large measure possess independence and inner completeness. Each such scene contains, as it were, the kernel of an independent work.

It is known that Pushkin intended to write a few more little tragedies, including two under the titles: *Kurbsky* and *Dimitrii and Marina*. These tragedies would undoubtedly have been a development of the respective scenes and characters of *Boris Godunov*.

Having conceived the idea of experimenting in the new genre of little tragedies, Pushkin chanced to read Barry Cornwall's *Dramatic Scenes*. This finally made him determine to carry out his idea. Pushkin highly valued the masterful originality of this English poet; but he did not follow him in the construction of his scenes. The main distinction between the little tragedies of Pushkin and the corresponding works of Cornwall is the former's richness of dramatic effect and complete absence of rhetoric which often overburdens even the great dramatic works of world literature.

It is difficult to find anything equalling Pushkin's little tragedies for beauty of language and verse. In them charm, vigour, musical elegance and brilliant, passionate expressiveness are combined into one harmonious whole.

Among Pushkin's great achievements is the hymn to the plague sung by the toastmaster of the public feast in *The Feast in Time of Plague*. In Wilson's tragedy there is no such hymn.

In *The Miserly Knight* an unforgettable impression is left by the monologue of the old baron when he descends to the cellar to feast his eyes upon his treasures, as he opens all his coffers and brilliantly illuminates the vault.

In *Mozart and Salieri* Pushkin contrasts two types of artist – the 'idle rake' Mozart who is free from all reflection, to whom his envious interlocutor says: 'You, Mozart, are a god and know it not!' and Salieri, who had made 'handicraft a pedestal of art' and put 'harmony to the test of algebra.' *Mozart and Salieri* is one of Pushkin's most profound poetical generalizations and is an integral part of Russian culture.

However, the most brilliant example of this genre is *The Stone Guest* which many authorities on Pushkin consider the most accomplished of all his works. There is no denying the subtleness of Belinsky's well-known utterance to the effect that according to Pushkin's idea the nemesis of Don Juan is contained in the first genuine passion which he conceived for a woman – for Dona Anna. This passion, though it is not unrequited, is Don Juan's ruin. The scene of Don Juan's death in Pushkin's *The Stone Guest* is full of powerful, poignant tragedy.

Pushkin had the idea of writing a few more little tragedies of which we know only the titles. In addition to *Kurbsky* and *Dimitrii and Marina,* which were mentioned before, Pushkin intended to write *Romulus and Remus, Jesus, Paul I* and a few others, but they were left unwritten. In the course of 1829-1832, while he was working on his little tragedies, Pushkin wrote *The Water Nymph,* a drama in verse, which was left in an unfinished and unpolished state. However, we have most of it in Pushkin's handwriting.

By its structure *The Water Nymph* reminds us of Pushkin's little tragedies; but it is distinguished from them by its Russian national colour. *The Water Nymph* was built up by Pushkin on material from Russian folklore. The heroine of the drama is a miller's daughter who is seduced by a prince. When heavy with child, she learns that the prince is marrying someone else, and throws herself into the Dnieper. The old miller goes mad. The daughter of the Water Nymph comes to the shore and entices the prince to the bottom of the river. The manuscript breaks off on the monologue of the prince who by some 'unfathomable power' is drawn to the familiar spot on the bank of the Dnieper and is met by the little nymph emerging from the water.

In a few instances the folklore material in *The Water Nymph* had been removed by Pushkin from the dramatic dialogue and given separately in the form of songs in which all the linguistic and rhythmic peculiarities of folksongs are retained. To date literary scholars have not been able to reach a final decision on the question of whether the Water Nymph's plaintive song (in the scene of the prince's wedding) is a genuine folk-song or merely Pushkin's stylization.

The little tragedies and *The Water Nymph* which should be included in the same category, notwithstanding their masterful dramatic style, form only a stage in the history of Pushkin's dramatic works. Pushkin himself regarded this genre as an experiment. Among the various covering titles which Pushkin wished to give to all his works of this genre, one was *Experiments in Dramatic Studies.* The monumental forms of drama continued to attract Pushkin and he returned to them not long before his death.

In 1835 Pushkin made several attempts to write a drama in prose, in monumental style, with a subject borrowed from Western European history of the late period of feudalism. Pushkin's premature death prevented the full realization of his idea. Apart from a few small drafts and an outline of a drama with the well-known legend of the woman-pope Jeanne as the subject, Pushkin completed about one half of a great drama which the publishers agreed to call *Scenes from the Days of Chivalry.*

The hero of this drama is Franz, the son of a clothier. Franz feels oppressed by his low station and cherishes the idea of becoming a knight. He leaves his father, by whom he is disinherited. The knight Albert makes Franz his equerry, but soon afterwards drives him out for his rudeness. Franz places himself at the head of a peasant uprising against the knights, is taken prisoner and awaits the gallows; however, at the request of Clotilde, Albert's sister, Franz's sentence is commuted to life imprisonment. To judge by Pushkin's notes, Franz was to gain freedom and attain his goal in the further course of the drama.

The struggle of the peasants against their feudal lords and the disintegration of feudal society form the main historical background of this drama. Interesting details in Pushkin's plot are references to the invention of gun-powder and printing. The concluding part of Pushkin's outline of the drama reads: 'The piece ends with the appearance of Faustus on the devil's tail (invention of bookprinting and new artillery).'

According to Pushkin's idea this fantastic scene was to symbolize the serious turn in the course of European culture which forms the principal subject of *Scenes from the Days of Chivalry*.

There is not the slightest doubt that Pushkin was guided here by definite analogies between Western European and Russian history. In the 1830s Pushkin considerably enlarged the range of his historical studies and was constantly reading all the latest publications of Western European historical literature. As an outcome of these studies we find various notes and fragments in which Pushkin made attempts to form a clear idea of the Russian historical process in the light of the history of the Western European peoples. The decay of the nobility, the rise of the bourgeoisie, the tense struggle between the landlords and the serfs – these were all subjects from the very substance of life around him.

Scenes from the Days of Chivalry was not completed. It is therefore difficult to form an opinion as to the conclusions which Pushkin would have drawn in this drama. There can be no doubt, however, on one point – the sense of historical objectivity and development according to natural laws would have been revealed in this last play of Pushkin's with still greater clarity than in his earlier historical works.

It is worth noting that Pushkin wrote his *Scenes from the Days of Chivalry* in prose. This should be ascribed to the general prose tendency which he developed in his last years of life. Mérimée's

Jacquerie was mentioned long ago as one of the patterns by which Pushkin might have been guided while working on this drama, but it is easy to see the essential difference in the style of the two writers, notwithstanding the similarity of their subjects. The main difference lies in the fact that in Pushkin's *Scenes from the Days of Chivalry* the idea of the historical regularity underlying the depicted events and the drama as a whole is brought out with much greater clarity. Pushkin in this drama is to a lesser degree than Merimee taken up with the picturesqueness of some of the episodes and with the typical details of 'local colour' of the life of those times. The action in Pushkin's *Scenes from the Days of Chivalry* centres around one group of ideas; and the whole piece, written in the usual, restrained, terse and lucid language of Pushkin's prose, is sustained in an original tone of historical generalization.

Thus we see that Pushkin's career as a playwright was versatile and rich with content.

It must be admitted that the development of Pushkin as a playwright never reached its culminating point. One may say with certainty that Pushkin's premature death deprived Russian drama of a number of important dramatic works which would have been written by Pushkin had he lived longer. But even the work done by him in the field of drama in his short life is more than sufficient to accord him an honourable place in the pantheon of the great dramatic writers of the world.

FRANK

LUCENT SORROW

S.M. Frank (1877–1950) was an outstanding Russian philosopher and theologian. Although attracted as a young man to Marxist ideas, he soon discarded them in favour of a philosophy which embraced a religious idealism based on traditional values. Expelled from Russia in 1922, he spent the rest of his life in the West, settling finally in England in 1945. Apart from many works on philosophical and metaphysical problems he also wrote a number of essays on Russian literature. The present essay, *Lucent Sorrow*, which first appeared in the journal *Renaissance*, Paris, 1949, is characteristic in its reflection of Frank's philosophical and religious approach to literary criticism. The critic is here concerned above all with reconciling two seemingly irreconcilable qualities in Pushkin: his passionate love for life, and his profound sense of its inherent tragedy.

The more you consider the spiritual world created by Pushkin, or rather, the more you let yourself be affected by it, the more clearly it strikes you how little the richness and depth of his talent have been valued and appreciated up to now. It is of course the very form of Pushkin's poetry which has partly determined this superficial attitude to his spiritual world. It is so finished and so perfect that it has an aesthetically compelling and bewitching effect on the reader and – curiously – distracts his attention from the depth and significance of its spiritual content; and it is for the most part so unpretentious and simple that superficially its meaning seems insufficiently serious.

It would of course be quite monstrous not to appreciate the perfection of this poetical form. But it is time we recognised that form is not something self-sufficient, something which can be analysed and assimilated without regard to what is being expressed. Its simplicity, its perfection and its bewitching charm together bear witness to that magic aura inherent in every revelation of the most profound spiritual truth. Lev Tolstoy's statement that 'where there is neither simplicity nor truth there is no greatness' can be put the other way round: 'where there is simplicity and truth – and where there is true beauty – there is always spiritual greatness and spiritual significance...'

In this short and, of course, fragmentary essay I should like to draw attention to one dominant theme in Pushkin's spiritual world, a theme which has generally been disregarded, even sometimes directly denied. It is customary to see Pushkin as a poet of 'joy' and to contrast the spirit of his poetry with the theme of tragedy, which dominated the rest of nineteenth-century Russian literature. It was Gogol who set the tone. His admiration for Pushkin's poetry culminates with the warning that 'Pushkin cannot be imitated'. The meaning of this warning becomes clear in the following words: 'Our poetry will lighten an angel's sorrow and will bring a vision of holiness to the coarsest of hearts ...' (Gogol forgot here that Pushkin used much the same sort of language when speaking about his own poetry: 'The poignant suffering of poetry strikes with untold force at people's hearts'. And if, following Mickiewicz's authoritative proof, convincingly confirmed by V. Solovyov, we acknowledge that, in his *Prophet,* Pushkin had the poet in mind, then the line: 'Set the hearts of men on fire with your word' should be seen as referring to the purpose of poetry). Gogol's view was to be repeated subsequently in countless variations. Khomyakov put forward the view that Pushkin's spiritual world lacked 'bass tones'. It is a well-known fact that Pushkin's spiritual world was ignored throughout the last half of the nineteenth century precisely because it lacked the theme of 'sorrow' (in particular, 'patriotic sorrow'). And even today K. Mochulsky has claimed, in his book on Gogol, that if the Russian spirit had followed Pushkin's path then we would have had a Maikov, but no great Russian literature. Whether Maikov was ever aesthetically close to Pushkin is somewhat dubious, but, leaving that to one side, is it not obvious that the greatest Russian writer after Pushkin, Lev Tolstoy, is, precisely in his capacity as an artist, the true, direct heir to the Pushkin tradition? But N.A. Berdyaev, not concealing his dislike of Pushkin, called him 'the sole example of the spirit of the Renaissance in Russia', by which he clearly meant that the spiritual world of Pushkin's poetry was bounded by the cult of the beauty and joy of life on earth, freed from all tragedy. And since insensitivity to life's tragic side is an unfailing sign of spiritual shallowness, then this prevailing view of Pushkin is equivalent to a negative or even supercilious evaluation of his work as a whole. Such a widely-held view of Pushkin's naive exuberance must of course have some basis – or, rather, there must be some tangible reason for its appearance. The most immediate reason is so obvious that it need be mentioned only briefly. Pushkin was indeed an exuberant person, temperamentally and spiritually. When he was a young man this was reflected in his anarchical gaiety, his unquenchable thirst for enjoyment, his liking for practical jokes and humour and his youthful high spirits. As he grew older it could be seen in his sociability, his sympathetic responsiveness and his revulsion against the puritanical and anything that was deliberately harsh or dour. According to Khomyakov his humour was as infectious as his poetry. Although this purely psychological characterisation of Pushkin needs to be qualified (contemporaries speak of his fits of melancholy, and he used to call himself a 'jaundiced character') nevertheless it remains generally true.

I will return later to the other, deeper and more material reason for this widespread view. For the moment I simply wish to point out that to form an opinion on the essential meaning of Pushkin's poetry only because this side of his character is reflected in it would be extremely shallow. Yet it is astonishing to see how little the *tragic* element in Pushkin's poetry has been noticed and taken account of. And yet – however paradoxical it might sound – it is possible to state unequivocally that a feeling for life's inherently tragic quality is, at the very least, one of the most important themes of his poetry. So as not to complicate the issue, we shall leave to one side the notes of 'depression' and 'despair' heard in his early Lycée period; we will accept Pushkin's own later evaluation of them as 'elegiacal diversions' (although I do not think that such an interpretation was exhaustive: a spirit such as Pushkin's could never, even when a very young man, simply imitate prevailing fashion, or describe purely fictional moods; and the organic link between these early themes and later ones is all too obvious). We shall take only Pushkin's mature lyrics, including the lyrical moments in his narrative poems. In asking the reader's permission to cite a few well-known lines of Pushkin, I am also asking him to follow the advice of one of Pushkin's few genuine admirers as well, M.O. Gershenzon, whose advice was to read Pushkin '*slowly and carefully*'.

'Thus do the errors vanish from my *tormented* heart.' 'My soul, as ever hourly filled with *anguished* thought'. 'My soul is free from the monotonous agitation of *gloomy* thoughts'. 'In their nakedness I see both light and life and friendship and love, I hate *melancholy* experience.' 'My poetry, the living sound of *depression*.' 'My heart is beset by *anguished gloom*.' 'By a *dark* path I crossed the *desert* of the world'. 'The *anguish* of *hopeless despair*.' 'The *world is not worth* our emotional *torments*.' 'The poet *sorrows* while the world sports.' 'In the *anguished* mind, *crowds a mass of heavy thoughts*.' 'I am wearied by the *melancholy* of life's *monotonous* sound.' 'The *sadness* of bygone days grows ever stronger in my heart.' 'Oh men! Pitiful stock, deserving tears and laughter!' 'My heart seethed with *embittered* feelings.' Wine gives '*momentary rest from bitter torments*.' '*There is no happiness on earth*, but there are peace and freedom'. 'He who has lived and thought cannot but inwardly despise people.' Pushkin described his most important and favourite work, *Evgenii Onegin*, as the fruit of the mind's dispassionate observations and the heart's sorrowful contemplation, and such a description can certainly be applied to many other works of his.

These few examples, taken at random, are sufficient to make us realise at once the essential part which the emotions of sorrow, melancholy, disillusionment and the awareness of life's inherent tragedy played in Pushkin's spiritual life. And this is quite understandable and natural. Pushkin was too intelligent not to take this self-evident fact into account and was too passionate and alive a person not to experience these emotions himself. As always with Pushkin, the truth of these poetical statements can be confirmed by the personal assertions he makes in his letters. 'Believe me,' he writes to Osipova, 'life, although a "sweet habit", is so full of grief that in the end it becomes disgusting.' And again:'I am an atheist, as far as happiness is concerned; I don't believe in it.' Or to Pletnyov: 'The devil suggested I rave about happiness, as if I had been created for it.' Or to Delvig, on the occasion of the latter's wedding: 'Be happy, although it is fiendishly difficult.'

Besides these lyrical, subjective confessions showing Pushkin's feeling for the tragic nature of life, there is also the significant part played by objective description of the tragic principle underlying human existence – and this also has not been sufficiently recognised. Evidence of this lies, above all, in Pushkin's dramatic gift, which in *Boris Godunov* achieves a Shakespearian power. All his smaller dramatic works show, in the same masterful way, the presence of dark, demonic forces in control of the human soul and destroying it. Of the long narrative poems – again leaving to one side the works of his youthful, Byronic period – the most mature and perfect, *Poltava* and *The Bronze Horseman*, are full of dramatic tension and end with the tragic death of all the characters. Pushkin himself said about *Poltava* that the figure of Mazeppa awoke such horror in him that it was only with great difficulty that he suppressed the desire to give up the whole idea. The atmosphere of *The Bronze Horseman* is summed up in the introduction: 'My tale will be a sorrowful one'. But most interesting in this respect is *Evgenii Onegin*. With all its multiplicity of themes and its 'half-comic, half-serious' comments and reflections, the novel has three figures as its compositional focus: Evgenii, Tatyana and Lensky, and describes the ruin of the lives of all three. Lensky dies a meaningless death as a result partly of the clash of his idealistic, immature nature with Onegin's cold cynicism and partly because of his false sense of shame before the 'idol of public opinion'. Onegin remains devastated and empty, losing all chance of happiness in life as a result of his spiritual indifference. And 'poor Tanya's' heart is broken for ever, although this tragedy is softened by the light of voluntary renunciation.

As far as Pushkin's prose is concerned, in *The Captain's Daughter* there is the tragic irruption of the horrors of the Pugachov rebellion (that 'senseless and merciless Russian uprising') into the peaceful life of good, simple Russians: *Dubrovsky* shows the tragic conflict between the all-prevailing injustices of life and the ideas of despair and revenge which it engenders. *The Queen of Spades* brilliantly depicts how a secret, depraved passion (for money) can bring a human being through crime and contact with occult forces to insanity. And even the comparatively idyllic *Tales of Belkin* include the demonic figure of Silvio (in *The Shot*), and a hopelessly pathetic story of human heartlessness and capriciousness which shatters the life of an old station-master.

I should like now to examine more closely the essential features of Pushkin's awareness of the tragic nature of life. In this respect there is a crucial distinction to be made between Pushkin and, for example, such a typical representative of the spirit of tragedy as Lermontov. Lermontov is such a subjective writer that he is never in a position to explain – either to himself or to his readers – exactly why he is suffering. Pushkin, on the other hand, is too objective and clever simply to complain about his suffering; he is aware of its objective basis and explains it. I might even say that in Pushkin something akin to a philosophy of the inherent tragedy of human existence can be seen. I want to show some specific examples of this, before turning to a systematic exposition.

Take for example *Stanzas* ('When I stroll along the noisy streets'). At first sight – and this it seems is the prevailing view – Pushkin is expressing, as always in beautiful verse, the commonplace idea that we are all mortal. But the true poet never expresses ideas in the abstract, there is always a vivid conception of reality. In *Stanzas* there appears a tense, distinct awareness of the fatal destiny of human life. It never occurred to Tolstoy's Ivan Ilich before his fatal illness that the syllogism he learnt at school – 'All men are mortal; Caius is a man; therefore, Caius is mortal' – had any vital or serious application as far as he himself was concerned. Is not all our everyday life based on the fact that we forget the reality of death? How often are we really conscious that we too, together with the multitude of all those we meet, will be lying dead under the ground at the most in a few decades' time? How often do we base our own lives and our relationships with others on this indisputable truth? The Church prays for the gift of an 'awareness of mortality' as a blessing which is essential for the enrichment of our spiritual consciousness. *It is precisely such an awareness of mortality which Pushkin is expressing here.* He sees all human existence overclouded by the black wings of inevitable death. If this in itself is not yet a religious conception of life, it is at least a precise and clear *metaphysical awareness* which is not present in the majority of people. As a result of this we have a picture of existence overhung by something which is not of this earth, something which can be both sad and yet suffused with light.

Or take the elegy 'The faded joy of mad years'. Its first four lines contain an entire philosophy of life – some original variant, as it were, on Schopenhauer's philosophy of pessimism. For Schopenhauer, as we know, happiness is simply a brief moment of satisfied desire, whereas it is suffering which is life's constant companion, for at the very heart of existence lie will, desires and aspirations, and that posits a state of dissatisfaction. Taken on its own, such a theory is a gross oversimplification and therefore a distortion of what actually occurs in the life of the heart. Pushkin, on the other hand, shows us a profound psychological experience. Sensual pleasures seem to evaporate, leaving behind a bitter sediment; but sorrow, arising from the recognition that earthly reality is inadequate to satisfy our souls, grows ever stronger, and is accompanied by man's spiritual enrichment. For this reason the only possible dignified and practicable aim of life is 'to live and to suffer'; and in the midst of this, 'midst grief, worry and anxiety', men can hope to be consoled by spiritual joys.

And finally, there is the lyric *Three Springs,* an exceptional pearl even for Pushkin, and one of the saddest poems in all literature. Life is a sorrowful desert; the people who pass through it are doomed to an unquenchable thirst. In this desert they come across three springs – but only as some kind of exception: the spring of carefree, youthful gaiety, the spring of poetic inspiration and the 'cold spring of oblivion' which 'more sweetly than anything else, quenches the fever of the heart'. (As always with Pushkin you can find a repetition of this idea. In the description of Tartarus in *Proserpina* 'slow Lethe's sleeping banks' are mentioned, a place where there is 'oblivion and unending delight'). The prerequisite for bliss is oblivion from earthly experiences, a renunciation of them.

This 'pessimistic philosophy' of Pushkin can be encapsulated in two basic propositions. The first says that the human spirit, in its cherished dreams and hopes, is alone in the objective world of reality. This objective world is first and foremost 'indifferent nature'. Human life ends in death, 'in the coffin'; both the beauty and the suffering of your beloved will disappear, but 'indifferent nature' will continue to radiate with 'everlasting beauty'. The tumbledown house where Parasha lived, poor Evgenii's 'dream' in *The Bronze Horseman,* has vanished under the evil onslaught of the flood, and Evgenii realises that 'our whole life is nothing but an empty dream, a cruel joke which fate plays upon the earth'; and yet by the next morning there are no longer any 'traces of yesterday's disaster; the evil has already been covered in crimson; everything is as it was before'. Pushkin's awareness of the 'indifference' of nature, the contrast between its existence and the hopes of the human heart, has an especial poignancy during the season of rebirth, spring, whose appearance is marked for him by sadness. As always, Pushkin has an objective explanation or even a whole series of explanations for this feeling, explanations which all nonetheless culminate in the same thought: 'With troubled minds we view nature's rebirth and contrast it with our inevitable fading' *(Evgenii Onegin,* Chapter 7). The 'sad season' of autumn, on the other hand, with its 'departing beauty', enraptures him, suggesting the fragile beauty of a young girl dying without a murmur.

But another part of this objective world and its indifference towards the human personality is formed by the crowd, the mass of the people and its way of life. In the same passage from *The Bronze Horseman* the insensibility of the forces of nature overlaps with the 'cold indifference' of the ordinary people walking along streets which have just experienced the flood's tragic onslaught. Pushkin's scorn and revulsion for 'the crowd', 'the rabble', 'the human herd' (it goes without saying of course that these are not social categories, but simply the community of human beings, the society of which he himself was a member) such feelings are so well known that there is no need to dwell on this point. His entire life and work are based on the acute awareness of the deep gulf dividing the inner spiritual life of man from the human community *en masse* and its society.

This is the first postulate in Pushkin's philosophy of 'pessimism' – the isolation of the deep recesses of the human spirit from the world. The second postulate stems from the first: the human spirit is vulnerable to attack from within itself as well – attack by irrational, chaotic and rebellious passions springing from man's heart and leading it on to destruction. This theme in Pushkin's spiritual life and work is widely known, especially since Merezhkovsky (in *Eternal Companions*) and afterwards Gershenzon (in *The Wisdom of Pushkin*) drew attention to it (although, in seeing it as an ideal, they both distorted its significance). The word 'rebellious' is one of the words most frequently used by Pushkin. The main strength of Pushkin's dramatic gift lies in his acute perception of the dark world of human passions, of their seductive and destructive nature. Passions, in their confrontation with implacable reality, lead to insanity; this is one of Pushkin's favourite themes (Maria in *Poltava*, Hermann in *The Queen of Spades*, Evgenii in *The Bronze Horseman*; Tatyana's 'prophetic dream' touches on the same theme.

Pushkin himself wrote a lyrical confession on the seductiveness of insanity ('God grant that I not lose my mind'):

I would sing in fiery frenzy,
And lose myself in a mist
Of wondrous, shapeless dreams . . .
And I would be strong and free.

Even better known is the lyric illustrating the demonic fascination the human soul feels for the idea of annihilation:

> There is an exaltation in battle,
> Or on the lip of an abyss...
> Everything that threatens disaster
> Contains inexpressible delight
> For mortal hearts...

And there are these lines on Tatyana:

> ...In terror itself
> She found a secret joy:
> For nature has made us
> Creatures of paradox.

The autobiographical significance of this theme has been confirmed by a whole mass of evidence and by Pushkin's own life. But this fascination with death is merely the high point in a whole range of themes showing the fundamentally seductive nature of dark, elemental, anarchic passions: 'How intoxicating is the language of mad, rebellious passion...' 'The wind, an eagle, a girl's heart know no laws... Be proud, poet, for such are you'.

Pushkin shows his unique mastery in describing these dark, destructive passions of the human heart. Dostoevsky with his tremendous revelations in this field was following a path already marked out by Pushkin. Smirnova tells us of Pushkin's view of the 'attraction of evil':

> This attraction would be inexplicable, if evil were not made to look beautiful and pleasant to the beholder. I believe all that the Bible has to say about Satan. There is a great philosophical truth to be found in the lines on the fallen spirit, who is beautiful and yet treacherous.

By depriving man of his stability and spiritual equilibrium, these dark, elemental passions are in themselves sufficient to lure him to destruction. Pushkin speaks of the 'insanely destructive nature of freedom'. 'And everywhere there are fatal passions, and there is no defence against the fates'. But there is yet another manifestation of the inherently tragic nature of the sinful human heart which especially interests Pushkin: the torments of remorse.

This is another aspect of Pushkin's work, it seems, which has not received the attention it deserves. Pushkin is unrivalled in Russian literature in his depiction of remorse and regret. It may seem strange, but Dostoevsky, who was able to depict brilliantly the *instinctive* reaction of the subconscious depths of the human soul to crime, nowhere describes the torments of conscience, a consciously moral remorse. On the other hand Pushkin's lyric 'When, for mortal man, day's clamour has ceased', his description of the remorse of Boris Godunov and Mazeppa, of Onegin's qualms of conscience after Lensky's murder – these are all classical instances in their artistic force and expressiveness and stand on a level with *Macbeth*.

Remorse is depicted most directly in its sense of agonising hopelessness; this is precisely why it is tragic. 'Reading with revulsion the pages of my life ...'; 'I would gladly run, but where can I go ... oh, horror! Pitiable is he, whose conscience is not clear'; 'He who has felt has been disturbed by the phantom of his irrevocable past ... by the serpent of memories: he is beset by remorse'. But Pushkin also knows that fruitless regret over the irreparable past can, if taken to its limit, be transformed into *repentance,* a sense of moral renewal and enlightenment.

'Laden with memories, full of sweet nostalgia', he returns, now a mature man, to the refuge of his blessed youth, the gardens of Tsarskoe selo.

> Thus the Prodigal Son, that foolish spendthrift,
> Having drunk to the last drop the cup of remorse,
> And seeing at last his native hearth,
> Bowed down his head and bitterly wept.

The culmination of this moral process is spiritual renewal.

> So from my tormented soul
> The sins fall away,
> And are replaced by visions,
> Of those early, chaste days.

But here we have reached the turning point in our discussion. Despite the tremendous significance of the tragic view in Pushkin's work, an approach to Pushkin based on this alone would give a distorted picture. With a clear and profound vision and knowledge of the tragedy inherent in human existence,

Pushkin is aware also that it possesses a depth of spirituality which goes beyond tragedy and whose essential quality is one of peace and a kind of lucent joy. He finds it in solitude, in peaceful contemplation and in creative activity. Together with words such as 'rebellious', 'languour', 'torment' and 'passion' we find 'solitude', 'endearment', 'silence', 'thought', 'pure', 'lucent' and 'clear', forming part of the basic Pushkinian lexicon. 'Far from the crowd the lyric muse sounds more sweetly, creative dreams appear more vividly'. 'In this majestic solitude ... my creative thoughts achieve a spiritual depth'; 'My heart is quiet once more. In solitude my wayward genius has found the desire for quiet work and contemplation'. He knows the 'beauty of lucent thoughts'. Of his past youth he holds dear only those 'moments of tenderness, of young hopes and inner peace', the 'fervour and sweet bliss of inspiration'. 'I knew both work and inspiration and sweet was the solitary fever of ardent thoughts'. 'Once again, delight, I feel your presence; my emotions are calm, my mind is clear'.

The desire for solitary contemplation and its enjoyment runs throughout Pushkin's life and literature, symbolised to a large extent in his cult of the *'penates'* (or *'lares'*).

Here too we see a philosophical grounding to Pushkin's spiritual mood. It can be found in his well known 'hymn' to the *penates* ('Yet one more important and exalted song'). In this Pushkin achieves the depths of mystical self-awareness. The fact that he clothes his thoughts in one of his favourite forms – the classical cult of the *penates* – is quite immaterial. As can be seen from the text of the poem, this is merely an undefined conventional symbol for the 'mysterious forces' with which the spirit of the poet comes into contact in the quiet of solitude.

Pushkin has found clear, precise words here to express a fundamental mystical experience, something which has been expressed, in various forms, by many mystics: in the words of St. Francis of Sales 'something supernatural', a 'spark' of divine light, appears to those wrapped in peaceful spiritual contemplation, unaware of the excitement and impressions of the external world.

It is this which distinctly marks the dividing line between the furthest reaches of the human spirit and the purely subjective – or, to use Nietzsche's words, 'human, all-too human' – emotional existence. The philosophical and religious distinction between 'spirit' and 'soul' becomes clear only when based upon such an awareness. In the emotional life of most people this distinction is generally felt only dimly, and both ideas are indistinguishably fused, merging into each other. As we shall see very shortly, in Pushkin, too, spiritual depth can be reflected in the life of the soul and radiates through it. Yet nevertheless for Pushkin there is a very sharp distinction between them. This was noted by many of his contemporaries. Pushkin himself was aware of this ambivalence within himself and pointed to the alternation of the two basically different spiritual conditions: 'Love has passed, my muse has appeared' and *The Poet* (1827). But equally characteristic was the way in which he incorporated within himself both these elements simultaneously. From this springs a fundamental duality in his life: a less than perfect moral sense together with an extraordinary inner power of insight and depth. During his youth, in his St. Petersburg and Kishinyov periods, he combined riotous revelry and the torments of impassioned love and jealousy with an almost hermit-like attitude of contemplation and moral reflection, the fruits of which can be seen, for example, in *The Village* and in *To Chaadaev* ('In a land, where I forgot the anxieties of past years', 'My heart is quiet once more', etc. Even the last days of his life, just before the duel, are permeated with the same ambivalence. Seething with a sense of wounded pride, he could write an outraged and insulting letter to Baron von Heckeren (founded merely on an unproven and, as we know now, unjustified suspicion), of the duel itself he could say things like 'the bloodier, the better' – and yet at the same time, Pletnyov tells us that 'he was gripped by a profoundly religious mood. He would speak about the destiny of Providence and exalt even above this man's ability to show love for all his fellows.'

Pushkin never achieved what less talented and passionate people sometimes manage to do: to spread the soothing wings of his spirit over his moral existence, to heal himself of his emotional rebelliousness (this has been pointed out, rather too severely, by V. Solovyov). Tyutchev expressed it very aptly: 'he was the living organ of the gods, but with black, hot blood in his veins.' It was only on his death-bed that he achieved final and complete moral purification and enlightenment.

Of course we are not interested here in evaluating Pushkin from a moral point of view – this is hardly relevant anyway, particularly in respect of a genius living such an intensely spiritual existence. We simply think it important to bring to light the fact of Pushkin's hidden spiritual depths.

The peace, harmony, inexpressible felicity and religious feeling of Pushkin's inner spiritual world endow him, by virtue of contrast, with the ability to recognise with a particular clarity and intensity both the tragic nature and the vanity and insignificance of human existence. This is on the one hand. On the other, this tragic awareness itself is coloured in light tones. It is precisely because of the religious nature of this inner spiritual world – an awareness, that is, of its ontological significance – that Pushkin is able to apprehend the religious and sacred significance of all creative activity, of all phenomena. The poetical apprehension of beauty – the beauty of a woman and the beauty of nature – becomes for him a simultaneously consoling and enlightening religious experience. Pushkin's rebellious eroticism – one of the main sources of his tragic apprehension of life – tends to spill over into religious eroticism. He is unable to 'look at beauty without profound emotion'; perfect feminine beauty is for him an expression of something standing 'higher than the world and passions', and in its contemplation he 'stands in reverent awe before the shrine of beauty'. His erotic sensibility is not confined within the limits of this earthly world; he implores his dead loved-one to return to listen once more to his profession of love for her, or looks forward beyond the grave to the promised kiss. The erotic religious sensibility of the Middle Ages is familiar to him *(The Poor Knight)*. The same applies to his apprehension of nature. In the sorrowful sound of the sea 'he hears a melancholy murmur, remote sounds, an abyss of voices'; he compares the sea to the spirit of Byron, who was 'as mighty, profound and sorrowful as you, and just as indomitable'. But in the same sea he can hear the 'deep and eternal chorus of the waves, singing a hymn of praise to the father of the universe'. The Caucasus can mean the revelation of nature's elemental forces *(The Caucasus);* and at the same time it can awaken in him religious feelings *(The Monastery on Mt. Kazbek)*. But the chief result of this inner spiritual existence and its reconciling 'immortal emotions' is the feeling of love for people in general, arising from the direct religious apprehension of the significance and sacredness of every human being, even the most worthless – the sense of the innate value of the human personality. This 'ability to show love for all one's fellows', an ability which, as Pletnyov has said, he placed higher than anything else in man, was something inherent in him to an unusual extent. This is evident from his letters, and it can be seen in his unfailing loyalty and kindness towards his school-friends. A whole host of witnesses testify to this. 'Pushkin's nature', said Vyazemsky, 'was one which was more inclined to show sympathy than revulsion; he possessed more love than anger'. Pushkin used to say: 'I find everyone interesting, from the humblest peasant to the Tsar'. (Smirnova's reminiscences according to Polansky). Pushkin used to say: 'Only fools and children are malicious' (Reminiscences of Mme. A.P. Kern). His review of Radishchev's book finishes with the words: 'Abuse is unconvincing; and where there is no love, there is no truth'. Characteristically tolerant and understanding is his attitude to a totally alien type of Muscovite – the followers of Schelling, of German metaphysical philosophy, something he hated. 'What can you do?' he would ask, to justify his relationship with them, – 'They're just a bunch of warm-hearted, obstinate chaps; the priest has his parishioners, the devil his'. Pushkin's direct joy of life is here transformed, through the spiritual strength emanating from the depths of his personality, into a conscious and morally enlightened attitude towards life. Because of this it is of course possible to forgive him all the shortcomings of his passionate and rebellious nature.

All this can be seen in Pushkin's work, in his typically loving attitude towards almost all his characters. The cold, malicious irony and the bitter satire, based on a sense of disgust, which we find in Gogol and frequently in Dostoevsky, is quite alien to him. Pushkin's irony is either sad, or good-naturedly joking, but always tolerant. The reader is made, if not to love, then at least sympathetically to understand almost all his heroes, even the wild and villainous Pugachov or the dark and criminally-minded Hermann. Exceptions – the chief one being Mazeppa – are extraordinary rare. This explains why he, almost alone in Russian literature, is able, artistically and truthfully and without the least idealisation, to depict simple and humble people, as they devotedly carry out their tasks.

Most interesting of all, however, is the reflection of this spiritual attitude in Pushkin's tragic sensibility. Unlike Lermontov or Dostoevsky, there is absolutely no sense of hardness, bitterness or outraged rebellion in him. Pushkin's tragic awareness is, on the contrary, a rueful *resignation* – a sadness, tempered by a sense of reconciliation. This is naturally not yet a genuine Christian submissiveness, but it is a step towards it. This mood of pure resignation comes across in one of his letters to Vyazemsky: 'Don't be angry with fate, for it doesn't know what it is doing. Imagine it as some huge monkey, which has been given complete freedom. Who will chain it up? Neither you, nor I, nor anyone else. There is nothing to be done; so there is nothing to be said'. This same resignation takes on a more comforting form in the good-humoured, wise and simple words of the well-known poem:

> If life has deceived you,
> Be neither angry nor sad;
> On a day of sorrow, resign yourself,
> A day of joy will surely come.
> The heart lives in the future
> For the present is depressing.
> All is transitory and will pass,
> And what has passed will seem sweet.

But the spiritual peace which Pushkin's tragic sensibility finds does not stop at a resignation based on a submissive acceptance of life's inevitable sorrows. Resignation is merely the first step on the road to genuine inner enlightenment. I have shown above how, in Pushkin, the sense of tragic remorse at what is irreparable culminates in the soul's spiritual enlightenment. His tragic apprehension of life undergoes an analogous spiritual process. If, as we have seen, nature's eternally self-renewing beauty stands in tormenting contrast to the transitoriness and sense of death which pervade human life, to man's everlastingly lost youth and the shattered dreams of his heart, then, on the other hand, the beauty of indifferent nature, just like the playing of 'youth at the entrance to the grave', is invoked as a kind of sorrowful consolation in the thought of death's inevitability. Bitter reflection is resolved in a harmonic minor chord. It is in this that the meaning and charm of the concluding scene of *Onegin* lies; Tatyana rejects Onegin's belated love, not out of some cold, proud and puritanical motive, but because she realises that the only way to achieve peace and salvation for her shattered heart is through self-denial and the fulfilment of her duty. This process of enlightenment can also be seen in Pushkin's erotic lyrics. Rebellious eroticism not only takes on a religious colouring, but merges with feelings of altruistic tenderness. While admiring a girl's beauty with voluptuous desire the poet blesses her and wishes her 'all life's joys, everything – even the happiness of her chosen one, the sweet girl's future spouse'.

This feeling is expressed most movingly when he describes the spiritual transformation of tormented and unrequited love into self-transcending tenderness:

I loved you so sincerely and so tenderly,
As, God grant, you will be loved by another.

This poem is perhaps one of the most morally exalted lyrics in world literature. Such a, for Pushkin, fundamental enlightening and transforming process is expressed in general symbolic form in the poem 'The passing storm's final cloud'. For this symbolic description of calm and enlightenment there is a corresponding formula when he describes the same basic idea in the life of the spirit, a formula which is astonishing in its concise expressiveness; in an early draft of one of his poems Pushkin expresses the desire that his heart be always '*pure, sorrowful and at peace*'. And finally this process of enlightenment culminates in the loving acceptance of all the tragedy inherent in life:

> All is good...
> Blessed is the day of cares,
> Blessed – the approach of darkness.

At first sight it might appear that this mood of resignation which is so forcefully expressed in Pushkin's poetry, and even this process of enlightenment, which culminates in the expression of tender reconciliation with everything, presuppose a passive acceptance of life's evil and inherent tragedy. But this is a false view. Pushkin was too passionately alive and possessed too active a spiritual nature for a purely passive attitude to become his ideal. What is true is simply that the total rebelliousness and the outraged rejection of the world of an Ivan Karamazov is quite alien to him. He has sufficient wisdom to see quite clearly the inevitability and omnipotence of what he himself in an observation defines as 'life's eternal contradictions'. But he also understands, both aesthetically and morally, that every tragedy must have its resolution and denouement and is meaningful only in such a perspective. He never revels in the idea of tragedy and never drowns in it passively. The sense of tragedy has been given to the human spirit so that it can be overcome – in one way or another. And Pushkin reacts to it extremely positively. When he is unable to master the passion raging within him and leading him on to a position of tragic hopelessness, he consciously seeks death – for this, after all, is also a way out. All witnesses agree scenes with her faithful hound and so on are none of them in the style of the popular fairy-tale which is far less rich in lyrical and other details.

The originality of Pushkin's fairy-tales in verse can be seen most clearly if they are compared with their popular sources. What does Pushkin bring into *The Tale of Tsar Saltan?* From him come the entire love story of Prince Gvidon and the Swan-Princess, Gvidon's 'melancholy anguish' concerning his father, and the scene of the mother's blessing – that is to say the tale's lyrical content. In *The Tale of the Dead Princess* the theme of Prince Elisei belongs entirely to Pushkin. Also his is the theme of the knights' matchmaking which demonstrates the princess's loyalty to her betrothed: 'But I am given for ever to another . . .'. (This is a theme which is sung). In the version related by Pushkin's nurse both the description of the princess's domestic skills and the scenes with the hound were missing. And all this comprises the heart of the tale. Into *The Tale of the Fisherman and the Fish* Pushkin introduces the themes of the old woman's ingratitude, her cruel treatment of her servants and her mockery of the old man. In *The Tale of the Golden Cockerel* the picture of Dadon's sleepy kingdom, the death of his sons and the catastrophic denouement were all Pushkin's own inventions. As far as plots were concerned, only *The Tale of the Priest and his Workman Balda* remains within the bounds drawn by his nurse's tales. Pushkin took the general outlines of the fairy-tale themes but combined them and elaborated them in his own fashion. Hence his fairy-tales cannot possibly be regarded as imitations. The legend of Don Juan was treated by Tirso de Molina, by Moliere, by Pushkin, and by Aleksei Tolstoy, but each of these works with the same theme is completely independent and bears the imprint of the personality of its author and the age in which it was written. Shakespeare did not generally think up his own plots: he took them from the historical chronicles and various stories or recast the plays of his predecessors. Goethe recast the legend of Faust. Can one on that basis possibly regard Shakespeare's dramas or Goethe's *Faust* as imitations?

Critics were right when they commented on the absence from Pushkin of that 'ingenuousness' which is typical of popular fairy-tales. Indeed, Pushkin's fairy-tales are far from ingenuous. Belinsky was right when he wrote of the impossibility and the pointlessness of 'recasting' and 'embellishing' fairy-tales, but he was mistaken when he took Pushkin's fairy-tales for 'recastings' and 'embellishments'. Pushkin was not making fun of the popular narrators of fairy-tales, was not dressing up in their costumes or undergoing a transformation. In his fairy-tales in verse he remained himself and his distinctive profile is clearly visible in them. Using Belinsky's terminology, Pushkin expressed in them 'that fundamental, impersonal and indefinable substantial element, which is usually represented by the mass of the people' (i.e. the unformulated national principle) and at the same time 'the formulated significance of this substantial element' which was developed 'in the life of the most educated strata of the nation' (i.e. the conscious, intellectual national principle). Here lies the basic distinction between Pushkin's fairy-tales in verse and the 'neutral' and 'impersonal' tales of his imitators which lack any individual physiognomy.

Pushkin's fairy-tales in verse found no direct continuation in Russian literature (unless one counts a few imitations appearing in the 1830's, among which only Ershov's *The Little Hunchbacked Horse* is of interest), but they provided models for the use of folk material and pointed to fresh literary resources, thereby contributing to the realist movement. A great part was played in this by Pushkin's enrichment of the literary language, a feature which was noted as early as 1845 by M.A. Maksimovich who wrote about Pushkin's fairy-tales:

> They are important in the history of our poetry because they were a true and timely pointer towards the popular style and colour which were destined to refresh the predominant time-worn mode of literary expression.

Without Pushkin's fairy-tales Lermontov could hardly have created his *Song of the Merchant Kalashnikov* with its contrasting of the rebel individualist, Kiribeevich, that sixteenth-century Pechorin, with the defender of the people's fundamental traditions, Stepan Kalashnikov. It is a poem with a highly individual idea arrayed in the costume of popular historical songs which were organically necessary to express the author's design.

It is not a question simply of language, however, but rather of the realist method of dealing with popular material. The popular character of Pushkin's fairy-tales in verse is not that of *Ruslan and Lyudmila:* it is more realistic. In the fairy-tales no place could have been found for such anachronisms and abstractions as Khan Ratmir's sentimental idyll or Ruslan's melancholy reflections on the battlefield. In the fairy-tales everything stands on firmly realistic soil and everything is in harmony with popular customs, notions and attitudes. Through the fantastic web of events looms an outline of various concrete features of old Muscovy, towards which all the historical *realia* tend. The lyricism, which occupies a primary position here and dominates the story-line (especially in the two purely lyrical fairy-tales), recalls folk-songs: longing for the parental home, choosing a bride, separation from the beloved, loyalty to a betrothed, etc. The behaviour of the heroes is in accordance with genuine folk customs and the true Russian character. Even in King Dadon we see a Russian who is sharply distinguished from the representatives of another, non-Russian world, the Arabian astrologer and the exotic Queen of Shemakha. Without concealing and glossing over the dark sides of patriarchal traditions, Pushkin at the same time picked out and underlined their positive aspect, namely their sound moral bases.

In Pushkin's hands fairy-tale fantasies acquired realistic outlines. The realism of Pushkin's fairy-tales in verse lies first and foremost in his deep understanding of the spirit of the people; and from this stem his realistic literary devices, the richness of concrete detail (the decorations in the knights' tower-chamber, and so on), the plastic fullness and typicality of his images, etc. The realistic manner is reflected also in the language, which is precise, sparing and articulate: words with a concrete and tangible meaning predominate, the syntax is simple and clear, and metaphorical elements are almost completely absent.

BLAGOI

PUSHKIN'S LAUGHTER

D.D. Blagoi (b.1893) is one of the Soviet Union's foremost literary critics. He started his literary career in 1917 with a critical appraisal of the poetry of Tyutchev, and since then he has published many works on numerous subjects and authors, from large-scale studies on the development of Russian literature and on problems of literary criticism, to small monographs on individual poets. He is best known, however, as a leading specialist on the life and work of Pushkin: his publications include *The Sociology of Pushkin's Work* (1929), *Pushkin's Creative Development* (1950) and *The Mastery of Puskin* (1955). Blagoi's works on Pushkin are characterised by his desire to view the writer in a contemporary light. This essay, *Pushkin's Laughter*, which first appeared in 1968, analyses the role played by parody and the 'light-hearted' in Pushkin's work, and sees these elements not just as frivolous devices but as of crucial significance in the poet's literary development.

'From early childhood our memories preserve a happy name – Pushkin' – this is how Alexander Blok began his speech, still remembered by many, in the Petrograd House of Literature on the occasion of the 84th anniversary of Pushkin's death. 'This name, its very sound', Blok continues, 'fills many days of our lives. The names of emperors, generals, inventors of weapons of slaughter, torturers and martyrs are forbidding. But next to them stands this light and elegant name – Pushkin. Pushkin managed to bear his creative burden very lightly and happily even though the poet's role is neither light nor happy, but tragic . . .' And this is how Blok ended his speech: 'I should like, simply for amusement, to proclaim three simple truths: There are no particular arts. One should not give the name of art to that which is really something else. In order to create works of art, one must have the ability to do so. To these happy truths of common sense, which we all sin against, we may swear by the happy name of Pushkin.'

As we can see, Blok's entire speech is framed within a view of Pushkin as a happy, light-hearted genius. But more than this: Blok held this view, formed in 'early childhood', right up to the end of his life (the speech was written in February 1921, and he died in August of the same year).

The claim that Pushkin 'managed to bear his creative burden very lightly and happily' is not wholly correct. Pushkin's life and creative work were by no means easy, but rather, using Blok's own expression, deeply tragic. Pushkin had his moments of despair, his outbursts of rage and many long hours of agonising, sombre melancholy. 'Boredom' and 'Russian spleen' – the conditions of contemporary life – possessed not merely Onegin but very often his creator as well. 'I am ... feeling anxious and melancholic (what an awful word!)', he wrote to Delvig on 4 November 1830. And in order to feel just how tragically difficult Pushkin found the process of artistic creation – and the more he wrote the more difficult it became – we need only read his poem *To the Poet* (1830). A little earlier, replying to Ksenofont Polevoi's perfectly correct observation that,'You meet at times in his works a sense of real happiness, something you will not find in any other poet', Pushkin said that the basis of his character was sad and melancholic, and if he did sometimes feel happy, such a feeling was very rare and it never lasted for long. Such feelings of melancholy and sorrow found their reflection in the multicoloured spectrum of Pushkin's creative process.

But according to the unanimous view of his contemporaries Pushkin really did possess a unique laugh: light, happy and with the infectious simplicity of a child. 'He would utter some biting comment, and then suddenly burst into peals of good-natured, artless laughter, revealing two rows of white teeth, like an Arab's' *(Reminiscences of V.A. Sollogub);* or there were these lines on Pushkin written by V.G. Benediktov in his poem *Reminiscence:*

> Onegin's impassioned creator,
> With his dark curls and fiery gaze,
> Would herald his approach
> With gay, resounding laughter.

And this was a characteristic not simply of Pushkin the man.

'The light and happy aspects' which, in our conception of the poet, have largely been overshadowed by the exceptionally serious and at times deeply tragic sides of the work of the founder of Russian literature, constitute one of the inalienable features and characteristics of Pushkin.

Pushkin put an extraordinarily high value on the presence in a writer of 'gaiety, this priceless quality, perhaps the rarest of gifts' (review of Zagoskin's comedy *The Dissatisfied,* early 1836). It was precisely his 'light-hearted shrewdness of wit, humour and lively style', a typically Russian feature in Pushkin's view, which made Krylov for him 'a truly Russian poet'. It was precisely the 'priceless quality' of gaiety which so delighted Pushkin in Gogol's first collection of stories: 'Have just read *Evenings near Dikanka.* They astonished me. Here is true gaiety, sincere, unforced, without affectation or primness', a 'gaiety' of which he once again, as in Krylov's fables, especially emphasised the democratic, popular qualities: 'I have heard that when the publisher entered the printing-house where the *Evenings* were being printed, the type-setters were choking with laughter.' 'Molière and Fielding', Pushkin adds, 'would doubtless have been glad to make the type-setters of their books laugh.' 'I congratulate the public on a truly exhilarating book,' wrote Pushkin on Gogol's first large-scale publishing venture. He repeated the same words in his review of the second edition of the *Evenings* with their 'light-hearted but subtle gaiety': 'How astonished we are at a Russian book which has made us laugh – we who have not laughed since Fonvizin's day'.

And our national poet, Pushkin, was generously endowed with just such a 'priceless quality' – 'true gaiety'. It appeared quite clearly in *Ruslan and Lyudmila* and emerged with full force in *Evgenii Onegin,* in its 'multi-coloured synthesis of half-humourous, half-sad' chapters in which every facet of the 'all-embracing' genius of Pushkin sparkles with an iridescent, diamond-like brilliance. Pushkin himself underlined the 'imprint of gaiety' and the 'light-hearted portrayal of human behaviour' in the foreword to the first chapter of his novel in verse. And in his polemics with A. Bestuzhev and Ryleev, who reacted to the first chapter of *Onegin* with undisguised disapproval, calling on the author to return to 'high poetry', to the genre of the long romantic poem, he had to defend hotly his right to such 'humour' and 'gaiety'. 'Bestuzhev is writing to me a great deal about *Onegin;* tell him that he is wrong: does he really wish to rid poetry of everything that is light and happy?' (Incidentally, was it from here that Blok took the words 'light' and 'happy' in his definition of Pushkin?) 'What has become of comedy and satire?' Pushkin continued. 'To be consistent we could have to get rid of *Orlando Furioso, Hudibras, La Pucelle* ... the best part of *Psyche,* La Fontaine's tales, Krylov's fables etc., etc., etc ..... This is a little harsh'. (Letter to Ryleev 25 January 1825. From Ryleev's reply of 12 February, 1825 it is clear that, although he calls the first chapter of Onegin 'wonderful', he shares A. Bestuzhev's basic position).

And, indeed, although in the chapters written after the tragic denouement of the Decembrist revolt this 'light and happy' facet became ever more shrouded in the mist of sadness, it shone in *Onegin* with such dazzling brilliance that at times it obscured everything else. This could be seen most sharply in the articles on Pushkin by N.I. Nadezhdin, a very significant critic for his time, who is viewed with some justification as the immediate precursor of Belinsky. In rightly seeing *Evgenii Onegin* as a work in which the most characteristic features of Pushkin's talent stood out in particular relief, he used just this point of view to declare all Pushkin's poetry *'simply a parody'* (the italics here and below are Nadezhdin's own). 'Pushkin's muse', he declared, 'is a mischievous young girl, who does not care tuppence for the world. Her element is to mock at everything, good and bad ... not out of spite or scorn, but simply out of the desire to poke fun. It is this which shapes in a particular way Pushkin's poetic process and clearly distinguishes it from *Byronic* misanthropy or the humour of Jean-Paul Richter ... There is nothing that can be done about it ... what is true, is true ... A master can mock and ridicule ... provided, of course, he has a sense of honour and proportion. And if one can be great in small matters, then it is perfectly possible to call Pushkin a genius – *at caricature!*' He makes roughly the same point in his article on Chapter 7 of *Evgenii Onegin.*

To see in Pushkin's poetry merely the 'elegance of a caricaturist', 'amusing prattle', the masterly ability to 'turn nature inside-out' and, as a result, to view him simply as a 'genius of caricature', a 'master of parody' is to misunderstand it completely. (Most of Nadezhdin's articles on Pushkin are an example of such a crude misinterpretation). But to reject, in the manner of A. Bestuzhev and Ryleev, the 'light' and 'happy' element in Pushkin's work or not to pay it the attention it deserves, means also to fail to understand the *whole* Pushkin, to ignore and to fail to appreciate one of the most characteristic traits of his genius, without which Pushkin would not be what he is.

The device of parody, in particular, plays a very large part in Pushkin's work and has a very important significance for his development as a realistic poet; it is this device, for the most part, which I shall be examining in this short study.

From early childhood Pushkin breathed the air of the Russian spirit of Voltaire, the reflected culture of the French eighteenth-century salons. He grew up in the atmosphere of witticism, pun, epigram and parody which prevailed in his parents' house and in the literary and semi-literary circles of Moscow generally. It is characteristic that, apart from some improvised plays in the spirit of Molière, the first extant literary ventures of the nine- and ten-year old Pushkin (written in French) took the form of an epigrammatic and 'heroic-comic' adaptation of Voltaire's *Henriade*. (Incidentally, the work which apparently proved to be Pushkin's last literary creation – an article, written for *The Contemporary* – was also a parody on Voltaire). A similar atmosphere coloured the activities of the first literary association in which Pushkin, albeit vicariously, played such an active role, *Arzamas,* with its parody of ritual, its humorous 'minutes', the mock 'birchings' of one of its members, the poet's good-natured but slow-witted uncle, Vasilii Lvovich. Epigrams and parodies against the literary opponents of *Arzamas* poured from Pushkin's pen while he was still at the Lycée and steeped in such works as *La Pucelle* and its Russian counterpart, Radishchev's *Bova,* Vasilii Maikov's heroic-comic poem *Elisei, or Bacchus Enraged,* Bogdanovich's parody *Psyche,* Krylov's mock tragedy in manuscript *Prince Trumpf* and the notorious I.S. Barkov's indecent parodies on the *Bold Horseman of Ardent Pegasus* . . .

The young Pushkin parodies not just the opponents of *Arzamas,* 'the friends of unenlightenment', 'the tattlers', but also writers who were at that time extremely close to him: his immediate predecessors and even his literary mentors – Derzhavin, some of Batyushkov (in *Shades of Fonvizin*) and especially Zhukovsky.

But Pushkin does not confine himself to his Russian predecessors. Beginning with *Evgenii Onegin,* he levels his parody against those very writers whom he himself considers to be most important, at times, even, against the greatest geniuses of world literature, writers such as Homer, Dante, Shakespeare, Voltaire, Byron, Goethe and Sir Walter Scott.

'I do not find it funny when some accursed charlatan

dishonours Alighieri with a parody'... These indignant words have achieved practically proverbial status. But Pushkin has put them into the mouth of the sullen, withdrawn, arrogant and covetous Salieri, a man who despises people and hates life, who dissects art like a corpse, and who never laughs (Can you even imagine him laughing gaily and freely like Mozart?). Far closer to Pushkin of course is the noble genius of Mozart, who rejoices that his music should have reached the simple people and who 'roars with laughter' when he sees the blind man at the inn scratching out his arias on a broken violin.

Nor did Pushkin himself find it funny when he came across works of authors who, he considered, did not show sufficient respect by 'dishonouring' a great writer. He reacted with great indignation to the portrayals of John Milton by Victor Hugo in his tragedy *Cromwell* and by Alfred de Vigny in his historical novel *Cinq Mars*. 'Milton is portrayed as a pathetic fool, and as an insignificant windbag by a man who, in dishonouring this great figure, probably did not know what he was doing', writes Pushkin, analysing Hugo's tragedy.

> No, M. Hugo, John Milton, the friend and champion of Cromwell, the stern fanatic, the austere creator of *Eikonoklastes* and *Defensio Populi* was not like this at all! The man who wrote that marvellous prophetic sonnet in honour of Cromwell, 'Cromwell, our chief of men...' would not have spoken in this way. The man who, *in evil times, the victim of evil tongues,* beset by poverty, persecution and blindness, preserved his inflexibility of will and dictated *Paradise Lost,* could never have been the laughing-stock of the dissolute Rochester or the court jesters. *(On Milton and Chateaubriand's Translation of Paradise Lost).*

Salieri's comment is clearly overshadowed by the anger and devastating force of these words.

It can hardly be said that Victor Hugo deliberately parodied the figure of Milton. But he portrayed him in such a way that what emerges is a 'meaningless parody', 'dishonouring a great figure'. Pushkin's parodies of 'great figures', for all their deliberate nature, contain nothing which can be called 'dishonouring' or 'discrediting'.

In the foreword which Pushkin intended to include in the chapter on Onegin's journey (as a separate publication before the novel as a whole appeared) he wrote: 'I was going to destroy the eighth chapter altogether. The thought that this light-hearted parody might be taken as a sign of disrespect towards somebody of great and sacred memory held me back. But *Childe Harold* stands in a position of such eminence that I could not conceive that it might be possible to insult it, whatever tone I might use about it'. The epithet 'light-hearted' can also be applied, as the most precise attribute, to Pushkin's parodies of all the other 'great figures' – of Shakespeare, of Goethe and of Dante.

And yet none of these parodies are purely light-hearted jokes; they also contain a very serious and significant element.

The profound and precisely formulated aim which Pushkin had already conceived by 1821, 'In enlightenment to stand on an equal footing with the age' (a task which has confronted the whole of Russian society and culture since the time of Peter the Great), was most intimately connected with his creative process as a writer. In order to stand on an equal footing with the age, with the contemporary world, it was necessary to have reached the same level, to have assimilated the experience not only of his Russian predecessors but also of the greatest achievements of world (at that time this meant mainly European) literature. It is just such a consistent and ever-widening assimilation of this experience which marks the basic stages in the development of Pushkin as a creative writer, stages which have so frequently and incorrectly been seen as imitations of Voltaire, Byron, Shakespeare, etc ...

It should also be said here that an invariable characteristic of Pushkin's creative intellect was his 'noble reliance on my own strength', that is to say an independence of view and critical judgement and the ability to maintain a critical distance between himself and the work of even those writers about whom he was at any given moment especially enthusiastic. In 1825, in the period when he was following in the footsteps of genius to discover new worlds and create his *Boris Godunov*, his admiration for Shakespeare was unlimited. And yet even this did not stop him from simultaneously parodying Shakespeare. He was parodying, it is true, a work which he himself called 'weak'. But the very fact that Pushkin is able to see in the work of a writer whom he worships the weak side as well as the strong is significant in itself; still more so is the fact that he found 'weak' points even in those works of Shakespeare which were the peaks of the latter's creative writing and which won him a place among the greatest masters of literature, namely his dramatic works. We remember what Pushkin was to say five years later: 'Shakespeare is great, *despite* his unevenness, carelessness and lack of polish' (the draft for his article *On Popular Drama and on M.P. Pogodin's 'Martha, the Governor's Wife'* 1830)...

'The reliance on my own strength' can also be discerned in Pushkin's reply in 1815 to the person whom he at that time valued more highly than any other contemporary Russian poet, Batyushkov, who was attempting to point Pushkin's poetry in what seemed to him the right direction: 'I am following my own path'. In the same year the meeting took place between Pushkin and his other direct literary mentor, Zhukovsky, with whose 'enchanting' romantic poetry he was then beginning to feel an especial affinity. From a letter of Zhukovsky to Vyazemsky it can be seen just how deeply Pushkin was affected by this meeting: 'I have made another pleasant acquaintance. With our young seer Pushkin. I was at his place in Tsarskoe Selo for a short while. What a wonderful, alive person! He was overjoyed to see me and firmly pressed my hand to his heart'... And yet it was just at this time that the young Pushkin was parodying Zhukovsky above all. The 'captivating sweetness' of Zhukovsky's poetry continued to enchant Pushkin even more strongly during the next few years. In 1818 he addresses an enthusiastic epistle to Zhukovsky beginning 'When to the world of dreams...'; in the same year appears his penetrating *Inscription to Zhukovsky's Portrait*. Zhukovsky's 'world of dreams', however, which Pushkin cherished so much from an aesthetic standpoint, was in essence profoundly alien to someone who was an admirer of Voltaire's *La Pucelle* and the author of free verse. And it was about the same time that Pushkin laughingly distanced himself from Zhukovsky with the sharpest and artistically most impressive parody he had yet written. The episode in *Ruslan and Lyudmila* – a work written by someone who still sees Zhukovsky as his literary mentor – telling of Ratmir's arrival at the castle of the twelve maidens, quite clearly parodies one of the most romantic poems of the great genius, of the 'confidant, guardian and custodian' of his (Pushkin's) muse. In ironically replacing Zhukovsky's 'charming falsehoods' with the 'truth' and his mysticism with erotica, Pushkin is here indeed 'discrediting' Zhukovsky's 'divine romanticism' which was later to be decisively challenged by the critical articles of the Decembrist writers. Pushkin's parody of Zhukovsky, far from offending him, most probably amused him. But Pushkin later characteristically reproached himself for it: 'It was unforgivable (at my age)', he wrote in 1830, looking back on his literary achievements, 'to parody an innocent poetic creation just to please the rabble' (his incomplete article, *Refutation of Criticism and Remarks on my Own Works*). And indeed there are no such sharp 'unmaskings' in the manner of Voltaire in any of Pushkin's later parodies.

Nevertheless it is this parody which reveals most clearly the special and very important function of Pushkin's use of such a device to reinterpret the most significant poetical achievements, both past and present. The latter must be assimilated if a writer is to stand on an equal footing with the age and at the same time preserve his independence, if he is not to be held 'in captivity' by their creators, and if he is to 'follow his own path'. For if Pushkin, in this light-hearted, romantic fairy-tale poem, rejected Zhukovsky's world of 'heavenly' romanticism, he here displayed very clearly for the first time the most characteristic features and qualities of his own talent and took the first step on the road towards *'realistic poetry'*, along which he realised all his most wonderful achievements, and gained his greatest victories in the field of literature.

This liberating function of 'gaiety', the device of light-hearted parody, emerges with especial clarity in Pushkin's so-called Byronic period. Byronism was the most typical and significant phenomenon in the spiritual life of Europe during this period, a period characterised by a loss of faith in the ideals of the Enlightenment, by the rise to greatness and the downfall of Napoleon, by the reactionary ideas of the Holy Alliance and by the establishment of a new bourgeois order. Byron's mighty talent was a unique expression of the psychology of his age and it therefore exerted a colossal influence on all European literatures and conquered the minds of all the leading intellectual figures. To ignore such a phenomenon meant not to stand on an equal footing with the age. It is not surprising that during his exile in the South the young Pushkin, in common with the majority of his contemporaries from practically every European country, became, as he himself put it, 'infatuated' with Byron's work. And yet Byron's *demonic* romanticism, which captivated him to an immeasurably greater extent than Zhukovsky's *heavenly* romanticism, was essentially alien both to his talent and to the basic principles underlying his development as a poet.

Pushkin brilliantly assimilated Byron's experience in his southern poems, rightly earning himself enthusiastic acclaim in

Russian romantic circles, which hastened to declare him the 'Northern Byron'. This same liberating use of parody helped Pushkin to leave Byron's sphere of influence and not to be a 'planet' in his 'system' – as Pushkin's significance was defined by certain critics, imagining that they were thereby praising him – but to win his rightful place as *the sun of Russian poetry*. This is precisely how his 'novel in verse' arose. In his foreword to Chapter 1 Pushkin himself emphasised the link between this work and, on the one hand, *Ruslan and Lyudmila,* ('several cantos or chapters of *Evgenii Onegin* are already finished, . . . they bear the imprint of gaiety, characterising the early works of the author of *Ruslan and Lyudmila'*) and, on the other hand, with *The Prisoner of the Caucasus* ('the hero's character is not unlike that of the prisoner'). The idea of placing a Byronic hero in an atmosphere of 'gaiety', something which was not merely uncharacteristic of him but wholly foreign to him, and of narrating his story in the 'light-hearted' tone of *Ruslan and Lyudmila,* was itself essentially a parodying one. The plot too of *Evgenii Onegin,* as I have already indicated, is an unmistakable self-parody of Pushkin's first romantic poem written in the Byronic manner and of its hero; the portrayal of Onegin, this Russian Byronic figure, this 'Muscovite dressed in Harold's cloak', as a figure of parody is stressed more than once during the course of the novel. 'Perhaps he is a parody?' Tatyana wonders, visiting in his absence Onegin's 'fashionable cell', a room adorned with a portrait of Byron and a bust of Napoleon, and acquainting herself with his literary tastes. The question remains apparently unanswered. But in fact the answer is in the next chapter on Onegin's journey which, as has already been mentioned, Pushkin calls in his preface a 'light-hearted parody' of one of Byron's most characteristic works. None of this indicates a desire to 'discredit' the wonderful achievements of Byron which stand on 'such a height', and Pushkin continues to render due homage to his 'wonderful lyre'; but Byron is no longer the ruler of his thoughts and inspiration.

The parody of Byronism extends, as we have just seen, throughout Pushkin's novel. But this of course in no way reduces the work's significance to one of parody alone. The light-hearted parody is here simply a means of escape from the 'prison' of Byronism, a device by which Pushkin can finally establish himself on his own truly innovatory path, the path of a Russian national genius, of a realistic artist and poet, providing in his novel the broadest panoramic view of contemporary society, an 'encyclopedia' of Russian life, and thereby creating one of the greatest works of world literature. Similarly, in *Count Nulin,* the parody of Shakespeare was simply one more device by which Pushkin established his creative method in the basic genre of his Southern poems: the creation of a light-hearted realistic story in verse in the place of long romantic poems.

The device of parody had one other important role to play in the development of Pushkin's talent. Pushkin wrote about parody: 'This kind of light-heartedness demands a rare flexibility of style; the good parodist will have mastered every kind of style' (the note 'England is the home of caricature and parody . . .' 1830). Pushkin possessed more than anybody else the ability to master 'every kind of style'. It was not for nothing that his contemporaries called him Proteus. And Pushkin's parodies clearly helped this ability, his protean qualities, to develop. Such works pointed to the poet's inner, creative ability to assimilate the 'style' and also the essence (which radically distinguished his parodies from mere stylizations) of the author or work he was parodying. A brilliant example of this is his variations on the theme of Dante's *Inferno,* about which the poet's young contemporary, Belinsky quite justifiably claimed that they enabled the Russian reader for the first time to understand the *Divina Commedia* and the true greatness of its creator. But then these variations are a parody not only of Katenin's unsuccessful translations from Dante but to a certain extent of the original as well. In early editions of Pushkin's works the editors entitled them *Imitations of Dante,* but they go beyond mere imitation precisely because of the subtle thread of light-hearted parody which runs through them. Similarly, in order truly to assimilate the 'style' (in the broad sense of the word) of Goethe's *Faust,* Pushkin had first to write the sketches for his *Faust in Hell.* Only when he had done this was he able to create his 'continuation' of Goethe's tragedy, his own *Scene from Faust:* following in the footsteps of a genius, he created a new world.

But this 'priceless quality of gaiety', which formed such an important part of Pushkin's spiritual world and which manifested itself so clearly in his masterly use of light-hearted parody, did not simply help him to establish himself as an artist and to progress swiftly along his 'own' path, led on by his 'independent spirit'.

Pushkin's laughter has another crucially important significance. 'Genius and villainy are two incompatible qualities'. Pushkin's enlightened words have firmly entered our consciousness. But we remember less firmly what Pushkin, as a very young man, said, in *Ruslan and Lyudmila:* 'Fear is incompatible with laughter'. These two phrases are at first sight unconnected and yet they possess an inner link.

With almost Dostoevskian force Pushkin felt, both within himself and in the outside world, the tragic paradoxes of life, the 'eternal contradictions of existence', and they are reflected in his work. We need mention only his lyrics which, in the impassioned words of Belinsky, are redolent with the 'outcry of universal suffering', and his *The Bronze Horseman.*

In May 1826, not long after the Decembrist catastrophe, the exiled Pushkin received a letter from Vyazemsky, who was deeply shaken by the event, and who had just suffered a tremendous personal loss: the death of his young son, the fourth such death in his family. To Vyazemsky's outcry, 'I am weary, sad, stifled and in deep distress', Pushkin, who was no less shaken, referred in his reply not only to Vyazemsky's personal tragedy but to the tragic fate of their entire generation: 'Fate is still playing tricks on you. Don't be angry with it, for it doesn't know what it is doing. Imagine it as some huge monkey, which has been given complete freedom. Who will chain it up? Neither you, nor I, nor anyone else. There is nothing to be done, so there is nothing to be said'. 'And there is no defence against fate', Pushkin had written earlier in the concluding section of *The Gipsies.* But he, as a great poet, did have a defence against fate. He was able to offset life's horror and tragedy, not simply by the steadfastness and power of the human spirit, typified by Walsingham, but also by the radiant, reconciling smile of genius; he was able to transcend and conquer 'fear' with 'laughter'.

Laughter and 'gaiety' are intrinsic elements in Pushkin's love of life and in his optimism, in the vital and invigorating strength which is to be found in the work of the author of *Evgenii Onegin.*

Blok was deeply influenced by this motif in Pushkin, expressed by Walsingham as the tragic delight in disaster, which, as many critics have remarked, became one of the basic themes of the later poet's work. But people rarely saw Blok either smile or laugh.

Fedin recalls that he only once saw Blok smile or laugh and adds: 'His laughter was fleeting, like a naughty schoolboy's, flaring up and then instantly dying away as if it had come from some other world, as if it had been disappointed in what it had seen and retreated swiftly to its point of departure. It wasn't gaiety, but a listless attempt to brush away boredom'.

According to those who were close to him, Blok too possessed a 'comic double'. But with extremely rare exceptions it never appeared in his work, which was largely tragic in nature. Could this not explain why Blok, whose whole being was filled with this tragic sense, was so drawn in the last months of his life to someone who was able to exorcise the 'terrible world' by laughter, to the light and happy genius of Pushkin?

INDEX

Aikhenvald, xvi
Akhmatova, 136, 224
Aksakov, S.T.,
  Family Chronicle, 48
Alexander I, 23
Alexander Nevsky, i
Alfieri, 140
Anacreon, 35, 125
Annenkov, iii, xiv, 177, 225, 231
Arina Rodionovna, xi, 53, 65,131, 238, 239
Arion, 150
Ariosto, 125
  Orlando Furioso, 246
Arzamas, ii, 247
Autumn, 141
The Avalanche, 141

Bakunin,
  Confession, 165
Balmont, 143
Barant, 89
Baratynsky, 25, 68, 178, 183, 224
Barbier,
  L'Idole, 166
Baring, v
Barkov,
  The Bold Horseman of Ardent Pegasus, 247
Batyushkov, 8, 65, 140, 158, 247, 250
Bazhov, 236
Beaumarchais, 125
Beethoven, 65
Belinsky, iii, vii, x, xiii, xiv, xx, xxiii, xxv, 25, 43, 51, 60, 61, 70, 110, 133, 142, 191, 203, 228, 239, 240, 246, 253
Bely, xvi, 140
Benckendorff, 90, 129, 133, 166
Benediktov,
  Reminiscence, 244
Beranger, 14
Berdyaev, 208
Bestuzhev-Marlinsky, ii, 25, 139, 141, 142, 143, 188, 245, 246
Blagoi, xix, xx
Blok, vii, xvi, xxv, 143, 243, 244, 246, 254, 255

Bogdanovich,
  Psyche, 16, 237, 247
Boris Godunov, x, 5, 20, 36, 47, 49, 50, 52, 53, 68, 114, 199-201, 202, 203, 210, 249
Bowra, iv
The Bridegroom, 47, 52
The Bronze Horseman, x, 68, 69, 138, 165-8, 211, 213, 214, 254
Bryullov,
  The Crucifixion, 90
Bryusov, xvi
Buddha, 92
Bulgarin, 129, 184
Bunin, viii, 224
  Arsenyev's Life, x
Butler,
  Hudibras, 246
Byron, i, 9, 20, 30, 65, 74, 78, 91, 92, 93, 101, 102, 136, 219, 247, 249, 251-2
  Childe-Harold, 249
  Don Juan, 21
  Caprice, 45, 46
The Captain's Daughter, viii, x, 47, 48, 51, 52, 68, 114, 117, 211, 225-34

Carlyle, 46
Catherine II, ii, 165, 229
The Caucasus, 291
Cervantes, 84
Chaadaev, iii, 45
Chaos and Cosmos, 128-30
Chateaubriand, 139-40
Chekhov, vii, 224
Chenier, 30, 31, 74, 125
Chernyaev, 172, 228
Chernyshevsky, xiv, xxiii, xxiv, 177
Chronicle of the Village of Goryukhino, 48, 52, 68
The Contemporary, 141, 192, 247
Cornwall,
  Dramatic Scenes, 203
Count Nulin, 60, 143, 253

Dante, viii, xviii, 92, 101, 109, 247, 248, 249

Divina Commedia, 253
Inferno, 253
D'Anthes, 108, 134
Dawe, 151
Decembrists, xiv, 23, 128, 163, 198-9, 246
Delvig, iv, 159, 175, 193, 200, 210, 244
The Demon, 16
Derzhavin, ii, 16, 136, 137, 247
The Miller, 16
The Devils, 47, 141
Diderot, 165
Dimitrii and Marina, 202, 203
Dobrolyubov, x, xiv
Dostoevsky, vi, vii, viii, xi, xv, xvii, xxi, 94, 109, 110, 111, 113, 117, 118, 119, 139, 154, 167, 168, 215, 216, 220
Crime and Punishment, 189
The Drowned Man, 47
Druzhinin, xiv
Dubrovsky, 48, 51, 52, 211
Ducray–Duminil, 179
Dudyshkin, xiv

Echo, 122
Egyptian Nights, 15, 69, 85
Eikhenbaum, xviii
Elegy, 41
Engels, 165
Ermakov, xviii, 154
Ershov,
The Little Hunchbacked Horse, 240
The European Herald, 33
Evgenii Onegin, v, x, 21, 34, 55-60, 77-82, 112-3, 121, 138, 143, 149, 210, 211, 213, 221, 229, 245, 246, 247, 252, 254

Fatov, 155
The Feast in Time of Plague, 85, 114, 115, 201, 203
Fedin, 254
Fet, 133, 136, 137, 143
The Field Marshal, 151
Fielding, 245
Flaubert, 110

Fonvizin, 245
Forster, xxv
The Fountain of Bakhchisarai, 11, 12, 30, 31-3, 60
St. Francis of Assissi, 92
St. Francis of Sales, 217
Frank, xxv
'Frost and sun, heavenly day', 47, 141
Futurists, xvii

Garshin, 110
German metaphysics, iv, 159, 220
Gershenzon, xvi, 142, 154-61, 209, 214
Gippius, V., 154
The Gipsies, 34, 74-7, 150, 175, 254
Glinka, 89
'God grant that I not lose my mind', 141, 214
Goethe, viii, ix, xix, 14, 33, 64, 65, 66, 67, 91, 92, 93, 101, 108, 109, 125, 135, 165, 182, 247, 249
Faust, 91, 239, 253
Gofman, 158
Gogol, ii, iii, vii, viii, ix, xii, xiii, xiv, xxv, 15, 43, 70, 73, 91, 111, 114, 139, 142, 167, 190, 208, 220, 224, 226, 245
Dead Souls, 42, 69, 169
Evenings on a Farm near Dikanka, 245
The Inspector-General, 42, 169
Goldenweiser, vi
Golikov, 194
Goncharov, ii, 110, 111
Goncourt, Brothers, 110
Gorchakov, 28
Gorky, 235
Griboedov, 21, 25, 59
Woe from Wit, 59, 198
Grigoriev, xv
Gukovsky, 233

Hafiz, 125
Hannibal, i
von Heckeren, 218
Hegel, 165
Heine, 22, 93

Herostratus, 108
Herzen, xiv, xxv, 224
Homer, viii, 9, 14, 64, 67, 101, 247
　The Iliad, 118
Horace, 35, 125
'How long have I left on this earth', 47
Hugo, 67, 93, 108, 109, 110, 139, 226, 228, 248
　Cromwell, 248
Hume, 226
Huxley, 223

'I am sad, Nina', 47
'I remember a wonderful moment', 172, 176
Imitation of the Koran, 85
Imitations of Dante, 253
Inscription to Zhukovsky's Portrait, 250
Invocation, 141
Ivanov, V.I., xvi

Jesus, 204
Journey to Erzerum, 193
Juvenal, 35

Karamzin, 49, 51, 52, 141, 182, 226
　History of the Russian State, 139, 200
　Letters of a Russian Traveller, 193
　Natalya, the Boyar's Daughter, 143
Katenin, 253
Kern, Mme., 220
Kharazov, 154
Kheraskov, 34
Khlebnikov, xvii
Khomyakov, 208, 209
'Kinsman John, when we start to drink', 83
Kireevsky, I.V., xiii, xiv
Koltsov, 25
Krylov, 42, 245, 246
　Prince Trumpf, 247
Kurbsky, 202, 203
Kuzmin, 136

La Fontaine, 246

Lady into Peasant, 142
Lamartine, 30, 31
Lao-Tse, 92
The Lay of Oleg the Wise, 34
Lazhechnikov, 51
Lemaitre, 119
Lenin, xvii
Leonardo da Vinci, 92
Lermontov, ii, v, 22, 25, 46, 70, 111, 117, 136, 166, 211, 220
　A Hero of Our Time, 112
　Song of the Merchant Kalashnikov, 117, 240
Leskov, 139, 224
Lessing, xix
Lezhnev, xx
Literary Heritage Vol. 16-18, xix, xxiii, xxiv
The Little House in Kolomna, 60, 143
The Lives of the Saints, 91
M.E. Lobanov's View of Literature, both Foreign and Russian, 180-1
Lomonosov, 16, 136
Lunacharsky, xviii

Machiavelli, 179
Mahadeva, 126
Maikov, V.I., 208
　Elisei, or Bacchus Enraged, 247
Maksimovich, 240
Mandelshtam, 136
Manzoni, 228
Marx, 164
Marxism-Leninism, xvii-xix
Mayakovsky, xvii
Merezhkovsky, xvi, 154, 155, 214
Merimee, iv, 66-7, 139, 205
　Jacquerie, 206
Merzlyakov, 10
Mey,
　The Maid of Pskov, 49
Mickiewicz, 24, 101, 102, 208
　Pan Tadeusz, 102
Mikhailovskoe, i, xii, 193, 199
Milton, 248
　Defensio Populi, 248
　Eikonoklastes, 248
　Paradise Lost, 248
Minsky, xvi

Mirsky, iv, viii, xix
The Miserly Knight, 67, 84, 201-2, 203
Mochulsky, 208
Modzalevsky, xviii
Moliere, 65, 239, 245, 247
de Molina, 239
The Monastery on Mt. Kazbek, 219
Monument, 42
The Moscow Messenger, iv, xiii, 159
The Moscow Telegraph, 34
Mozart, v, 65, 129, 184, 223, 248
Mozart and Salieri, 114, 115-6, 159, 201-3
Muravyov,
  A Journey through Tauris, 193
de Musset, 138

Nadezhdin, 246
Nadson, 110
Napoleon, ix, 38, 93, 96, 118, 166, 189, 251, 252
Narezhny, 141
The Negro of Peter the Great, 51, 225-6
Nekrasov, 46, 136
  Village News, 46
Nicholas I, ii, xii, xiv, xx, 23-4, 164, 166, 168
Nietzsche, 92, 217
Notes of the Fatherland, 43
Novel in Letters, 228

Odoevsky, *Mnemozina,* 34
Ogaryov, 46
On Classical and Romantic Poetry, v
'On Georgia's hills', 141
On Mme. de Stael and Mr. A. Mukhanov, 184
On the Memoirs of Vidocq, 184
On Milton and Chateaubriand's Translation of 'Paradise Lost', 248
On Popular Drama and on M.P. Pogodin's 'Martha, the Governor's Wife', 250
On Style, 139
Ormuzd and Ahriman, 92, 159
⋯ova, 210
⋯vsky, 52, 111

The Thunderstorm, 50
Ovid, 23, 125
Ozerov, 198

Parny, 74
Pasternak, vii
Paul I, 204
Pecherin, 166
Peter I, i, 22, 64, 73, 86, 95, 164, 166, 249
Petrarch, xix
Pindar, 35
Pirogov, 224
Pisarev, x, xiv, xxv, 94, 133
Pisemsky, 48, 110, 111
Plato, 92
Plekhanov, xvii
Pletnyov, 137, 172, 210, 218, 219
The Poems of Alexander Pushkin, (1829). 8
The Poet (1827), 98, 130, 151, 218
The Poet and the Crowd, 96-8, 141
Pogorelsky,
  The Nun, 191
Pokrovsky, 164
Polevoi, K., 244
Polevoi, N.A.,
  History of the Russian Poeple, 179
Polezhaev, 25
Poltava, 138, 149, 165, 211, 214
The Poor Knight, 219
Potemkin, 179
The Prisoner of the Caucasus, 11, 12, 27-9, 137, 252
Proletkult, xviii
The Prophet, 98-9, 208
Proserpina, 213
Pugachov, 20
Pushkin (For works see individual entries)
  Aesthetic Sense, vi, xii-xiii, 6, 9, 36, 101-6, 123, 144, 207-8, 219, 223
  Ancestors. i
  Aphorisms, 177-83
  Aristocratic spirit, i-vi, xxiii, 14, 93-9
  Childhood and schooldays, i-ii, 121, 197, 209, 247

Vyazemsky, xi, xxiii, 31, 33, 96,
    172, 182, 220, 250, 254
  To a Solitary Beauty, 172
  The Water Nymph, 15, 47, 50, 114,
    204
  What I think of Shakhovskoy, 197
  'When for mortal man day's
    clamour has ceased', 141, 216
  'When I stroll along the noisy
    streets', 141, 212
  'When to the world of dreams', 250
Wilson, 202, 203
  The City of the Plague, 202
  'Winter. What can we do in the
    country?', 47
Yakubovich, 227

Yazykov, 237
Zagoskin, 51, 245
  The Dissatisfied, 245
  Roslavlev, 51
  Yurii Miloslavsky, 51
Zamyatin, viii
Zhukovsky, iii, vi, 8, 34, 90, 136-7,
    154, 158, 171-6, 247, 250-1
  'I would meet the young muse',
    173
  Lalla-Rookh, 172-3, 175
  Ode to Voeikov, 137
  The Raphael Madonna, 174
  To the fleeting familiar spirit,
    175
Zola, 110